Nick Bryant is one of the BBC's most trusted and senior foreign correspondents. He has been posted in Washington, South Asia, Australia and, most recently, New York. He is a regular contributor to several Australian magazines and newspapers, including *The Australian*, *The Spectator* and *The Monthly*, and the author of *Adventures in Correspondentland* (Bantam, 2011). Nick studied history at Cambridge and has a doctorate in American politics from Oxford. He now lives in New York City with his wife and children.

THE RISE AND FALL OF AUSTRALIA

How a great nation lost its way

NICK BRYANT

BANTAM
SYDNEY AUCKLAND TORONTO NEW YORK LONDON

A Bantam book
Published by Random House Australia Pty Ltd
Level 3, 100 Pacific Highway, North Sydney NSW 2060
www.randomhouse.com.au

Penguin
Random House
RANDOM HOUSE BOOKS

First published by Bantam in 2014
This edition published in 2015

Random House Books is part of the Penguin Random House group of companies whose addresses can be found at global.penguinrandomhouse.com.

National Library of Australia
Cataloguing-in-Publication Entry

Bryant, Nick, 1968– author.
The rise and fall of Australia / Nick Bryant.

ISBN: 978 0 85798 902 4 (paperback)

Australia – History.
Australia – Politics and government – Social life and customs.

994.072

Cover art and design: Design by Committee
Typesetting and internal design by Midland Typesetters, Australia
Printed in Australia by Griffin Press, an accredited ISO AS/NZS 14001:2004 Environmental Management System printer

Random House Australia uses papers that are natural, renewable and recyclable products and made from wood grown in sustainable forests. The logging and manufacturing processes are expected to conform to the environmental regulations of the country of origin.

To my favourite Australians,
Fleur, Billy and Wren

CONTENTS

PREFACE TO THE UPDATED EDITION

OBSERVING THE CHAOTIC SCENES in Canberra since the publication of *The Rise and Fall of Australia* has been like watching the book get made into a movie. The rolling regicide of the Rudd-Gillard-Rudd years has continued into Tony Abbott's bungling prime ministership. Volatility has become the new normal in Australian politics. Over the past 13 years there have been 64 leadership changes at the federal and state level, a startling, Italianite figure. The country's era of reform has given way to an era of revenge.

The excessively adversarial nature of day-to-day politics is bad enough. The excessively oppositional character of the body politic is a larger cause for concern. Political leaders with an eye on power have little incentive to come up with constructive policies or programmes, because elections are won in a blaze of negativity. Often all they have to do is to wait for their opponents to self-destruct. When new governments take charge, the cycle repeats itself because so little thought has gone into preparing for government.

The system, rather than nurturing strong prime ministers, tends only to breed effective opposition leaders. Tony Abbott is the latest to suffer from that problem. As public discourse has reached new lows, public discontent with politicians has reached new highs.

Since the publication of this book midway through 2014, the fall of Australia has been more noticeable than the rise. Its subtitle, how a great nation lost its way, also resonates more strongly. Some commentators disputed it back then. Few, surely, would do so now. Because politics has long been in a state of disrepute, much of what has unfolded was predictable enough. More unexpected has been the speed of the country's regression. Even in the midst of so much bloodletting, it seemed unlikely, for instance, that Tony Abbott would face a 'spill motion' less than 18 months into his first term. In titling one of the chapters 'The Slow Death of British Australia', I never imagined that Prince Philip, the Duke of Edinburgh, would be made an Australian knight, which suggested that true decolonisation still had some way to go. Having lamented the bellicose and inflated language of parliamentary invective, it was shocking nonetheless to hear a prime minister attack the opposition for causing a 'holocaust of jobs'.

Inevitably, events have dated certain passages of the book, whose pages have been left largely unaltered. Richard Flanagan had not then published his haunting novel *The Narrow Road to the Deep North*. Rolf Harris, the 'Australian washboard virtuoso' as Robert Hughes once memorably called him, had not been convicted of indecent assault for molesting young girls. No children were then detained at Australia's offshore detention centre in Nauru.

Overall, however, the thesis has not only withstood the passing months, but been strengthened by what has unfolded.

What delighted me most about the reception to the book was that it was interpreted primarily as a love letter to Australia. This revised edition remains just that. But it comes with a new afterword that doubles as a warning: that the political recession, having already pummelled Australia's reputation, runs the risk of consigning the country once more to the margins, when it should be front and centre.

Nick Bryant
New York City
July 2015

PROLOGUE

WHEN FIRST I ARRIVED in Australia it seemed strange, if not faintly ludicrous, to see maps that positioned the country in the centre of the globe, where a Briton would ordinarily expect to find the Greenwich meridian or the Cape of Good Hope. Among the places I have seen them hanging are the prime minister's suite of offices at Parliament House, the walls of the ABC headquarters and, with ever more frequency, those trendy nursery shops that you find in up-and-coming inner-city neighbourhoods, which offer a more accurate pointer of the fashions of the day. Though Australia could be forgiven these cartographic selfies, they were obviously at odds with how outsiders looked upon this distant land. More tellingly, they hardly aligned with how the country viewed itself. Australians seemed reconciled to observing the centre from the fringes, a role assigned to them by geography and history. Nor did they seem perturbed with their country's unofficial name, 'the Land Down Under', even though its corollary was remoteness and unimportance. Rather, they continued to embrace it with affection.

The then Prime Minister John Howard, instead of fully embracing the Asian century, was determined to prolong the American century and also to reach back to the British century, such was his attachment to Washington and the Windsors. In the national conversation, the idea of proximity had not yet dislodged the longstanding sense of isolation.

Nowadays, those maps with Australia as the centrefold look more plausible, because the country itself feels more central. With the shift in the locus of global economic activity from the Atlantic to the Pacific has come the realisation that Australia is in the right place at the right time, a phrase with the potential to become a new national mantra. Though it still takes 23 hours to fly from Sydney to London and New York, the relatively short time it takes to sail to China has arguably become more relevant. Besides, the internet, and the absence of a geographic digital divide, has made Australia *virtually* close to everywhere. In an ever more interconnected world, in which foreign books, TV shows and films are almost immediately available, there is no longer the same sense of cultural lag, nor that nagging feeling that Australia is always playing catch-up with the global zeitgeist.

At the outset of the Asian century, few countries are as well positioned, well endowed or well connected. Label it the Indo-Pacific century, a more precise description because it also encompasses America, and Australia enjoys even more competitive advantages because of the concentration of resources west of the 129th meridian. Even if this country is not in the same tier as emergent nations such as China, India or Brazil, it is part of the same story: the rise of the rest in a world where American hegemony is no longer a given, and where power is being reapportioned from the north and west to the south and east. It is hard to think of a nation that has benefited quite so richly, with so little upheaval, from the global economic realignment of the millennial years.

Australia is the planet's 12th biggest economy, with a GDP larger than Saudi Arabia, Turkey, Spain or Indonesia. After avoiding the last three global downturns, and having become the only westernised nation to avoid one after the 2008 crash, it can also boast the world's most stable developed economy. Australians would not recognise the term 'the Great Recession', adopted in America to describe the post-2008 slump. Those under the age of 30 would not even have any recollection of a mild national recession. A currency once derided as the 'Pacific Peso' has regularly been at parity with the greenback. Few countries have such a strong balance sheet, or have retained their AAA credit rating. In 2008, government debt was 4.9 per cent of GDP. In the UK it was over 60 per cent while in Japan it was over 180 per cent. Australia has a mandatory minimum wage twice that of America and one-and-a-half times higher than the European Union. International retailers, because of the rich bounty on offer from local consumers, refer to Australia now as 'Treasure Island', a far cry from the 'banana republic' of which the then Treasurer Paul Keating warned in 1986 when the economy was in the process of being levered open.

Just as enviably, Australia can claim to be the lifestyle superpower of the world. In 2013, it completed the hat-trick of topping the OECD's Better Life Index, a measure of national happiness, for the third year running. Melbourne, that urban overachiever, was judged by *The Economist* to be the world's most liveable city, again for the third year in a row, and was one of four Australian cities in the top ten. Sydney, the serial underachiever, ranked as the world's favourite city among tourists, according to *Condé Nast*

Traveller, the 12th time it had topped the poll. Its beauty, safety, financial stability and all-round reputation also made it most 'reputable' city. Even Adelaide made *Lonely Planet*'s top ten cities to visit list. Following a global survey, a study from the Boston Consulting Group reckoned Australia had the world's best national brand. Only Norway edged it out in the UN Human Development Index, which is regarded as the ultimate yardstick of national wellbeing.

Naturally, then, people want to ape the Aussie way of life. Australian cookbooks occupy ever more shelf space in British and American bookstores. Foodies queue in Notting Hill to taste Bill Granger's scrambled eggs. In New York, Williamsburg hipsters form long lines to taste flat whites brewed by Australian baristas. Even the lowly Ugg boot is a prized buy on Bond Street and in TriBeCa, where the signage on the stores reads 'UGG Australia', even though the company is American-owned. Australia is not known for selling its inventions around the world. But its lifestyle has become a major export. So much so that a country long derided as overly imitative has now become emulative.

Nor is Australia's appeal and influence limited to the Anglosphere. Asked which country topped their bucket-list, the Chinese put Australia on top. In the global ranking of must-visit holiday destinations, it edged out Hawaii, the Maldives and France.

Aussie creatives are in particularly high demand. The American style guru Martha Stewart poached the former editor of the Donna Hay cooking and lifestyle magazine to edit her own glossy. Until recently a Sydneysider served as the global trend-spotter for the giant US retail brands Abercrombie & Fitch and Victoria's Secret. The Melburnian advertising executive behind the groundbreaking 'Antz Pantz' campaign is now the creative director of the global powerhouse JWT in New York. Australia's nonchalant sense of style fits the informal spirit of the times.

My own employer, BBC News, like most other international news-gathering operations, would struggle to function without its squadron of Aussie cameramen. Two of our three most brilliant cameramen travel the world on passports emblazoned with the emu and kangaroo. They bring with them qualities one would normally associate with this country: bravery, ingenuity, an up-for-it optimism, likeability and sense of fun. But the traits that often set them apart are their creativity and emotional intelligence. As with the lifestyle, it is another intangible export: the Australian approach.

Small wonder that Australia can boast such a disproportionately large and impactful diaspora. Out of a population of 22.5 million, roughly a million Australians are abroad at any given time, the vast majority living long-term overseas. Unlike the past, it is not that Australians necessarily are looking to escape, a condition once diagnosed as 'expatriatitis'. Rather, the trend has been towards the boomerang effect of the 'rolling diaspora', where people leave for a period but fully expect to return to their homeland of plenty. A talented diaspora, much in demand, its members have ended up running everything from McDonald's to Ford Motor Company, Pizza Hut to British Airways, the World Bank to WikiLeaks.

When after the global financial crisis it emerged that 2700 Aussies were leaving the UK each month – lured home by the expanding economy – *The Times* urged them not to go. We 'need all the Australians we can get. Would they please not go back where they came from?' At that stage, *The Times* was not yet edited by Robert Thomson, a native of Torrumbarry, Victoria, although it was owned, of course, by the country's most powerful expat and the world's most influential media mogul, Rupert Murdoch. Though the passport may well be American, his mindset remains obstreperously Australian.

The world not only likes Australia, it is increasingly reliant on it. It is the world's biggest exporter of coal and iron ore and boasts the largest known recoverable reserves of uranium. Sometime over the next ten years, Australia could overtake Qatar as the biggest exporter of natural gas. By the end of the decade, it should also be home to the Southern Hemisphere's largest solar energy plant, while it has the potential to be the world leader in geothermal 'hot rock' power generation. On the food and drink front, it is the world's fourth largest exporter of wine and, more importantly, the fourth largest exporter of wheat. When wheat riots erupt in Egypt or pasta protests are held in Italy, the empty grain silos of rural Australia partly explain why.

Never before has the country enjoyed such commercial clout, a heft that extends beyond traditional heavyweights like BHP Billiton and Rio Tinto. Macquarie Group, the Sydney-based 'Millionaires Factory', has quietly become the world's largest non-governmental owner of infrastructure. Globally, it owns all manner of things, from the Chicago Skyway to Thames Water in London, from the Indiana Toll Road to Red Bee Media, a company better known in its previous incarnation, BBC Broadcast. In retail, Westfield has become the world's biggest shopping-mall owner, with a heavy footprint in the US, UK and even Brazil. Just as the queue of coal ships lining up outside Newcastle, which on a busy night resembles a twinkling seaborne suburb, has become a reliable barometer of Asian economic activity, Westfield's annual report has become a useful gauge of America's recovery. In a sector where location, location, location is all, its malls occupy some of the world's most prized retail real estate, from Olympic Park in London to the new World Trade Center in New York.

Overall, Australia has become a bellwether economy, not least because the order books of its resources giants provide early warning signs of the health of the Chinese economy. The personal wealth of Gina Rinehart, Asia's richest woman, is another useful indicator, not least because it tends to rise and fall depending on the price of iron ore, again a measure of China's wellbeing.

Diplomatically, Australia no longer has a punch more powerful than its weight, but one that is commensurate – that of the beefy middleweight in a world of few heavy-weights. It has earned its new monicker as a 'middle power plus'. From APEC to the G20, both of which in recent years have become more consequential bodies, Australia's rising influence has been institutionalised. Both also bear the stamp 'Made in Australia'. Bob Hawke was instrumental in the creation of APEC, while Paul Keating elevated it into a leaders' forum, attracting presidents and prime ministers. The former treasurer Peter Costello was a chief architect of the G20, a grouping that since the global financial crisis in 2008 has come to rival the more exclusive G8. Its elevated influence came about largely as a result of an intense lobbying campaign by Kevin Rudd in the wake of the collapse of Lehman Brothers.

It has now become a job requirement that Australian prime ministers should impose themselves on the international stage. John Howard, alongside George W. Bush and Tony Blair, became a key figure in a post-9/11 'War on Terror' triumvirate. Especially close was his relationship with George W., whose four nights in Sydney during the APEC summit in 2007 was the longest stay in an overseas city of his entire presidency, and intended as a favour to his host. Kevin Rudd had the same mind-meld with Barack Obama, and was singled out by senior administration officials as the world leader with whom the president felt most closely aligned. 'Not since Singaporean Prime Minister Lee Kuan Yew during the Vietnam War has a leader had a bigger behind-the-scenes impact on American thinking on Asia than Mr Rudd,' wrote Kurt M. Campbell, the Obama administration's one-time point man in the region.

Mindful of the 'Kevin 747' jibes that dogged her jet-setting predecessor, Julia Gillard deliberately never set out to be such a commanding presence. Still, lawmakers on Capitol Hill invited her to address a joint session of Congress, and she came to enjoy a close and tactile personal relationship with Obama.

When President Obama announced his much-heralded 'Asian pivot', he did so on Australian soil. With it came the deployment of US marines at the Top End, a further indication of this country's heightened strategic importance. So pleased was Washington with Canberra that its former ambassador Jeffrey Bleich described the relationship not just as special but 'perfect'.

This is a far cry from the past. During the White House dinner in 1971 at which Prime Minister William McMahon's wife, Sonia, wooed Washington with her racy, flesh-revealing evening gown – a fabulous statement of Australianness – Richard Nixon had to ask how to pronounce her husband's name. On the same trip, when it was suggested to the singer Eartha Kitt that she serenade the visiting prime minister during her set at the Waldorf Astoria, she made the humiliating mistake of sidling up to an American security man.

In country-to-country relations, talks with China have now been placed on an annual footing, as is the case with Britain. Though Australia still has a tendency of lapsing into its deferential diplomatic default position – and never more so than in its Yankophile relationship with Washington – at least there is now a greater sense of parity with its former colonial master. No longer would an Australian diplomat observe that 'one needs very good peripheral vision to see Australia on the world map', as Owen Harries, the one-time planning head at the Department of Foreign Affairs, did in 2003. When *Monocle* magazine compiled its soft power index in 2011, Australia ranked fifth. (Because of its harsh treatment of asylum seekers, it slipped four places in the following year's ranking, but still ranked third in education and fourth in culture.)

Capping its diplomatic rise, Australia became one of only ten non-permanent members of the United Nations Security Council, and took up the rotating presidency in September 2013. That month, the busiest at the UN since the run-up to the war in Iraq, its mission based on 42nd Street showed no sign of stage-fright. Not many Australians realise that in 1946 their country chaired the first ever meeting of the UN Security Council. Then it came by virtue of its position in the alphabet. Nowadays, it owes its place to its position in the world.

In other ways, too, Australians have shown themselves to be good, dependable and knowledgeable global citizens. Though Gareth Evans, the foreign affairs minister under Paul Keating, is best remembered in Australia for his affair with Cheryl Kernot, the one-time leader of the Australian Democrats, his global renown stems from being the author of the doctrine of responsibility to protect, the idea that the international community should intervene when government themselves cannot look after their own people. David Kilcullen, a product of Duntroon and a former officer in the Australian army, is widely regarded as the world's foremost authority on counterinsurgency operations. The retired justice Michael Kirby recently chaired the UN inquiry into war crimes in North Korea, a report so painstaking and forensic that it has now become the model for international investigations.

In the arts, the cultural creep, a growing appreciation of Australia's artistic exports, has replaced the national contagion first diagnosed by A. A. Phillips as the cultural cringe. Just consider the success of *Tropfest*, which began in 1993 with 200 people descending on the Tropicana Caffe in Sydney's Darlinghurst. Nowadays it is the world's largest short film festival. Audiences have flocked to Tropfests in Abu Dhabi, London, New Zealand, Toronto, Bangkok, Las Vegas and New York. It has also colonised the internet. Its YouTube channel has attracted more than 14 million views. Whisper it faintly, but Australian culture is enjoying greater international success right now than Australian sport – although it comes at a time when the country no longer craves international validation to assuage its artistic status anxiety.

Unlike their predecessors 30 years ago, cultural celebrities no longer feel the need to distance themselves from home, either physically or mentally, to taste success abroad. Hugh Jackman's greatest success on Broadway came from singing, emblematically enough, 'I Still Call Australia Home'. Jackman does, too, as do Cate Blanchett, Geoffrey Rush and Russell Crowe. Their tickets to Los Angeles are normally returns. Happy in their Australian skins, countless local actors, singers, painters, writers, dancers and architects have perfected, to borrow Phillips's graceful phrase, 'the art of being unconsciously ourselves'. Cate Blanchett, in accepting her second Oscar for a startling performance in *Blue Jasmine*, spoke of how her years at the Sydney Theatre Company had made her a more complete actress and described her husband, Andrew Upton, as 'a legend', an unapologetic Australianism.

There has also been a shift in how the country looks upon successful Australians who leave. Whereas in the past, the country felt diminished by the departure of figures like Clive James, Robert Hughes and Germaine Greer, nowadays its national self-esteem is nowhere near as fragile. The novelist Peter Carey may live in New York, but he continues to write with a uniquely Australian voice. Just as important, he now does so blamelessly, without his compatriots feeling any sense of betrayal. Do many people realise, still less care, that one of Australia's brightest literary talents, Anna Funder, lives in Brooklyn? Once seen as a negative, the heavy international footprint of Australia's artistic diaspora is now viewed as a national strength. When the Lowy Institute carried out research on attitudes towards the country's expatriates, only 10 per cent agreed with the statement they 'let us down by leaving Australia'. Eighty-six per cent rejected it.

As for the 'Great Australian Emptiness' described so caustically by Patrick White when he returned after World War II, it is now crowded with thriving universities, book festivals, local publishers, TEDx conferences, and a website called The Conversation, where academics vacate their ivory towers to address topical issues of the day, which attracts more than 1.5 million unique visitors a month. Australia can boast the third most universities in the global top 100, beaten only by America and Britain. It has also emerged as a powerhouse in the lucrative foreign student market, which has quietly become the country's fourth most money-spinning export. In the sciences, Australia has won four Nobel prizes over the past eight years. The latest went to Brian Schmidt, an unassuming scientist who, though American-born, goes by the quintessentially Australian Twitter handle of 'Cosmicpinot'.

The Australian intelligentsia no longer sounds oxymoronic. The mind is no longer the 'least of possessions', as White witheringly claimed. Nor does the country any longer represent, as Donald Horne put it, 'a victory of the anti-mind'. No editor would put 'intellectual' in inverted commas when juxtaposed with the word 'Australian', as Horne insisted while in charge at *The Bulletin.* The notion that the country is artistically allergic is ridiculous.

Just as Australia no longer suffers from the tyranny of geographic or mental distance, it no longer falls victim to the felony of neglect. When I arrived here as the BBC's Australia correspondent in 2006 at the fag end of the Howard years, we were the only international broadcaster with a permanent presence. After postings in Washington and South Asia, covering Afghanistan, India and Pakistan, I was worried about suffering from relevance deprivation syndrome. But from my first week, when Steve Irwin was lanced in the heart by a stingray, to my last, when Kevin Rudd came back from the dead, the tumble of news came thick and fast. By the time I left in 2013, Al Jazeera and Sky News had also set up shop, *The Wall Street Journal* and *Financial Times* had bolstered their presence and *The Guardian* had even launched an Australian edition, soon to be followed by the *Daily Mail. The New York Times* also has a resident correspondent, a far cry from the days when the author Bill Bryson first started to research his bestseller *Down Under* in the run-up to the Sydney Olympics. Back then, as Bryson wryly observed, Australia only got a measly 20 mentions in the world's great newspaper of record over the course of the year. Albania racked up 150, more than seven times that number. Nowadays, Australia gets that many mentions each fortnight. Few peaceful countries receive such per capita exposure.

The nature, as well as the scale, of international coverage has also changed. Time was when Australia only made the headlines when there was a bizarre outback crime to report or a skateboarding koala 'And finally' story. It was as if foreign correspondents and the London-based editors viewed the country through a fairground hall of mirrors, with all its frivolous distortions and exaggerations. Traditionally the role of foreign correspondents in Australia was to serve up what was expected rather than to look for surprises. Nowadays, they treat it more seriously, whether analysing the much-vaunted 'wonder from down under' economic success story, or watching for signs of climate change. The Great Barrier Reef, in all its fading glory, has come to be viewed as a gauge for the effects of global warming. Likewise, few countries offer a better vantage point from which to view the rise of China, with the conflicted sense of fortune and foreboding it engenders.

For sure, British and American news editors have not weaned themselves off novelty Australian stories. Mockery remains an irresistible temptation. But whereas once the tone of coverage was almost universally condescending, today it is often admiring, even fawning. *The Economist* dubbed Australia 'the next Golden State', an especially welcome accolade for a country that has traditionally measured its international success metallically.

An irony is that during this phase of national success, sport, the country's usual gold standard, has been a field of comparative disappointment. At the London Olympics, Australia finished tenth in the medal table compared to fourth in Sydney. The once all-conquering swim team, with its misfiring 'Missile', James Magnussen, is still searching for a new 'Thorpedo'. The Wallabies have not lifted the Bledisloe Cup in more than a decade. In cricket, the age of Warne was followed by the long national nightmare of Hauritz, Krejza, Hogg, Casson, McGain, Beer, White, Agar, Smith and Doherty. Yet as the moustachioed Mitchell Johnson and his teammates showed in the most recent Ashes, Twain-like obituaries of Australian cricket are frequently precipitate. Besides, there has been no shortage of success elsewhere.

Because of the dominance of the Kangaroos, rugby league remains a unipolar sport. In golf, Australia has rarely been stronger, with Adam Scott slipping into the green blazer at the Masters in Augusta, a jacket even Greg Norman never got to wear. In cycling, Cadel Evans came away with the yellow jersey in the Tour de France, an 'Aussie first' that briefly turned Australia into the 'Lycra Country'. Sports fans have also been able to gorge on Black Caviar.

The fall of Australia comes not in sport but politics. The national story, which tends to get judged globally in terms of gross domestic product, stands in stark contrast to the Canberra story, with its gross domestic politics. Debate has been reduced to base sloganeering, crude name-calling and intemperate rants. The quarrels have become so repetitive, the rhetoric so recurring, that it would hardly be a surprise if Punxsutawney Phil, the furry star of *Groundhog Day*, emerged from the grassy knoll that covers Parliament House. Diabolical policy problems, most notably the boat people issue, have produced even more diabolical politics. Parliamentary life, whether judged by the rancour on display in Question Time or the childish refusal to grant 'pairs' for absent colleagues, is a national embarrassment.

The chronic insularity of the Capital Circle takes that well-worn phrase 'all politics is local' to the point of absurdity. At the very moment when the rest of the world has shown more interest in Australia, the present crop of Australian leaders has displayed a bewildering indifference to the rest of the world. Julia Gillard, speaking from Brussels in one of her first television interviews as prime minister, purposely admitted that she much preferred to be in an Australian classroom than on the international stage. Tony Abbott has shunned most interviews with the international media, after telling a columnist with *The Wall Street Journal* that 'Oz pollies who think the world is interested in them have tickets on themselves'. Intended for domestic consumption, both were calculated statements of political parochialism.

The stock analogy has it that politics has become a soap opera. Such is its brutality and goriness that the metaphor works only with Quentin Tarantino as writer and director. Because of the high casualty rate, political coverage has come to resemble triage: a sifting of the wounded and slain. Yet how can a polity with such limited human resources afford to knife so many leaders? The Canberra talent pool now has the depth of a drought-ridden billabong. The mental list I compiled over the years of impressive Australians bore little resemblance to the roll call of Australian parliamentarians. Because of this shortfall in talent, politics not only looks alarmingly brutal, but scandalously feckless.

The more serious indictment is the extent to which policy has become hostage to politics. Canberra is not only hobbled by its brutopia but its myopia: the narrow focus on a small number of suburban constituencies, many of them in the western suburbs of Sydney. The great reform era, ushered in by Gough Whitlam's election in 1972 and accelerated in the 1980s and 1990s, was marked by bold initiatives that required political bravery and public elucidation, whether it was John Howard's unpopular decision to introduce the GST, Malcolm Fraser's open door policy towards the Vietnamese boat people, Bob Hawke's end of protectionism or Paul Keating's superannuation reforms. Nowadays, policy typically involves a political fix, as with the retreat from the mining tax in the face of a concerted campaign by the resources sector, or a political deal, as with the introduction of the carbon tax, the price tag of the Greens' support for the minority Gillard government. Overall, Australian politics is suffering from a crisis of overpoliticisation.

Consequently, the cultural cringe has been surpassed by the political cringe, as Australians are embarrassed by the inferior quality of daily Canberra fare. Lampooned around the world, what happens in and around Parliament House now vies for the 'Only in Australia' slots once reserved for those ravenous crocs and rampaging cane toads, whether it be Tony Abbott denying that he was the 'suppository of all wisdom', Kevin Rudd shaking his sauce bottle, Craig Emerson performing karaoke in the courtyard of Parliament House, Troy Buswell sniffing chairs, or that Queensland MP sending a 'dic pic' showing his penis dunked in red wine, an episode which captured some of the madcap flavour of the present political vintage.

To outsiders, this rapid decline is hard to fathom. After all, the country with the most stable economy in the developed world has over the same period experienced the most volatile politics. Perversely, however, the two are entwined. Had the country confronted larger problems, such as a recession or some other national convulsion, it could not have afforded the extravagance of so much leadership speculation and overall silliness. Presumably, medium-sized problems, like a rise in the number of boat people, would not have been presented as national emergencies – an 'INVASION', as Sydney's *Daily Telegraph* dishonestly headlined it. Rather, as the country has grown stronger, its politics have become nastier and more adolescent.

In *The Lucky Country*, the nation's best but also most misunderstood book, Donald Horne never argued that Australia's good fortune merely flowed from its wealth of resources. Rather, he claimed success resulted from its institutional inheritance from Britain, whether in the form of its parliamentary democracy or legal system. He called it 'the luck of our historical origins'. In his follow-up *Death of the*

Lucky Country, he was more explicit: 'In the lucky style, we have never "earned" our democracy. We simply went along with some British habits.' It meant that its second-rate leaders, who shared the nation's luck, did not have to strive that hard to create a viable and thriving society.

Now, the latest generation of leaders, for whom the description 'second-rate' also seems appropriate, benefit from the policy inheritance from the reforming prime ministerships of Bob Hawke, Paul Keating and John Howard. Bequeathed such well-attuned policy settings, whether in the form of tariff reforms, the floated dollar, the independence of the Reserve Bank, superannuation or the GST, modern-day politicians have not had to engineer major changes to prolong Australia's economic success. The Australian model has helped make the country recession-proof, but just as crucially it has helped make it politician-proof.

So Canberra makes a mockery of the sophisticated, modern, relevant and thrusting country evident in so many other areas of national life. In a progressively more consequential country, politicians have made themselves increasingly irrelevant. Australians find themselves in the anomalous situation of witnessing simultaneously the rise and fall of their country.

Chapter 1

WHAT THE WORLD GETS WRONG ABOUT AUSTRALIA

THE NEW YEAR OPENS not only with a bombardment of pyrotechnics but also a barrage of images, broadcast globally, which imply to the rest of the world that Australia is uncomplicated and unchanging. The fireworks illuminate a harbour crowded with pleasure cruisers and yachts, along with the faces of fun-loving Aussies who appear to be living up to type by enjoying a drink and a party. The Land Down Under seems to be at its factory setting, which is to say carefree and revelling in the good life.

At the next fixture in the national calendar, when the revelry switches from Sydney's harbour to its cricket ground, Australia again lives up to expectations. Long before the first ball is bowled, thousands of sports fans converge wearing singlets, thongs and green and gold sombreros, with zinc cream smeared across their faces, like tribal decorations. The occasional cry of 'Aussie, Aussie, Aussie, Oi, oi, oi' will ring from the stands, although the crowd will seldom chant and never sing. Someone will occasionally shout, 'Have a go, ya mug,' largely out of a vague sense of colloquial tradition. If the visiting team is from England, doubtless a few expletives will echo as well, as fans succumb to the Tourette's-like syndrome so impossible to suppress whenever confronted by the Old Enemy during the Ashes.

As the Australians take the field they will touch the flag, as if it were some sacred shroud. During the first fielding session of the match, they will all don the Baggy Green, another holy piece of cloth. Fans will drink beer that is overpriced and understrength. Bob Hawke has made it a tradition to skull a schooner of beer like some superannuated rock star coming out of retirement to perform his most celebrated song. Observing this ritual at the Ashes Test in 2014, the *Daily Mail* noted, '[i]t was a moment that couldn't have been more Australian,' especially since he was egged on by dozens of fans wearing beige sports jackets who had come dressed as Richie Benaud.

Attendance for the prime minister of the day is also mandatory. They will perform commentary duties on both Channel Nine and the ABC, partly to demonstrate that they understand the sovereignty of sport in national life, and partly to demonstrate they are game to have a go.

January also sees bushfires ablaze across large swathes of this sun-dried continent, blackening thousands of hectares of forest-land and threatening rural towns and hamlets. Parts of Queensland will also be inundated by murky floodwater, launching the usual flotilla of tinnies. These extreme weather events, which often occur simultaneously, are a reminder not just of the harshness of the landscape and the vastness of the continent, but also the resilience of its inhabitants. 'No worries, mate,' will often be the response if you put a microphone in front of a bush-dweller confronted by a wall of flame on the smoky horizon, or a Queenslander sitting on his veranda sucking on a Castlemaine XXXX as the floodwaters rise around him. Even when firefronts have been bearing down on their properties, I have witnessed homeowners exhibit this same laconic air. 'She'll be right,' they will sometimes say, as if reading from a dog-eared script that has been handed down through the generations.

The month draws to an end with another celebration, this time to mark Australia Day. Sydney Harbour, with its ferry races, aerobatics and military helicopter dragging a massive flag of Aussie colours, but North Korean scale, again provides the most telegenic backdrop. Yet the true focus is the backyard and beach. Once more, Australia comes across as self-satisfied, self-confident and half-cut. The country, in John Howard's famed summation, does indeed seem relaxed and comfortable.

In some ways, the Australian New Year brings to life the scene from *The Adventures of Barry McKenzie*, in which the upper-crust British presenter Joan Bakewell introduces Bazza onto the fictional late-night review programme, *Midnight Oil*. 'Most of us Europeans think of Australia as a tough, uncompromising land stricken by drought and flood and inhabited by kangaroos and tough, insensitive, foul-mouthed beer-swilling bores . . .' Certainly, these summer rituals reinforce the sense that outsiders know and comprehend Australia already, and suggest there is little need for further inquiry. The quest for understanding rarely gets past the stereotypes and clichés, even though so few of them withstand close scrutiny. Australia is a kingdom of the mind. Many feel that they know it intuitively, even without ever visiting.

What these New Year rites truly show, however, is a country hiding in plain view, and a nation starkly at odds with its stereotype. The pyrotechnics may well have a hedonistic air, but New Year's Eve also reveals the country's inclination towards order and over-regulation. Crowds gathering on the harbour foreshore with their Eskies, beach towels and picnic blankets are confronted by signs declaring a strict prohibition on alcohol, a policy enforced with near zero tolerance by police officers dressed in dark-blue boiler suits, as if on standby for mob violence rather than a riot of colour.

Historically jarring though it seems to crack down on alcohol consumption at Sydney Cove, the site of modern Australia's inaugural booze-up following the arrival of the First Fleet, it is also historically faithful. To North America, British settlers brought a stern morality. To Australia, they bequeathed a code that was penal rather than puritanical. In the official mind, which has always been censorious, it could be the fireworks alone are seen as fun enough. After all, pyrotechnics are banned across Australia, and public displays are the only time they can legally be set off.

Elsewhere around the harbour are further signs of Australia's unexpected officious streak. Consider the notice erected near the cliffs at the Heads, where tragically over the decades hundreds have taken their lives. It threatens jumpers with fines of $150 should they leap from the cliff-top. If the sign has ever acted as a deterrent, and put someone off committing suicide, then we should applaud the genius of the official who came up with it. But I suspect it came from the more mind-numbing reaches of the bureaucratic imagination that also came up with rear-to-curb parking, and the hefty fines meted out to drivers guilty of the cardinal crime of parking in a non-conformist way.

Even the harbour's great landmarks, which provide such a staggeringly beautiful stage, are deceptive. The simplest interpretation of the Sydney Opera House, the Sagrada Familia of the south, is that it bears testimony to Australia's rising post-war self-confidence. Certainly, the appointment of Jorn

Utzon, an unknown Danish architect without a major project to his name, was a sign of a new spirit of adventurism and a less insular outlook. This internationalism was evident, too, in the global competition that attracted more than 200 entries from around the world, and also in the role played by its most influential judge, the American architect Eero Saarinen, who reputedly plucked the Dane's revolutionary design from the pile of rejects and instantly declared it the winner.

In another sign of the building's multilateralism, new immigrants from southern Europe provided much of the manpower for its construction. In November 1960, Paul Robeson, the black American singer, even performed an impromptu concert amidst its scaffolding and cranes, his sonorous 'Old Man River' a musical foreshadowing of the end of the White Australia policy.

However, the Opera House is a structure of multiple entendre, which actually symbolises the country's internal contradictions. Glorious on the outside, but humdrum on the inside, it is the unhappy result of two architects with antagonistic philosophies. Though oft-told locally, few outsiders know the backstory of the enforced resignation of Utzon, and his replacement by a local architect who was handed the torrid task of delivering a cut-price fit-out. Whereas Utzon was obsessed with form, Peter Hall, the head of the government team, was preoccupied with function and cost – he had authored a study on architectural costing techniques. Initially, the Sydneysider turned down the job out of sympathy and solidarity for the sacked Dane, but eventually he came to regard Utzon as a prima donna, interested only in architecture as a means of self-expression. Hall's principal goal was more mundane: to design a building that worked. Utzon, after exiting the country, could never bring himself to return to see how the building had been disfigured.

Utzon's sacking, and replacement with Hall, showed that a dreary provincialism was still hard to shake. The Dane, after all, was not only seen as profligate and fantastical but unfathomably foreign. So, too, did the treatment meted out to Eugene Goossens, the English conductor of the Sydney Symphony Orchestra who had lobbied so hard after the war for a new concert hall that did not have the rinky-dink acoustics of Sydney Town Hall. After carrying on an intense affair with Rosaleen Norton, a woman known as the 'Witch of Kings Cross' because of her interest in the occult and erotica, he was arrested at Sydney Airport. The police had obtained passionate letters between the two lovers, and judged them to be pornographic. In other ways, however, the building speaks of the country's licentiousness. After all, it was funded by a lottery.

The building's ambiguities do not end there. It was opened by the Queen, but in a ceremony that included indigenous ritual. Its opening celebrations in 1973 not only featured Sir Charles Mackerras conducting the prelude to Wagner's *Die Meistersinger von Nürnberg*, but also Rolf Harris singing 'Tie Me Kangaroo Down, Sport', which offered a populist counterpoint. Ever since, it has been the home to low-brow culture as well as the high. It has been a focal point of national celebration and of protest. It has provided the backdrop both for papal visits and Spencer Tunick's mass nudity installations, been a venue for the Olympics and also the final of *Australian Idol*, and has hosted George W. Bush four years after one of its shells was daubed with the graffiti injunction, 'NO WAR' – Utzon afterwards sent the protesters signed photos of his creation, presumably as an endorsement.

Even its very name is misleading. The Sydney Opera House is primarily a concert hall. Its opera theatre is so cramped that the percussion and brass sections have to be housed in the orchestral pit behind perspex screens, like spectators at an ice hockey match, so as to avoid impairing the hearing of the strings and woodwind. When the theatre hosts ballet, the dimensions of the stage are so restrictive that hands have to wait in the wings, much like a cricketing slip cordon, waiting to catch dancers hurtling towards the walls. For all its foibles and larger imperfections, persuading successive governments to finance the much-needed improvements has been disconcertingly challenging. That, above all, is why the Opera House is such a perfect national symbol: though incomplete and not fully realised, Australians seem not to care.

Nor is the Sydney Harbour Bridge, the beloved 'Coathanger', quite the monument to Australian ingenuity that it first seems. The Queensland-born engineer J. J. C. Bradfield might be regarded as the father of the bridge, but Sir Ralph Freeman, a Briton, oversaw the intricacies of its final design and construction. It was built by the Middlesbrough-based firm, Dorman Long. Almost 80 per cent of its steel came from Britain. Its distinctive stone pylons were designed by a Scottish architect. Even its design was filched from the Hell Gate Bridge in New York.

Those pylons are also structurally superfluous. To the architectural critic Robin Boyd, the author of *The Australian Ugliness*, who bemoaned the country's often slavish imitation of foreign styles, such as the faux Greek columns and Palladian ballustrades on suburban homes, the towers exemplified a broader problem: Australia's derivative tendencies. To him, they represented 'a spectacular example of Featurist irrationality', and even a lie of 'Goebbelian proportions'.

Boyd may have gone too far in expressing his contempt for the bridge – 'Goebbelian proportions', please – but his description in *The Australian Ugliness* of 'the pervasive ambivalence of the national character' is hard to outdo.

Arguably, he is better at describing Australians than the buildings they inhabited.

> Here also are vitality, energy, strength and optimism in one's own ability, yet indolence, carelessness, the 'she'll do, mate' attitude to the job to be done. Here is insistence on the freedom of the individual, yet resigned acceptance of social restrictions and censorship narrower than in almost any other democratic country in the world. Here is love of justice and devotion to law and order, yet the persistent habit of crowds to stone the umpire and trip the policeman in the course of duty . . .

> The Australian is forcefully loquacious, until the moment of expressing any emotion. He is aggressively committed to equality and equal opportunity for all men, except for black Australians. He has high assurance in anything he does combined with a gnawing lack of confidence in anything he thinks.

These vacillations are especially evident throughout January.

Like the Opera House and bridge, the New Year's Test match at the Sydney Cricket Ground can be easily misconstrued. Once again, the same constabulary of fun policemen is on duty, dressed in their blue fatigues. They are on hand not only to pluck inebriates from the crowd but also to identify fans with the temerity to launch Mexican waves. Two hundred police cameras are trained on the bleachers, with a rewind capability, so that the waves can be replayed and their instigators ejected from the stadium. Beer snakes are also verboten. Even bouncing around a beach ball, that most blameless of summer sporting activities, is frowned upon. 'The act of hitting inflatable beach balls can lead to patrons becoming over enthusiastic and resulting in the others being injured or their view of events impaired,' reads the SCG rulebook. If ever one encroaches on the playing field, it is punctured by a steward, to the pantomime boos of the crowd. And woe betide a streaker sprinting across the playing surface. The fine now can be as high as $5,500 (a repeat offender who bared all at the State of Origin in 2013 was sentenced to three months in jail). So when the Barmy Army joins together to sing 'You all live in a convict colony', to the tune of 'Yellow Submarine', it doubles not only as a taunt but also half-decent social commentary.

Even members of the SCG, who are not normally renowned for their unruliness, are seen as potential troublemakers. Before purchasing drinks – the limit here is four per round – they have to remove their sunglasses to prove to a watchful steward they are not completely inebriated. On the final day of the 2013–14 Ashes series, when Australia completed a 5–0 whitewash, even members were only given fifteen minutes of drinking time to celebrate before bar staff called last orders. We tend to think that Australia is granted national holidays on such occasions, but here the fans weren't even allowed another watered-down beer.

This kind of restrictiveness also has an historical antecedent: the wowserism of the six o'clock swill, when the hotels shut early to prevent excessive drinking – a policy that survived until the mid-fifties in New South Wales, the mid-sixties in Victoria and 1967 in South Australia, the last state to abolish it.

Judging by this spirit of prohibition, one would naturally presume that Australia is a land of beer-swilling drunks. But that is also a wrong-headed view. For all the binge-drinking on display in city centres late on a Friday and Saturday night, the country has actually become more abstemious in recent decades. Now it ranks a lowly 44th on the worldwide alcohol consumption ladder, well behind Britain at 17. Champion piss-pots continue to be venerated – Bob Hawke for downing a yard of ale at world record speed and the cricketer David Boon for swigging 52 stubbies of beer on a long-haul flight to London in 1989 – though modern-day acts of heroic drinking are harder to find. In the first mini-scandal of the Rudd years, which came with the tabloid revelations that he had once been ejected from a strip club in New York after a night of overindulgence, he sheepishly admitted that he had rarely before been drunk.

Let us also forever scotch the notion that 'Foster's is Australian for lager', as most of my British compatriots have been urged by marketeers to believe. Never have I seen it on sale in an Australian hotel. Besides, tastes remain fairly parochial, with Victoria Bitter dominant in Melbourne, Tooheys the beer of choice in New South Wales, Coopers in South Australia, Castlemaine in Queensland and Swan Lager in Western Australia. This is a country divided by its love of beer.

At the cricket, the authorities not only seek to control what goes into a fan's mouth but what comes out of it. Ahead of the 2006–07 Ashes series, as part of a laudable attempt to banish racism from the stands, Cricket Australia even went as far as to consult the Australian Human Rights and Equal Opportunity Commission on whether the word 'Pom' or 'Pommie' was a term of abuse. After careful consideration, the Commission ruled that 'Pom' was 'not hurtful in isolation', but crossed a line when used in conjunction with other words that were 'racist, offensive or humiliating'. Fans caught in an act of flagrant conflation risked being ejected from the stadium, much to the bemusement of a cabbie interviewed on the BBC, who told us that the Barmy Army were 'the kind of Pommie bastards who don't mind being called Pommie bastards'. However, in the face of this authoritarianism, the supposedly anti-authoritarian Australians are unexpectedly meek and acquiescent. Australia may not celebrate heroes of law enforcement, in the same way that Americans esteem Elliot Ness, but they obey them nonetheless.

A day at the cricket, which has always offered something of a crash course in Aussiedom, yields other surprises. For sure, the crowd can be hostile to visiting teams. With good reason, the SCG's most famous barracker, Yabba, is memorialised in bronze, in the stand that now occupies what used to be The Hill. But the crowds can also be generous, sporting and even tender-hearted. During a Test match against South Africa in 2009, the Proteas' skipper, Graeme Smith, emerged from the pavilion with a broken arm in a last-ditch attempt to earn a draw, an act of gritty bravery that earned a standing ovation from all corners of the ground. Often the biggest receptions reward less talented players, the underdog prepared to dig in and battle it out.

Fans can also be unexpectedly hostile to their own side. Michael Clarke, whose early Beckham-lite celebrity proved a turn-off, was booed by his fellow New South Welshmen at the SCG when he strode to the wicket against England in 2011. They did not take kindly to cricket culture being contaminated by celebrity culture. Nor did the Australian sporting public appreciate the manner in which Ricky Ponting's team celebrated a last-ditch victory over India in 2009. Winning in the penultimate over of the match, when Clarke somehow spirited three wickets in five balls, the players cavorted around the field like a syndicate of 'garbos' who had just won millions on the Powerball lottery. Amidst their celebrations, however, they neglected to shake hands with the departing Indian batsmen. When in the post-match news conference the Indian captain, Anil Kumble, reprised Bill Woodfull's famous line from the Bodyline series, 'There was only one side out there playing the spirit of the game,' many Australians agreed.

Contrary to the view widely held in my homeland, Australians have never been win at all costs. Cricket fans still lament the unsportsmanship of the infamous underarm delivery in 1981 that denied the New Zealand team the chance to hit a six off the ball in a one-day international at the MCG. Greg Chappell, the captain who ordered his brother, Trevor, to roll the ball along the ground, speaks of the incident in such anguished terms that it is almost as if he is recalling some heinous offence. To him, and other Australians, it was one of the cricketing crimes of the century.

Australian teams play tough and hard, but they are also expected to adhere to the country's fairness doctrine, an unwritten code regulating national behaviour. Take a walk along the parade of champions outside the MCG, where alongside the statues of a snarling Dennis Lillee and the swaggering Shane Warne stands the sculpture of the world-record-breaking miler John Landy. It does not show him crossing the finish in first place, nor overtaking a rival on the final bend. Rather, it memorialises the moment at the Australian National Championship prior to the 1956 Melbourne Olympics when he stopped, mid-race, to help his fellow competitor Ron Clarke, who had tripped and fallen. Another celebration of fair play comes each year with the awarding of the Brownlow Medal in the AFL. Players guilty of disciplinary offences are excluded from consideration.

Much of Australia's sporting traditionalism on display at the New Year Test is a modern invention. Consider the famed 'Baggy Green'. The practice of taking to the field together wearing the cap dates back only as far as the Gabba in December 1996. Before that, many ex-players discarded their sweat-bleached Baggy Green in the loft or garage, rather than encasing it in glass and mahogany.

The Ashes rivalry is also misunderstood. The common mistake is to interpret the rivalry as hostility, when the contest is more a celebration of a shared cultural and sporting heritage. Donald Bradman, the scourge of English bowlers, referred to England as 'home', as did many of his compatriots, and even those who had never set foot in the country. Arriving in Austerity Britain in 1948 on his final tour, he brought with him 19,000 food parcels donated by Victorians. Harold Larwood, whose life-threatening leg-theory bowling almost caused a riot in the stands at the genteel Adelaide Oval, eventually emigrated to Sydney. A large portion of his early board and lodging was paid for, unbeknownst to him, by the former Prime Minister Ben Chifley. Modern-day tours, for all the snarling gamesmanship, still have the feel of a reunion of kindred spirits.

Unquestionably, the days when Australia viewed the Ashes as a moment of national self-validation, with teams setting out to balance some imaginary historical ledger, are long gone. Yet Britain still likes to think Australia suffers great convulsions whenever it loses to the Old Country at cricket. My editors in London were continually disappointed by the muted public response when England won the Ashes. They expected footage of news anchors breaking down, Cronkite-like, on air, of flags at half-mast atop the Sydney Harbour Bridge and of newspaper front pages framed in funereal black. Again, they were thinking of Assumed Australia.

Test matches are actually one of the few occasions, outside of the Olympics, when the whole country rallies enthusiastically behind a national team. Though sport has long been viewed as a springboard for Australian nationalism, whether it be the nation-unifying joy of Bradman sticking it to the Poms, or Australians doing disproportionately well at the Olympics, it has a surprisingly divisive effect. Most outsiders do not realise that during the winter months the sporting public goes its separate ways. Often I find myself citing the story I heard soon after arriving of a businessman overnighting in Melbourne who turned on the television hoping to see the rugby Bledisloe Cup, but instead saw Julie Andrews in *The Sound of Music*. In place of the All Blacks chanting the haka, that dignified expression of controlled rage, the Von Trapp children were singing Do-Re-Mi. Having long suspected this might be apocryphal, a few years later I had a similar experience, when Channel Seven's Melbourne affiliate, which held the terrestrial rights to the game, broadcast *Cool Runnings*, a movie about the Jamaican bobsleigh team, rather than the Wallabies. From that moment on, I banished the mistaken notion that when an Australian sports team takes to the field the entire nation watches spellbound resplendent in green and gold shell-suits, however many times the then prime minister reached into his well-stocked wardrobe.

Stronger sporting passions are unleashed by the interstate enmity between New South Wales and Queensland during the State of Origin rugby league series than the trans-Tasman rivalry between the Wallabies and All Blacks. Likewise, a match between Carlton and Collingwood will arouse a more emotional response in Melbourne. With the footballing codes trying to encroach on each other's turf, those lines are being blurred. Thirty years ago, the notion that the Sydney Swans could win the AFL grand final would have seemed fantastical. Yet for all the attempts to spread the AFL gospel – a game first known as Melbourne Rules, then Victorian Rules and finally Australian Rules – ten of its 18 professional teams are still to be found in Victoria. In rugby league, too, the Melbourne Storm has emerged as a powerhouse. Still, its average attendance remains below 17,000, pitiful in sports-mad Melbourne, which speaks of the ongoing regionalism of sport.

Even the cricket team brings to the surface regional rivalries. Each time an Australian squad is announced there are grumbles in Melbourne about the over-representation of New South Welshmen and the selectors' long-standing neglect of Victorians.

National teams do not have a natural home venue, and tend to flit peripatetically between the state capitals. For the Wallabies, this means Sydney, Brisbane, Perth and even Melbourne. For the Socceroos, it means Olympic Park in Sydney, the 'G and Docklands Stadium in Melbourne. In other countries, national teams tend to play their home games in the national capital, but that rarely happens in Australia. Canberra had to wait until 2013 before hosting the Australian Kangaroos, and then it was a gesture from the NRL to mark the city's centenary celebrations.

From the three different railway gauges that didn't marry up to the siting of the compromise capital, north of the Murray in New South Wales but a hundred miles from Sydney, the fragmentary nature of national life was understandable at that fledging moment of Federation. The passion for unification, as was reflected in the low turn-out of the polls in 1898 (30 per cent) and 1899 (43 per cent) which brought it about, was never that strong. More unexpected is how this lack of unity persists to this day. The centenary of Federation was a revel in search of a cause. The neo-classical rotunda that marks the spot in Sydney's Centennial Park where the country formally came together is the home of early morning personal trainers, with their yoga mats and discarded boxing gloves. For dogs, which routinely ignore the exclusion zone that it is encircled by, it is a place not of reverence but of relief. It is a far from glorious monument solemnising a far from glorious event.

Edmund Barton, the country's first prime minister, may well have proclaimed 'a nation for a continent, a continent for a nation', but the fact that he was memorialised with a suburb in Canberra rather than anything more grandiose spoke volumes about the resonance of that phrase. To this day, the states continue to be 'set in their ways', according to *The Oxford Companion to Australian History*, 'and as suspicious of each other as they were before the union was declared'. As David Malouf noted in an essay 'The States of the Nation': 'We are easiest with "Australia" when what we are referring to is a national team.' There was an Australian cricket team, of course, before there was an Australia.

More than a hundred years after Federation, what constitutes the national interest is far from settled. Veterans of the travel industry tell the extraordinary story of the time when state-based tourism agencies reluctantly banded together to mount a national advertising campaign. Deadlocked over which of the country's major landmarks and attractions should receive top billing, they eventually arrived at a compromise. They would only use footage that was geographically unidentifiable, so that Queensland's Great Barrier Reef would never be in competition with the Northern Territory's Uluru or Victoria's Twelve Apostles. With one generic shot following another, potential visitors were left wondering where the bloody hell they were. That interstate competitiveness persists today. Only Queensland, remember, is beautiful one day and perfect the next.

Canberra, the vital centre of federal government, lacks pulling power as a capital. The description from 1909, the year compromise was reached, still stands: it is 'a bush-capital in no-man's land'. It was originally designed by an American, the Frank Lloyd Wright protégé Walter Burley Griffin, and influenced by a British baron, Sir William Holford, who based it on the soulless British new town concept. The joke has it that it is a group of stray suburbs looking for a city. But I sometimes wonder whether Australia is a group of stray states looking for a genuine capital. Certainly, Canberra has never lived up to the boast that it 'would rival London in beauty and Athens in art'. As the political journalist Christian Kerr has written: 'The city that was supposed to be a focus for the nation has no focus at itself. Canberra does not represent the nation. It is a place most Australians neither know about nor care about. And with good reason, too.' If Canberra engendered more of an emotional or awe-inspiring pull, might not Australia be more cohesive?

Partly because of Canberra's limitations, power is dispersed. Melbourne is the literary and intellectual capital. It can also lay claim to being the sporting capital, even though the headquarters of the Australian Olympic Committee overlooks Sydney Harbour. Sydney is the home of major commerce and fashion. Perth is the resources capital, even if BHP Billiton and Rio Tinto's corporate headquarters are in Melbourne. Banking cannot seem to decide. Westpac and the Commonwealth Bank are headquartered in Sydney, while NAB and the ANZ reside in Melbourne. Artistically, it is probably a draw between the two great rivals, even though the National Gallery, the National Portrait Gallery and the National Library are located in Canberra. This national diffusion brings to mind that hoary joke: Australia has a great opera house, but its exterior is in Sydney and its interior is in Melbourne.

'Tasmelbawalqueen' was the ridiculous acronym that someone came up with when Canberra was searching for a name ('Olympus', 'Paradise' and 'Spamb' were other proposals). But it works as a portmanteau for the geographic dispersion of power.

The media, far from being a consolidating force, remains balkanised. And that, seemingly, is how Australians prefer it, going by the circulation of the country's two national newspapers, *The Australian* and the *Australian Financial Review*. They rank only eighth and ninth in terms of readership, behind, in ascending order, Melbourne's *Herald Sun*, Sydney's *Daily Telegraph*, Brisbane's *Courier Mail*, *The Sydney Morning Herald*, *The West Australian*, the Melbourne *Age* and the Adelaide *Advertiser*. Newspapers, for all the recent attempts of News Limited and Fairfax to exploit cost-cutting economies of scale by nationalising its content, tend to be local in focus.

On television, the Channel Nine evening bulletin starts each night with a lie: the deceit, proclaimed on a mock banner trailed through the Sydney CBD, that it is a national news show. Yet the New South Wales edition is anchored in Sydney, just as the Victoria edition comes from the Melbourne studio. The same is true of all the commercial networks.

ABC has come a long way from the days when it used to have to fly its *Four Corners* programmes around the country, showing them on different days. But some of that spirit still persists. Though most of its flagship news programmes come from Sydney, it would never call its headquarters in Ultimo a national newsroom. Its News Channel starts the morning on the sofa in Melbourne, before Sydney takes over mid-morning, and then hands over to Canberra in the late afternoon. Like the commercial networks, its evening shows are hosted from the state capitals by anchors who are unrecognisable elsewhere.

On radio, too, shock jocks and radio hosts tend to have citywide rather than a nationwide following. Many

Sydneysiders would not have heard of Jon Faine or Neil Mitchell. Most Melburnians would struggle to pick out Ray Hadley or Richard Glover. In the run-up to the 2007 election, I posited a theory that John Howard's decline was partly a result of Alan Jones's waning in the wake of a biography by the journalist Chris Masters, which among other things outed him as a closet homosexual. Yet readers in Melbourne and elsewhere got in touch saying they had never heard of the elderly shock jock. Jonestown is a place in Sydney.

The fragmentation of the media stands in the way of a truly national conversation. The weekly debate show on ABC-TV, *Q&A*, which has become such a Monday night fixture, is played out on tape delay in parts of the country, meaning that viewers who do not live on the east coast cannot participate in what host Tony Jones calls the Twitter conversation at #QANDA. The programme tries to get around this by occasionally venturing out onto the road, but often these excursions highlight the regional divide. On *Q&A*'s first visit to Perth, the opening question asked whether Western Australia should secede.

Extreme weather events bring the same regionalism to the fore. The floods of 2011, which international reporters like me breathlessly reported covered an area equivalent to the landmass of France and Germany, produced an outbreak of 'Queensland exceptionalism'. Residents of the Sunshine State depicted themselves as a breed apart, a band of 'super-Australians'. Anna Bligh, then the state premier, set the tone in a teary rumination on the uniqueness of her fellow Queenslanders. 'I want us to remember who we are,' she said, as she fought to contain her emotions. 'We are Queenslanders. We're the people that they breed tough, north of the border. We're the ones that they knock down, and we get up again.'

Even within Queensland, however, there were stark divisions that revealed Australia's separatist tendencies. Residents of Rockhampton, who were some of the first people to be affected by the rising waters, got a few laughs that week contemplating how 'city slickers' in Brisbane would deal with heavy flooding. How they would have enjoyed the pictures we filmed the following week in Rosalie, one of the trendier inner-city suburbs of Brisbane, where a barista carried his beloved espresso machine to safety, cradling it as if he had a newborn baby in his arms. The floods, then, revealed intra- as well as inter-state rivalries, and in particular the gulf between bush and urban Australia.

Bushfires, which are outside the experience of most city dwellers, tend to do the same. After all, almost 90 per cent of Australians live in the cities, and the vast majority will go their entire lives without ever seeing the flames of a bushfire, even if some might occasionally whiff its smoke. For all the folkloric myths about the bush and outback, this is one of the most urbanised countries in the world.

Even Australia Day, that final New Year ritual, is far from straightforward. Because it marks the moment of British colonisation, many Aborigines refer to it as 'Invasion Day'. Sometimes, as in 1990, Australians do not even all celebrate on the same day. That year, New South Wales, Queensland and the Australian Capital Territory celebrated on a Friday. Victoria, South Australia, Tasmania and Western Australia waited until Monday.

Rarely does Australia Day come around without some kind of divisive controversy clouding the celebration. In 1998, it was Pauline Hanson, the leader of One Nation, moaning that the indigenous athlete Cathy Freeman had been made Australian of the Year and Tan Le, a Vietnamese refugee, had been made Young Australian of the Year just to spite her. 'I do believe it's because of me,' she cried, in narcissistic fury. 'It's rubbing my nose in it.' In 2007, a row erupted when the organisers of the pop festival the Big Day Out asked revellers not to come wrapped in the Australian flag because, in the aftermath of the Cronulla riots, they viewed it as a racist gesture. In 2013, it was the Australia Day melee outside a restaurant in Canberra, where mainly indigenous protesters besieged Tony Abbott. The following year, it was a t-shirt sold by the chain Aldi, which was emblazoned with the slogan 'Australia Est. 1788', that provided the customary controversy, and, on the morning itself, the graffiti daubed on an 18th-century cottage that once belonged to the family of Captain Cook: '26th Jan Australia's shame.'

Australia Day, with its fabricated fun, can also feel unspontaneous and manufactured. Prominent Australians – and also some not-so-prominent ones – are dispatched to small towns in the bush to deliver nation-building orations. The government invests heavily in advertising campaigns that exhort Australians to have fun. In one campaign, a chirpy bureaucrat toured the suburbs looking for backsliders who failed to celebrate with sufficient fervour. 'Listen,' he said, 'Australia Day is your chance to say thanks for beaches, lamington drives, Kylie, and our democratic right to give dead arms.' His Australia Day checklist included overcooking a selection of meats on a semi-hygienic barbeque, doing a 'reverse horsey' in an inflatable pool, making some disparaging remarks about English cricket, and 'doing something cultural, like watching the fireworks'. The jollity surrounding Australia Day is approached with the utmost seriousness. Besides, the Great War revivalism of the past decade also means that Anzac Day has come to be regarded as a more rightful – and righteous – national day.

The Australian of the Year ceremony in Canberra is another rather contrived attempt to vest the day with loftier meaning. But the history of the award provides another case study in

Australian separatism. Rather than being proposed by the national government, it was the brainchild of the Victorian Australia Day Council. Thus, for 20 years, a five-member panel that included the archbishop of Melbourne, the premier of Victoria, the vice-chancellor of Melbourne University and the Lord Mayor of Melbourne chose the recipient. Irked by this Victorian bias, the Canberra Australia Day Council decided in the mid-1970s to set up a rival Australian of the Year award. Melbourne hit back by calling its awardee 'the real Australian of the year'. The stand-off between the two rival committees only came to be resolved when Malcolm Fraser's government established the National Australia Day Council, a tautological delight. Even now, the award is a state versus state, mate versus mate affair, with the winners of the state accolades vying for the national prize.

Australian of the Year has, at least, served the useful purpose of demonstrating what an eclectic bunch Australians are. The list of the 50-plus winners is both reinforcing and revelatory. At the Australians of the Year Walk alongside Lake Burley Griffin in Canberra, where each winner is commemorated with a plinth and an anodised aluminium plaque, you will find figures straight out of central casting: Paul Hogan, Steve Waugh, Allan Border and John Farnham. But also there are Manning Clark, Sir John Crawford, the economist seen as a prime architect of the country's post-war growth, Lowitja O'Donoghue, the inaugural chairperson of the Aboriginal and Torres Strait Islander Commission, and the Aboriginal boxer Lionel Rose. As one might expect, sporting figures feature most prominently, with 14 winners. But the arts do well, too, with ten winners, as do medical sciences with eight.

A national identity debate, with its welter of angst-ridden and self-absorbed prose, is the other great staple of Australia

Day. It is not so much an exercise in deconstructing the country but in trying to assemble it into a whole. A common failing of these kinds of columns is that they insist on defining a singular Australia rather than acknowledging that there are many Australias. This, after all, is a nation that defies neat encapsulation.

To fly from Sydney to Alice Springs on the morning of Australia Day, as I did a few years back, felt like touching down in a distant land. In a grungy bar late that night at the side of the Stuart Highway not far from Tennant Creek, the only small hint of any celebration marking the national day was a white man dressed in a replica Kangaroos shirt supping rather joylessly on an icy beer. The surrounding township, home to the local indigenous population, remained unnervingly quiet.

Travelling the country, I regularly felt the same sense of separation that was mental as much as geographic. To arrive in Melbourne on a Saturday, and to be surrounded by scarf-draped AFL fans observing the weekly liturgies of their secular religion, felt like visiting an independent city-state. Doubtless, some Melburnians feel the same about touching down in their nemesis Sydney. In South Australia, I recall watching in astonishment as a local advertisement for a national fast food chicken chain championed the historical fluke that the state had not been colonised by convicts.

Prosperous Western Australia, where the secessionist spirit as we have seen has never fully been extinguished, already felt like it was enjoying an economic form of independence. In Perth, people seemed too busy making money to pay much attention to the rest of the country. Tim Winton captures this sense of isolation in his novel *Eyrie*, describing his native state as a 'philistine giant eager to pass off its good fortune as virtue, quick to explain its shortcomings as east-coast conspiracies, always at the point of seceding from the Federation. Leviathan with an irritable bowel.'

Tasmania, the country's forgotten sixth state, has its own islander approach. The western suburbs of Sydney are a very different place to their eastern counterparts and the Northern Beaches. All countries are obviously a conglomeration, especially ones the size of Australia, but for a country that we expect to be nationalistically compact such stark dissimilarities are jolting.

The contradictions so evident in national life also make it harder to arrive at a singular definition. Australia is fiercely patriotic yet bereft of a homegrown head of state. It venerates the bush and the outback yet is one of the world's most urban and suburban countries. It is a coast-hugging nation with a landlocked capital. As the British film writer Jan Dawson once put it, it is 'a baffling mixture of arrogant nationalism and self-deprecatory comment'. The nerdy Kevin Rudd for a time reached levels of popularity not seen since the rascally Bob Hawke. But who best personifies the national character: Rudd, who looks more like a Nordic finance minister, or the 'Silver Bodgie', who describes himself as a 'dinky-di Australian'? To the outside observer this might seem a no-brainer, but the answer is by no means clear-cut.

Just as ideas about the archetypal Australian are changing, so, too, are notions of the 'average Australian'. When the Bureau of Statistics came up with its own description based on the latest census data it not only avoided the usual clichés but also demolished them. They came up with a 37-year-old woman. The mistaken tendency is to think of Australia as a dominantly male and macho country, partly because historically it was. In the years after British settlement in 1788, the sex ratio was six men to one woman because so many convicts and their guards were male. The gold rush in the mid-19th century maintained this large excess of males, as did the early waves of post-war immigration because of an influx of men from southern Europe. But in 1979, women finally overtook men. Australia has become a demographically more feminine country. Since women live longer, this will continue in perpetuity. Only in Western Australia do men still outnumber women, because of the modern-day gold rush effect of the mining boom. Leviathan with a Y chromosome.

To those who know the nation, perhaps the biggest surprise about the 'average Australian' was that both of her parents were born in Australia. When the Bureau of Statistics repeats the exercise in a few years' time, surely she will be of immigrant stock.

Australia has become one of the world's great polyglot nations, which brings us to Australia Day's most eloquent statement on national identity: the pluralism of the citizenship ceremonies that now proliferate. New immigrants, who believe there is no better way to celebrate Australia Day than to become Australian, throng them. The statistics are now well known, if not widely accepted. A quarter of Australians were born overseas. Forty-six per cent have at least one parent who was born abroad. Those citizenship ceremonies, then, offered proof, as the political commentator George Megalogenis once put it, that 'middle Australia is becoming more brown than white'.

By some it is argued that multiculturalism acts as a bar, and that these displays of diversity thwart the development of a unitary identity. My sense, however, is that multiculturalism makes it easier, because all you have to do is ask these new immigrants what attracted them to Australia. They will tell you it was the lack of pretention, the belief in social mobility, the emphasis on egalitarianism, the optimistic spirit, the informality, the belief in self-sufficiency (rarely are immigrants a burden on the state), the love of land and sea, the life abundant. They can define the national identity because they came here to embrace it. Moreover, the social commentator Hugh Mackay was correct when he said that the defining characteristic of Australia is now diversity itself.

Such sentiments found expression in an Australia Day speech written for Kevin Rudd by his speechwriter James Button, the son of John Button, the much-respected Labor minister. Rudd was due to speak at a ceremony on the shores of Lake Burley Griffin in Canberra at which citizenship would be conferred on 61 new Australians. Ahead of the ceremony, they had written down why they wanted to be Australians, and Button weaved their stories into the speech. A Scottish man had written, 'It's fresh, it's vibrant, it's optimistic – ooh, and it's hot.' A Chinese woman had said that 'the opportunities here are still true, and if you work hard you will get what you want in life'. An Italian who had apparently dreamt of Australia since childhood, rhapsodised, 'I loved the idea of the ancient land and the strength and vitality of its people.' A woman from Northern Ireland, whose new neighbours had lent her a fridge and furniture while her belongings were delayed for three months en route, commended the 'welcoming spirit'. Alas, not a word from Button's draft made it into the final speech.

Only up to a point is it true that Australia is defined by these Australian values, because they present an idealised view of national identity that can be at odds with elements of the national character. Australia is a country that prides itself on its egalitarianism which champions the underdog, and trumpets the 'fair go', but has not always extended those precepts to its original occupants and some of its most recent arrivals. It is a fun- and larrikin-loving land but also exhibits that zealous streak. The comedian Paul Hogan, who was pursued relentlessly by the Australian Tax Office, can attest to both. It is a 'no worries' nation in which one in five people suffer from a mental illness, most commonly depression and anxiety disorders, and where the consumption of anti-depressants has tripled over the past decade. Australia is a laid-back country, but one where more than 14 per cent of employees work 'very long hours', significantly more than the OECD average of 9 per cent. The world's driest inhabited continent, which is recovering still from the effects of a once-in-a-century drought, The Big Dry, is also home to some of the planet's most ardent climate-change sceptics. Few people in the world can be at once so welcoming to foreigners and seemingly intolerant. Even the very word 'mate' has dual meaning when expressed verbally: it can be a statement both of genial camaraderie and snarling menace.

On Australia Day in 2003 *The Australian* declared that 'the days of great unifying statements that define national identity are probably gone forever', adding, 'there is no point in lamenting if we cannot find any form of words which explains our nation's history, defines its values and sets out its aspirations for the generations to come'. It was a problem identified by the historian Manning Clark at the time of the Bicentenary: 'if anyone asks us who we are and what we want to be, we lapse into the great Australian silence'.

Australia is hardly an unsolvable riddle but it does face a problem. The world continues to get Australia wrong because Australians themselves do not always get it right. This is as much a problem of language as of understanding. The country has a national vocabulary that is no longer fit for purpose, and a frame of thinking that is starting to look like a derelict shell.

Chapter 2

RETHINKING THE LAND DOWN UNDER

NOT LONG AFTER ARRIVING in Sydney, I ran into an ambitious young Australian architect who sketched out an outlandishly heretical theory, that the surest way to improve the quality of local design would be to demolish the Sydney Opera House. The structure had a paralysing effect, he reckoned, since homegrown architects had resigned themselves never to producing a building of comparable outward beauty. In his mind, at least, it had a dulling rather than inspirational effect. It restrained the imagination.

The same could be said of what is arguably Australia's most influential post-war book, Donald Horne's *The Lucky Country*. It has become such a literary landmark that it has produced a kind of analytical paralysis. Sitting down to write the first draft after lunch on a summer Sunday afternoon in December 1963, Horne wanted to set down on paper ideas that had been percolating since the war, and that he had first outlined in a book proposal in 1948. Approaching the project with no great ambition, he saw his book as a transient snapshot of post-war life, which would read like a field guide rather than a scholarly treatise. However, Horne's thinking was so brilliant, and his pen portrait of post-war Australia so bull's-eye accurate, that his opus has been difficult to improve upon or challenge. The title, the brainchild of the publisher rather than the author, proved a masterstroke. Although an early review predicted that the book would not last the season, the first print run sold out within just nine days. In the 50 years since, it has sold more than a quarter of a million copies.

Over that time, 'lucky country thinking' has come to have as emasculating an effect as 'cringe thinking'. Horne and the Melbourne-based critic A. A. Phillips, his contemporary who coined the phrase 'cultural cringe', framed the national debate so rigidly that it was hard for dissenting intellectuals to break free.

On a flight from Sydney to Perth, I devoured *The Lucky Country* in one sitting, marvelling at how neatly it captured the vast and often confounding land down below. Though the book is best remembered for its most oft-quoted phrase, 'Australia is a lucky country, run by second-rate people who share its luck,' it is a treasure trove of gems. Barbs, too, a large portion of them directed at politicians. 'Many of the nation's affairs are conducted by racketeers of the mediocre,' he notes, 'who have risen to authority in a non-competitive community where they are protected in their adaptions of other people's ideas.' His prologue reads like it could have been penned at any stage over the past five years: 'Much of its public life is stunningly bad, but its ordinary people are fulfilling their aspirations.'

On Australian egalitarianism, he is particularly strong: 'The cult of informality derived from a deep belief in the essential sameness and ordinariness of mankind.' Noting the absence of an Australian Orwell, he wrote that it reflected a 'failure to take Australian life seriously', along with a 'hollowness and hesitation in attitudes'. Again, that rings true today.

I was reminded of the book's indispensability when I set out to write a piece arguing that the 'Australia in the Asian Century' debate provided an opportunity to break free of 'lucky country thinking'. Suffice to say, I had forgotten that Horne's introduction begins on the terrace of the Carlton Hotel in Hong Kong, with whisky in hand, discussing China, a country that even then loomed large in the Australian psyche. 'Be careful of the Chinese,' his host warned, which provides the prelude for a riff on regional relations that could have been written yesterday. 'Australia's problem is that it now exists in a new and dangerous power situation and its people and policies are not properly re-orientated towards this fact,' he wrote, which offers a tidy summation of a dilemma that continues to haunt foreign policy thinkers.

His thoughts on Australia's ambivalence towards its near neighbours also echo down the decades. 'If the impression has been given that no one in Australia ever thinks of Asia, it should be pointed out that this is now far from true. There has been a huge shift in attitudes. Sensations burst into the newspapers, seminars are held, articles are written. But the interest is sometimes that of someone momentarily attracted to an idea.'

For all that, much of Horne's thinking sounds dated, as indeed it should. The forgotten subtitle of *The Lucky Country*, after all, was 'Australia in the Sixties'. It is wrong to say that 'the world is not very interested in Australia'. Nor is there 'a cult of optimistic improvisation, of the slapdash and the amateurish'. Australia strikes me as a belts-and-braces sort of place. I would also challenge his view that intellectual life is 'fugitive' and that 'Australians get bored with serious talk unless it is expressed in the most laconic terms'. Maybe then, but not now, which explains the modern-day popularity of book and ideas festivals. He would also be surprised at the extent to which Australia has become a truly creative nation. Back in 1964, he wrote: 'In an imitative country no one has to be creative; the creative person is likely to be confronted with distrust.' Still, not many paragraphs go by without Horne producing a turn of phrase that twirls still today. 'Much energy is wasted in pretending to be stupid,' sounds positively clairvoyant, given the then Labor minister Craig Emerson's bizarre performance of 'Whyalla Wipeout' in the courtyard of Parliament House.

Horne, as is well known, went to the grave ruing that his epithet 'lucky country' had been so misappropriated and his thesis so misinterpreted. In 1976, he even went as far as to publish a follow-up entitled *Death of the Lucky Country* that was intended to kill it off: 'When I invented the phrase in 1964 to describe Australia, I said: "Australia is a lucky country run by second rate people who share its luck". I didn't mean that it had a lot of material resources . . . I had in mind the idea of Australia as a derived society.'

By then, however, the book had become a foundation stone for post-war thinkers. The distorted version of his misread thesis, that Australian national success was primarily the product of its abundant resources, became as durable as it was debilitating. In its most recent iteration, Australia's insulation from the global downturn is solely down to the mining boom.

Nor is it simply a case of *The Lucky Country* being so good. Much of its enduring appeal flows from public debate in Australia being so bad. Too much intellectual energy has been taken up with the history and culture wars, the fights over the interpretation of the country's sometimes baleful past and what sort of values and knowledge to pass on to the next generation. They have become the dreariest of trench battles. Kim Williams, the former head of News Corp Australia and also the chairman of the board at the Opera House, aptly described them as 'the often tiresome parades of intellectual conceit between "left" and "right"' and their 'descent into simplistic binary views on politics and society'. Again, this analytical void continues to be filled by Horne.

Thankfully, the realisation is dawning that, after successfully avoiding the last three global recessions, there might be more to Australia's success than serendipity. Belatedly, the idea is taking hold that bold economic reform, judicious regulation and well-calibrated policy settings have played a larger role. At the forefront of this intellectual push-back have been two of Australia's leading political journalists, Peter Hartcher and George Megalogenis.

According to Hartcher, the country has found its 'sweet spot'. Megalogenis has crowned this 'The Australian Moment'. Both have produced a compelling counter-narrative to Lucky Country thinking that might even lead to a shift in the national paradigm – although to put it in these terms is to invite the kind of piss-taking that has traditionally militated against national self-congratulation and self-reflection.

The last journalist to interview Donald Horne before his death in 2005, Hartcher describes his book as a response to *The Lucky Country*. However, it reads more like a rebuttal to its bastardised thesis. In *The Sweet Spot: How Australia Made Its Own Luck – And Could Now Throw It All Away*, Hartcher reminds us that Australia managed to avoid the Asian financial crisis in 1997 and the dot.com collapse in 2000, well before the effects of the mining boom trickled down to the rest of the economy. 'By the time the commodities boom of the 2000s began its first phase in 2004–2005,' he notes, 'Australia had already developed a flexible, high-performance economy that was consistently outstripping US growth.'

Others had noticed this, as well, not least Paul Krugman, the Nobel prize-winning American economist and mainstay of the *New York Times* editorial page, who observed as far back as 1998 that Australia was 'the miracle economy of the world financial crisis'. Again, that is long before Perth Airport became congested early on a Monday morning with itinerant mine-workers dressed in the colours of the competing resources giants about to head north to the Pilbara.

This national success is all the more remarkable, argues Hartcher, given that modern Australia got off to such an inauspicious start. At the moment of white settlement in 1788, Australia seemed 'destined to fail' because of its geographic remoteness, 'fragile environment', population of 'criminal outcasts', and 'racial discrimination and exclusion'. In the space of just 200 years, however, it became a model nation, even a global exemplar. 'Australia today is closer than it has ever been to fulfilling its promise as a golden land,' he writes, 'even the most golden of all lands.'

Perhaps because he, like Horne's publisher, came up with such a pithy title, George Megalogenis's book has become the more widely read of the two. In *The Australian Moment*, he rejects the derisive notion that luck and resources explain Australia's affluence in the face of such economic misery elsewhere. 'An American or a European might think it is easy for us to gloat when we are blessed with the world's biggest quarry in China's backyard,' he writes. 'But China didn't get us through the initial phase of the GFC. The communist stimulus only kicked in later in 2009, well after the first phase of ours had done its job.' Echoing Krugman, he calls this an 'Australian miracle'. Four decades of almost continuous reform had made the country 'more versatile today than any other first-world nation'.

Striking to both authors is the dearth of self-congratulation for this national achievement. Success 'does not fit with the humble story we have been telling ourselves since federation', says Megalogenis, 'that we are a spoilt people in charge of a minerals-rich continent, a quarry with a view'. The 'laconic side' of the national character 'wants to downplay the achievement', he adds, while the 'insecure side assumes that we will succumb soon enough'. A 'self-sabotaging streak' is overlaid by an aversion towards 'self-reflection', which leads the country to personify itself in the Olympic gold medallist, Steven Bradbury, the journeyman speed skater who managed to remain upright, not just in the final but the semi-final as well, while everyone in front of him tumbled on the ice.

Hartcher, in making the same point about the Australian tendency to denigrate its own non-sporting success, uses a similar metaphor. 'If this were a sporting triumph, Australians would have erupted in a frenzy of celebration,' he wryly observes. 'Perhaps we need a medal ceremony to get people's attention?'

As well as a failure of self-awareness, I would suggest there exists also a problem of self-expression. Australia needs to update its national vocabulary, because the language, tropes and clichés commonly used have become so obsolete. However much Australians want to present a different, renovated image of their country to the world, an outdated national vocabulary herds them in. In the absence of new ways of describing Australia, there is a tendency to use language that typecasts the country. Compounding the problem is an over-reliance on a frame of rhetorical reference that seems almost antique. The country will not get its narrative right until it dispenses with its dated vernacular.

The language of Australian remoteness is a case in point. Terms like 'antipodes', which grew from being at the opposite end of the earth's surface to Britain, and its popular derivative the 'land down under' which first appeared in the 1880s, seem redundant. In this the Asian century, both decontextualise the country they describe. The phrase 'the tyranny of distance' comes from another book title that has outlived its usefulness. It more rightly belongs in a Merchant Ivory movie.

At least the vocabulary of peripheralism is slowly being discarded from the diplomatic lexicon. No future prime minister would ever say, as Paul Keating did in a private conversation with Bob Hawke prior to entering The Lodge, that Australia is at the 'arse end of the world'. Nor is Australia a 'strategic backwater', which Kim Beazley said was an apt description of the country during the Cold War. 'Now things are different,' Beazley observed when he took up his post as ambassador in Washington. 'We are the southern tier of the focal point of the global political system which, for the foreseeable future, will be the Asia-Pacific region.'

Eliminating anthropomorphic language to describe Australia's national development, the linguistic corollary of being settled by the 'Mother Country' may well take longer, because its use is so widespread. It is still not uncommon to hear phrases like 'colonial upstart', 'rebellious teenager' or 'aggressive adolescence', which imply stunted development and an inability to achieve full maturity. Frequently, Australia experiences 'a coming of age', as it did at the Sydney Olympics in 2000 but also during the Melbourne Games 44 years earlier. Australia has had almost as many 'coming of ages' – the opening of the Sydney Harbour Bridge, the Melbourne Olympics, the completion of the Snowy Mountains dam project, the 1967 indigenous referendum, the opening of the Sydney Opera

House, the Bicentennial celebrations and Sydney Olympics – as America has had losses of innocence. Australia might not yet be fully realised – which nation is? – but to describe it as immature or in some way adolescent is absurd. For a start, it can boast one of the world's oldest democracies. It was in the forefront of female suffrage, minimum wage legislation and old-age pensions, and invented the secret ballot. The Americans called it 'The Australian Ballot'. As Clive James observed on the eve of the Olympics, 'it was only the belief that was lacking, never the maturity'.

'Mother Country-speak' has spawned other familial expressions. We talk of an 'umbilical relationship' with Britain, of the need to 'cut the apron strings'; or, as Horne put it, to enact some 'final casting off'. All these expressions imply that Australia is struggling still to overcome a childlike fear of abandonment. All speak of an Anglocentric mindset that, with each iron ore shipment to China, seems antiquated.

This language is particularly problematic for republicans pushing for a 'mate as the head of state'. It perpetuates a familial and sentimental attachment to Britain that has buttressed the status quo. It also implies that Australia somehow remains reliant on Britain performing a parental, or matriarchal, role. When Professor Patrick McGorry, the then Australian of the Year, delivered the 2010 National Republican Lecture, he spoke of the country emerging from its 'prolonged adolescence' into 'the full flower of independent adulthood'. Irked by its language and tone, James Curran, the co-author of *The Unknown Nation: Australia After Empire*, called for a 'rhetorical reset'. He opined, 'It might be a requirement for all future republican advocates to swear that they will henceforth dispense with these tired, creaky old anatomical metaphors. The republican debate need not be permanently riddled with this strain of rhetorical arthritis.'

The phrase 'punching above its weight' could probably do with being pensioned off because it implies again that Australia is not yet fully formed and that it is only a bantam nation. Yet it's a super-heavyweight in sport, trade, economics and, increasingly, the arts. 'Per capita', a term often placed in close proximity to 'punching above its weight', should stay, if only so Australia can safeguard its status as the country that most mentions per capita per capita. We need to talk, though, about 'she'll be right', a phrase that made its debut in the *Adelaide Mail* in 1940, unbefitting of a country so industrious and creative. Yet, as the database at the Australian National Dictionary Centre in Canberra reveals, 'she'll be right', with the flukey good fortune implied, gets at least two outings a week in Australian newspapers.

'Tall poppy syndrome' has also been a weekly fixture for years, even though Australians have become a lot less resentful towards successful fellow countrymen. Even Nicole Kidman and Russell Crowe these days get a good press at home. As Sarah Ogilvie, the former director of the Australian National Dictionary Centre, noted before heading off to join Google in Silicon Valley: 'People are still using phrases which to an outsider seem anachronistic.' Thankfully, we no longer hear much of 'the convict stain'. It is as much a historical relic as Ned Kelly's skeletal remains, but it took decades to die out.

Much like Washington reporters overuse the '-gate' suffix, Australian journalists have the same dependence on variations of 'the lucky country'. Like biographers straining to pinpoint the single characteristic or mannerism that captures their subject, they struggle to decide what should be the correct adjective. Likewise, a glance through the shelves of any decent bookshop also reveals the difficulty of definition. There you will find titles such as *A Secret Country* (John

Pilger), *Strange Country* (Mark Dapin), *Bipolar Nation* (Peter Hartcher), *The Unknown Nation* (James Curran and Stuart Ward), *Advance Australia Where?* (Hugh Mackay) and *Looking for Australia* (John Hirst). To borrow a phrase that the economist John Kenneth Galbraith once applied to India, Australia would appear to be in a perpetual state of 'suspenseful indecision'.

So much of its vernacular describes the old Australia rather than the new, it is as if Australians want to use idioms and phrases comporting with how outsiders view it, rather than setting out to articulate a fresh, more sophisticated identity. Often the 'land down under' is deployed when Australians are trying to make their country intelligible to Americans. So, too, is 'g'day', as in the 'G'Day USA' marketing campaign. And consider the language that Julia Gillard used during her speech to the joint session of Congress, when she described herself as a 'true mate' of America, and stressed that Washington had a 'true friend down under'. During the same visit, she presented a Sherrin football to Barack Obama and engaged in some presidential banter over 'vegemite'. It is akin to a former pupil returning for a school reunion and reverting to the personality they had in Year 9.

Mimicking her language, Obama, too, spoke of the countries being 'great mates'. When the president visited Canberra, and made a lighthearted speech at a dinner in the Great Hall of Parliament House, it was peppered with what he thought were Aussie colloquialisms. To encouraging if not wholly enthusiastic laughs, he spoke about having a 'chin-wag' with the prime minister, and avoiding an 'ear-bashing'. After making the mandatory vegemite gag, he then added that the Australian alliance was 'deeper and stronger' than it had ever been. 'Spot-on. Crackerjack. Top nick.' Clearly the president thought he was charming his guests, which he undoubtedly did, but it sounded as if he had dispensed with the services of his speech-writing team and outsourced the task to the maître d' at the nearest Outback Steakhouse.

Even more cringeworthy were the words of welcome that Obama received in the House of Representatives the following morning from the Speaker Harry Jenkins. He wished the president a safe return home to 'your cheese and kisses, that's the missus, the wife. And to the billy lids, the kids, your children.' Obviously, modern Australians do not speak like that, but Jenkins happily carried on the long tradition of using the language of self-caricature when people here describe their country to Americans.

The same tendency was also evident when Australia took up the month-long presidency of the Security Council in September 2013, when pies, sausage sandwiches and lamingtons were served to the diplomatic dignitaries. Likewise, the end-of-presidency party featured the low-pitched rasp of the didgeridoo and a fluorescent yellow sign in the lobby outside warning of the threat from kangaroos for the next 50 kilometres. Throughout that month, a startlingly lifelike toy kangaroo was placed in the office next to the Security Council that goes with the presidency. According to Australian diplomats at the UN, it yielded unexpected dividends, because it brought to the surface warm feelings towards Australia. But are they not patronising feelings as well? What makes this cartoonish national persona all the more passé is that Australia is being taken far more seriously on the international stage. It no longer needs these props.

National self-stereotyping is a recurring problem. Baz Luhrmann's movie *Australia* provoked something of a critical backlash partly because it was as if the country itself had emerged from central casting. 'Welcome to Ozzstrayleeeah,' slurs Hugh Jackman's character, speaking fluent ocker, when he greets an English aristocrat, played by Nicole Kidman. It grated on the Australian ear, but Luhrmann had pitched his movie for American audiences.

Australia, the art show at the Royal Academy in London, also drew criticism for typecasting. 'If the exhibition encapsulates Australia, as the title wants us to believe,' asked the cultural commentator Peter Conrad, 'what notion of the country does it proclaim to the wider world? The show consists of landscapes, mostly of the bush or the desert, despite the fact that Australia is the most urbanised nation on Earth.' Conrad concluded that the exhibition was a 'stunning' piece of theatre, but that the thesis underpinning it was flawed. 'At its most trite,' he wrote, 'this emphasis on scenery lapses into the adjectival flummery of the tourist brochure.'

In peddling clichés and outdated views of the country, Tourism Australia is, indeed, the biggest serial offender. Here, the success of Hogan's celebrated 'Come and Say G'Day' campaign acts in much the same way as Horne's *The Lucky Country*. Tourism chiefs have found it hard to improve upon. 'Australia – a different light', the bold new campaign launched in 2004, fell flat. As the marketeers have learned to their cost, playing to your strengths means playing to your clichés. 'Koala Australia' will always trump 'Cool Australia'. 'Dumb blonde Australia' is of more appeal than anything more multi-hued.

The latest campaign, 'There's Nothing Like Australia', ended up being a real 'ocker shocker', featuring kangaroos skipping playfully through the bush, a barbie on the beach, a brace of surfers waiting for the first big wave of the day, a local pub 'where everyone's your mate', a sea plane skimming over the Great Barrier Reef, an Aboriginal elder stood in front of Uluru, a ferry carving through Sydney Harbour, with the Opera House and bridge in the background, and, of course, the requisite koala. And all to the bouncy refrain of a catchy new song, 'There's Nothing Like Australia'. It prompted one commentator to ask: 'When will we shake these dowdy, 50-year-old stereotypes?' Under the headline 'Stone the crows, are they fair dinkum about this flamin' ad?', Rick Feneley complained in *The Sydney Morning Herald* that the new ad 'casts us as a nation of tone-deaf bogans caught in a '70s time-warp'. The blogosphere weighed in with 'bogan pride at its best'.

In fairness to Tourism Australia, its role is not to distil the essence of the nation. A tourism advertisement is a tourism advertisement: a marketing device rather than a 90-second summation of national identity. But it speaks of the broader failure in Australia to come up with new and different ways of describing itself that these campaigns have become inadvertently meaningful. As with *The Lucky Country*, they fill a vacuum.

Though the political class should not be expected to carry the full burden of national self-expression, this generation of leaders has been especially inarticulate. The overriding aim on both sides has been to assassinate the character of political opponents rather than describing the new personality of the nation.

Kevin Rudd's victory speech in 2007, on a night that Labor celebrated the end of 11 years of conservative rule, was a passion-killer, memorable only for a lame joke about 'Iced VoVos'. His national apology to indigenous peoples, a good speech not a great one, lingers in the memory for the power of three words: sorry, sorry, sorry. When he was ousted from office in 2010, and delivered the first draft of his own obituary from the prime ministerial courtyard in Parliament House, he outlined his legacy in tearful bullet points. A politician known for his linguistic skills had trouble speaking

English. When writing speeches, he evidently stuck to a seven-point plan on how they should be drafted. With lyricism beyond him, he lapsed into impenetrable jargon – 'points of stability', 'commitment periods', 'interim targets', 'steering points' and 'scientific endpoints' – and faux colloquialisms. He is probably best remembered for a line purloined from 'Bazza' McKenzie: 'Fair shake of the sauce bottle'.

As for Julia Gillard, her main rhetorical contribution was a rant rather than an oration – the misogyny speech started out as a printout of Tony Abbott's most sexist quotes. When she tried to produce something more thoughtful, at the Labor Party conference in December 2011, her address was pilloried for the self-satirising soundbite, 'We are us.'

Abbott, as a young journalist writing for *The Bulletin*, exhibited a deft turn of phrase, but he became a political sloganeer. 'Stop the boats.' 'A great big tax on everything.' Like Rudd in 2007, his victory speech in 2013 lived about as long in the memory as a one-day cricket international.

Parliament is largely bereft even of half-decent speechmakers, while the few blessed with a verbal capacity have generally fallen short. Malcolm Turnbull, during his short spell as opposition leader, tended to address parliament as if it were a courtroom. Listening to Bob Carr, a talented orator, often felt like speed-dating in a room full of classicists and American history trivia hounds. So packed were his speeches with references and allusions that they sounded blustery and tangential.

In the main, political speeches, with their mandatory evocations of the fair go and mateship, sound like hotel-lobby muzak: background noise easily ignored. The overuse and repetition of this vocabulary of egalitarianism has rendered it almost meaningless.

But then, Australian leaders are not expected to deliver

rousing oratory, since there is not much of a rhetorical tradition. Children probably leave school with a vague sense of six prime ministerial speeches: Curtin's New Year's message in 1941, Ben Chifley's 'Light on the Hill', Robert Menzies's 'Forgotten People', Gough Whitlam's 'Men and Women of Australia', Paul Keating's Redfern speech and Kevin Rudd's national apology. But I wonder how many can actually quote from them. Australians are better acquainted with quotations from Lincoln, Roosevelt, Churchill, Kennedy and Obama than their own prime ministers.

Nor is there a national occasion, more's the pity, that demands great speechifying. Campaign launch speeches are little more than a collation of slogans, arranged haphazardly like those randomly worded fridge magnets. When prime ministers are sworn in, they are merely expected to read out a roll call of new ministers. The old adage has it that campaigning requires poetry and governance involves prose. In Australia, however, on both sides of election day the language is usually listless and banal. Budget night, the parliamentary set-piece of the year, is an exercise in national accounting. Australia Day speeches usually sound like they have been farmed out to a junior-ranking member of the prime-ministerial speech shop.

Successive prime ministers have made more of an effort on Anzac Day, but then the intention is to draw meaning from the past rather than plot a national future. It nurtures what the historian James Curran calls 'sentimental nationalism', as opposed to something more dynamic.

Nor has outsourcing 'the vision thing' produced anything more vivid. The Asian Century white paper, which was entrusted to a team led by the economist Ken Henry, was a work of 'bureaucratese' – more PowerPoint than poetry.

Unlike America, where the words of the Declaration of

Independence still echo down the generations, stirring words are absent from Australia's founding documents. As Manning Clark once put it: 'No one has ever drawn up for us a list of self-evident truths.' The Australian constitution is bone-dry, though it was written, as Don Watson reminds us, in the uninspiring midst of 'a drought, a rabbit plague, an economic depression and a British war in South Africa'. Devoid of ringing phraseology, it speaks of 'an indissoluble federal Commonwealth firmly united for many of the most important functions of government'. Listening to Radio National one afternoon, I almost veered off the road when I heard the presenter declare, without apparent irony, that horizontal fiscal equalisation, the payments that flow from federal to the state government, is 'the glue that holds the nation together'. No American would ever say that.

Australia would reject the imperious grandeur that unfolds on the Washington Mall, where the US Capitol Hill serves as the most magnificent of presidential pulpits for the inaugural address, even though the lawns of Parliament House have at least some of the same symmetrical trappings. Sometimes I wonder, though, whether Australians would embrace the equivalent of a third way – something, in automotive terms, between the prime ministerial white Holden and president's black Cadillac limousine, the so-called 'Beast'. A prime ministerial speech offering a clearer and more impassioned expression of where the country stands and where it is going. An occasion, without the pomp, religiosity and grandiloquence of the inaugural, focused not so much on national renewal as national definition. All too often, attempts to tell and retell the national story get caught up in the culture and history wars.

Certainly, the sentimentalism on the left around the 20th anniversary of Paul Keating's Redfern speech and a similar wistfulness on the right for the 70th anniversary of Robert Menzies's 'Forgotten People' address shows an appetite still for landmark speeches.

When Barack Obama delivered his second inaugural he spoke evocatively of an American journey, marked with milestones like Selma, where black civil rights protesters were beaten with billy clubs by Alabama state troopers, and Stonewall, the violent disturbances in 1969 which followed a police raid on a gay bar in Greenwich Village, New York. The 'Australian journey', with the right words and history attached to it, also has the potential to be evocative. Alas, presently it sounds like a backpacker excursion or an attraction at a Gold Coast theme park.

Lacking redolent words to describe themselves, Australians have a tendency of identifying compatriots who personify the nation's character. The individual is deemed to sum up the collectivity. This trend was noticeable in the response to the death of Steve Irwin, the famed 'Crocodile Hunter' who in September 2006 was lanced in the heart by a stringray. For a foreign correspondent who arrived in Australia determined to demolish its outdated national stereotypes, I admit to regarding his death during my first week in the country as something of a personal disaster. After all, Irwin was a marauding cliché. His death seemed to offer proof that mythic Australia was alive and well, and initially I found myself covering the typecast view of the country that I was so desperate to avoid. The liturgy of his memorial service at the Crocoseum in Queensland, which culminated with Irwin's mud-splattered ute being loaded up with his surf board and croc-hunting gear and driven slowly out of the arena, was so emphatically Australian. It could not have been staged in any other country. As John Williamson reprised 'True Blue', zoo hands dressed in tight khaki shorts even set down flowers that spelled out his catchcry, 'CRIKEY'.

Unexpectedly, Irwin's death ended up being the perfect introduction to Australia because his dead body became a proxy battleground for the latest clashes of the culture wars and national identity debate. Bizarrely, his death could even be described as an intellectual event, as argument raged over whether he was the human embodiment of Aussie values or an absurdly caricatured version. The stereotypes themselves became the story.

First out of the blocks was Russell Crowe, who called his mate 'the Australian we all yearn to be', a view which found an echo in the bush and on the right. Andrew Bolt spoke witheringly of a 'cultural class that feels threatened by blokes in work boots who shout "crikey"'. When Germaine Greer weighed in from London, complaining that Irwin had spawned a 'generation of kids in shorts seven sizes too small' who would 'shout in the ear of animals with hearing ten times more acute than them', the response was vituperative. The Queensland novelist John Birmingham called her 'a feral hag' and a 'poorly sketched caricature of a harridan'. Then he went after the inner-urban elite for whom Irwin was 'a fucking moron' and a 'cashed-up bogan'. In the New South Wales parliament, the Liberal MLC Charlie Lynn even introduced a motion condemning Greer as a 'radical, left-wing hairy-arm-pitted feminist' on the hunt for publicity. 'It was a sad and sorry day for the left-wingers and terrorists,' he harrumphed. 'They hate anything to do with Australia, and they cannot understand what it is to be Australian.'

Irwin, it emerged in the eulogies, was intensely proud of his larger-than-life persona, seeing himself not only as a wildlife warrior but a cultural warrior, a conservationist not just of Australian animals at his Australia Zoo but also the Australian vernacular. His grandfather and great-grandfather, he said back in 2003, had fought and died for Australia, and he uttered every strewth, crikey and fair dinkum in their honour. 'They didn't fight on the frontline and get shot at by the enemy for us to forget who we are,' he said. 'They weren't saying holy smokes or goddamn. They were saying crikey, strewth, fair dinkum, have a go ya mug. That's what they were saying, mate.'

Countless others, however, did not see Irwin as a 'dinkum Aussie'. Never was he cynical enough to satirise the Aussie stereotypes as Barry Humphries had done to woo foreign audiences, but he saw no problem in amplifying the stereotypes to make it in America. This was problematic for many people, for the Crocodile Hunter presented such a travestying image of their homeland to the rest of the world. Despite Russell Crowe's thoughts on the matter, he was not the Australia they wanted to be, nor the Australian by whom they wanted to be defined.

This tendency to locate Australia in a single personality was also evident during the ceremonies celebrating the sanctification of Mary MacKillop, the country's first saint. 'Mary MacKillop is the vernacular saint for a people who deify the battler, are democratic, tilt against authority and are yet traditional,' wrote Tom Dusevic of *The Australian*. Deification was not enough. She also had to be defining. And not just for Australia's five-million-strong Catholic community, but also for the country as a whole.

The Australian of the Year award also encourages the idea that an individual can be the guardian of national identity. In their cricket captains, too, Australians like to see their country. Steve Waugh was cast as the battler's battler. Mark Taylor was the likeable Australian everyman. Allan Border exemplified the toughness and no-nonsense resilience that Australians like to see in themselves. Michael Clarke was initially a harder sell because the sporting public failed to see in him a personality trait that characterised the nation as a whole. Rather, they only saw vapid celebrity. Curiously, the remaking of his public image started when he ditched his one-time fiancée, Lara Bingle, the star of the 'Where the Bloody Hell Are You?' campaign and the poster girl of 'Dumb Blonde' Australia. To make too much of this runs the risk of over-extrapolation, but breaking from Lara Bingle, and her 'famous for being famous' stardom, certainly set him on the path to being a more substantial figure, which in this context meant a more substantial Australian.

Perhaps Ricky Ponting never achieved the same level of popularity as Waugh, Border or Taylor, because in 'Punter Ponting' fans perceived a national vice, gambling, rather than a national virtue. Tellingly, Shane Warne was never given the captaincy, partly, one suspects, because the messier aspects of his private life barred him from becoming the kind of national role model that Cricket Australia is now expected to appoint.

More so than other nationalities, Australians tend to mine the personalities of their deceased countrymen and women in search of universal character traits. It was not enough for Joan Sutherland to be a great singer, she also had to be a great Australian. Thus, she was portrayed as the Australian anti-diva – an 'Australian Diva' would be oxymoronic, after all – who rejected the airs and graces ordinarily associated with operatic stardom. A hard-working lass, who had laboured years for her overnight success, she fitted the battler mould as well. Also fearless, she happily took on many of the great bel canto roles that filled other sopranos with dread because of their high degree of musical difficulty. If her singing reached the highest pitch, her manner was reassuringly down-to-earth. While she sang like an angel on stage, she spoke fluent Aussie 'strine in the wings.

But Sutherland's personality also hinted at Australia's darker side – not that it was fashionable to say so in the aftermath of her death. At a luncheon in 1994 held by the Australians for Constitutional Monarchy, she bemoaned not having a British passport any more and resented having to go to the post office to get a new one where she was 'interviewed by a Chinese or an Indian'. 'I find it ludicrous,' she harrumphed. She was also regarded as a philistine. Too low-brow for his tastes, Patrick White described her as 'a wound-up Ocker Olympia'. Dame Joan made the mistake of telling him over dinner that she had never read any of his novels, but loved *The Thorn Birds*. Needless to say, the very qualities that riled White were the same attributes that gave her such broad public appeal.

The death of the racing driver Peter Brock, which came as the nation was still absorbing the shock of Steve Irwin's passing, also highlighted this inclination towards Australianising the dead and departed. Known as 'The King of the Mountain' for his domination at the Bathurst 1000, Brock was cast as the quintessential Aussie, a V8 Supercar Hall of Famer who was the 'rev-head of the masses'. But Brock's personality was more complex. After giving up booze and cigarettes, he became a vegan who believed in New Age thinking on how crystals and magnets could improve the performance of a car. It showed that 'quintessential Australians' often end up being just as complicated and confounding as the country itself.

Nothing speaks more powerfully of the need to recognise Australia in a single personality than the canonisation of the Aussie digger. The soldier, wearing the trademark slouch hat, is egalitarian mateship made flesh and blood. And when that blood is shed, the whole nation is expected to nurse wounds. I know of no other country, for instance, where the awarding of military honours creates so much news. Corporal Ben Roberts-Smith, the giant of a man granted the Victoria Cross in 2011 for singlehandedly charging and destroying two Taliban gun emplacements, was portrayed as a thoroughbred among thoroughbreds, a champion of the breed.

Likewise, I know of no other country where the death of a member of the armed forces draws both the prime minister and the leader of the opposition to the funeral. In Australia, a country that tends to downplay the ceremonial, it has become politically sacrosanct.

It also explains why Anzac Day has defied the predictions of those in the early 1970s who thought they were witnessing its last gasps to become the de facto national day. Its enduring appeal lies in the simple truth that it remains, as Horne noted in the early 1960s, 'an expression of the commonness of man'. However, is not Anzac revivalism also an expression of a country that finds it hard to express itself? It is comforting to locate the country's foundation story in the blood and senselessness of Gallipoli, with all the myths that have grown up around that period of national trauma. But is it not also a tad intellectually lazy? Once again, mythic Australia is easier to define than the real thing.

Doubtless for many older Australians, Anzac Day also helps maintain the link with an essentially Anglo-Australia at a time of disorientating demographic change. Its appeal for the young, who flock to Gallipoli in such huge numbers, is more intriguing. One possible explanation is that the commemorations have come to fill a vacuum: the void left by the failure to define Australia in a less maudlin, sepia-tinted or mateship-orientated manner. Whereas for older generations Anzac Day has become a firm anchor, for the young it shows their sense of national identity to be somewhat adrift. They need to travel to the cliffs of Pine Cove to go in search of their country.

At least the Australian digger usually offers a positive role model. All too often, the country allows itself to be defined by the 'Ugly Australian'. The bogan. The vulgarian. The thugs who beat up Indian-born taxi drivers in Sydney and Melbourne. The rioters at Cronulla. The senior defence personnel who posted online horribly sexist messages and photos denigrating women, which in 2013 embroiled the Australian Defence Force in yet another scandal. In all of these instances, however, characters appeared as a counterpoint, more representative of Australia as a whole. During the attacks against taxi drivers, it was Mia Northrop, a thirty-something web designer, who organised the Vindaloo against Violence, where thousands of her fellow Melburnians went out for a curry to show their solidarity with Indian immigrants. In the scandal involving the Australian defence personnel, it was commander Lieutenant-General David Morrison, the head of the Australian army, who posted a video to his troops with the stirring rejoinder: 'The standard you walk past is the standard you accept.' In Cronulla, it was the members of the local surf life saving club who launched a campaign to recruit Muslim members. This initiative led to the invention, by an Australian, of the burqini, a swimsuit in which Islamic women would feel comfortable at the beach.

Australia is Pat Rafter, the most likeable successful sportsman I have ever had the pleasure of meeting, more so than Lleyton Hewitt. It is Hazem El Masri, the brilliant Lebanese Australian footy star, more so than the legion of hard-drinking, hard-hitting boofheads who have brought dishonour on their code. It is John Eales rather than Quade Cooper. It is the loveable, irascible and extravagantly gifted Shane Warne, rather than the errant child with a roaming eye and a roaming mobile. But again, Australia all too easily lapses into negative stereotyping. Australians could be talking themselves up, when the preference is often for talking themselves down. Again, a failure of language is partly to blame.

Asked to assess the performance of Julia Gillard during her prime ministership, members of political focus groups would regularly complain about the Welsh-born leader's voice. More land of 'strine than land of song, her speech seemed to originate from her nasal passage rather than her larynx. Also, she had a tendency to add extra syllables even to monosyllabic words. When making public statements her delivery was often halting and ponderous, as if reading a scary story to a classroom full of pre-schoolers. Though fluent as a deputy prime minister, when she spoke at regular pitch and pace, she struggled to find a prime ministerial voice, partly, it seemed, because she had made such a conscious effort to do so. For those random focus group participants the problem was not how the voice sounded to them, but rather the impression it created internationally. 'The Kath and Kim voice feeds this idea that we're a nation of Shane Warnes,' says Rebecca Huntley, the social commentator who carried out the research. 'Twenty years ago it was the cultural elites who used to cringe at the stereotypical Paul Hogan, Steve Irwin and Shane Warne view of Australia. Now that's part of a much broader discussion. People are very aware of what the world imagines Australia to be, and what we really are. We want our national profile to reflect our lived experience. They're open to a more complex and sophisticated view of what Australia is.'

The irony is that words and new expressions are the first indicator of cultural change and that academic lexicographers usually have to race to catch up. Australia at present seems to defy that lexicographical rule.

Thankfully, a new vocabulary does appear to be slowly emerging that reflects the nearness of Australia. Gillard and Wayne Swan talked repeatedly about being in 'the right place at the right time'. Bob Carr, the former foreign affairs minister, regularly used the phrase 'Asianised' to describe the country he represented on the international stage. Tim Harcourt, the self-styled 'Airport Economist', talks now about the 'power of proximity'. In a shrewd inversion, the foreign policy thinker Michael Wesley has spoken of the 'tyranny of proximity', because of the potential threat posed by emergent China.

Even internationally, where clichés die hard, the phrase 'down under' is used less commonly. In the 13,000-word special report in which *The Economist* dubbed Australia the 'next Golden State', the words 'down under' did not appear. In the wake of the Obama administration's Asian pivot, Charles Emmerson, a scholar at Chatham House in London, referred to 'the pivotal country', eschewing the conventional Lucky Country. *The New York Times* located the country in China's 'strategic backyard'.

Still, nothing underscores the failure of the national vocabulary more than the rise of the term 'un-Australian'. Even though the term was first used in the 1850s, and has been uttered intermittently ever since, it re-entered the lexis in the mid-1990s, mainly in reference to asylum seekers, Asian immigrants or anyone who refused to adhere to the dominant culture. In 1995, the word was used in metropolitan newspapers 68 times. By 2004, it was 571. When the Macquarie Dictionary first decided to use the word, they said it was in response to a 'burst' in its usage from John Howard and Pauline Hanson. But it is remarkable how the word is now used on the left as well as the right. Indeed, some turned the language back on Hanson, and said her immigration policies were 'un-Australian'. Now, its use is wholesale.

The rise of 'un-Australian' shows, above all, that Australians have become much more adept at describing what they are not rather than articulating what they truly are. It speaks of the need for a rhetorical rethink.

Chapter 3

AUSTRALIA'S POLITICAL CRINGE

MEASURED IN THE BLOOD spilt in leadership challenges or the bile spewed daily in parliament, the developed world's most stable economy has produced the most volatile and petty politics. To outside observers, who have marvelled at the 'wonder from down under' economy, this is hard to fathom. As the prime ministership passed from John Howard to Kevin Rudd to Julia Gillard to Rudd again and then to Tony Abbott, they looked on askance, like freeway rubber-neckers passing the scene of a major pile-up made all the more inexplicable because the driving conditions seemed so perfect at the time.

This high political casualty rate has made Canberra the coup capital of the democratic world. Australia even has its own unique language for leadership changes – 'the spill', 'to be rolled' – which spoke of the problem. From late 2006, when the caucus room turned on Kim Beazley, the ALP had five different leaders in seven years. Between 2007 and 2010, the Liberal Party had four different leaders: Howard, Brendan

Nelson, Malcolm Turnbull and Abbott. Managers of the premier league football club Chelsea enjoy greater job security. Of the six national ALP and Liberal Party leaders who lost their jobs, Howard was the only one turfed out solely by the electorate. In the space of three especially manic months in 2013, Australia had three different prime ministers.

At the state and territory level, too, there has been a hurtling turnover of leaders. In just seven years, the New South Wales Labor Party had five: Bob Carr, Morris Iemma, Nathan Rees, Kristina Keneally and John Robertson (as I write, I am Googling that list to make sure I have not omitted a stray name). Even leaders who won elections were not spared. In the Northern Territory, after securing a long-awaited victory bringing 11 years of ALP rule to an end, Terry Mills survived just six months in the job. In true coup style, he learned of his sacking via a telephone call while conducting a trade mission to Japan. Ted Baillieu, the premier of Victoria, survived longer, just over two years, but resigned as leader when scandal engulfed his office. Mike Rann, the long-time premier of South Australia, also had to relinquish power a year and a half after voters returned him to office because of a party room revolt. The state's Liberal leader, Isobel Redmond, who had once volunteered to be tasered by police, was at more risk from colleagues, who ended up felling her. It looked furiously cannibalistic, but these swift leadership changes were usually the product of cold calculation.

No two words more neatly encapsulated the prevailing mood in Canberra than those uttered by Julia Gillard, her first in the well of the House of Representatives as prime minister, when Tony Abbott approached to offer his congratulations: 'Game on.' Politics was sport. Her boast to ABC's *Australian Story*, during an interview in 2006, also ended up being prescient as well as apposite: 'I'm not naive, you know,

I'm not Doris Day who's just somehow parachuted into Canberra. I had to fight hard to get preselected, I had to play a factional game to do that, I had to count numbers, I had to make deals and I'd do all of that again tomorrow if I needed to.' Again, her words spoke of the ruthless and unprincipled spirit of the times, and also its political myopia.

As for Abbott, the choice of title for his autobiography-cum-manifesto typified his approach: *Battlelines*. So, too, did his promise earlier in his career to be a 'junkyard dog savaging the other side'.

Too many politicians appeared to have taken Paul Keating's acid dictum at face value: 'If you're in politics, you're in the conflict business.' However, there was more to Keating than barbs and bromides. He was in the nation-building business. That is a key behavioural shift. Though aggression has always been central to Australian politics, it has not always been the sine qua non. Moreover, the bellicosity of times past arose out of a genuine battle of ideas. Passion lay behind firm-held beliefs. Now, politics is politics.

Visiting Parliament House for the first time in 2006 I experienced first-hand the ferocious political gamesmanship, and also the awe in which its most accomplished practitioners were held. After a particularly fiery Question Time, I attended a dinner in the Members' Hall where I was seated next to a Labor MP who had been ejected that afternoon from the chamber. Throughout supper, as he sipped on his chilled chardonnay as if it was vintage champagne, admiring colleagues came up to slap him on the back and to offer congratulations. After his spell in the parliamentary 'sin bin', he was the hero of the hour. New to Capital Circle politics, I thought my dinner companion must be the kind of professional troublemaker that every parliament throws up. The jester. The loveable rogue. But the lawmaker in question was

Joel Fitzgibbon, who would soon take on one of the most grown-up ministerial portfolios going, that of running the defence department. The irascible Fitzgibbon, though not unlikeable, typified the modern-day Canberra politician: aggressive, hyper-partisan, scheming, and a headkicker very much in the 'Game on' mould.

That early Canberra visit also brought me into contact for the first time with Kevin Rudd, the then shadow foreign affairs minister. Rudd was part of a panel discussion I had to chair that also featured his front-bench Labor colleagues Lindsay Tanner and Martin Ferguson. Rudd was charmless to the point of outright rudeness, and I was more impressed by Tanner, who seemed just as sharp but more human. Over dinner, I rhapsodised about the member for Melbourne, assuming, naively, that he, rather than Rudd, must be the coming man. But my dinner companions quickly pointed out the error of my ways. By then, Rudd, who had built up such a strong personal following on the *Sunrise* breakfast show, was deemed more electable. Tanner, by contrast, came from the wrong faction. Few in the ALP warmed to Rudd – many loathed him, even then – but it mattered not. He was a vehicle to regain power, however joyless the ride. It provided a valuable early lesson in the overlapping importance of polls, factionalism and the cold-bloodedness of Labor chieftains.

Thereafter, one of the biggest challenges in covering Australian politics was to make sense of Rudd's Hawke-like approval ratings – which were made all the more inexplicable because he was so unlike Hawke. Each time he uttered one of those faux larrikinisms or ended a press conference with that nerdy pay-off, 'I've gotta zip,' I was reminded of what Mark Twain once said of the music of Richard Wagner: it was better than it sounded. Kevin 07 felt like a personality cult without a personality. But therein lay another lesson:

Rudd seemed so good, because his fellow parliamentarians seemed so bad.

On the Liberal side of politics, Malcolm Turnbull benefited from the same phenomenon. Following him around a Sydney shopping centre in his eastern suburbs constituency of Wentworth during the 2007 campaign, where he faced a tough fight to retain his seat, he seemed too self-conscious for retail politics. For a start, he apologised to voters for exposing them to a camera crew – the act of a gentleman, but not a natural campaigner. His political weaknesses also became evident throughout his short-lived spell as leader between September 2008 and December 2009, and were exposed most starkly during the disastrous Godwin Grech Utegate affair, when he arrogantly thought he could bring down the Rudd government with what turned out to be a forged email from a wayward Treasury official. Still, Turnbull continued to be popular with the public, if not Liberal colleagues, partly because the alternatives were so unattractive. Maybe he was liked precisely because he was not particularly adept at politics, but brought other non-political strengths, not least his stellar curriculum vitae.

Covering this phase in political life, and comparing it to what was happening elsewhere in Australia, it was impossible not to be struck by the discrepancy between the national story and the Canberra story. Over this period, Australian political life suffered from a crisis of overpoliticisation. It came to be exemplified by the rise of a political class overexposed to politics and sequestered in the capital from everyday life.

Excessive partisanship became the order of the day. Gone was the spirit of collegiality that marked a healthy parliament. In a move that crystallised the lack of basic decency, the opposition barred the then arts minister Simon Crean from attending the memorial service of one of the country's beloved artists, Margaret Olley, by refusing to grant him a voting 'pair' – allowing him to leave parliament without endangering the government's thin majority. Craig Thomson, the disgraced former Labor MP, initially was not even allowed a pair to attend the birth of his second child. The historian John Hirst has spoken of a 'democracy of manners', meaning that Australians 'talk to each other as if they are equals' and 'blot out differences when people meet face to face'. Suffice to say, he was not referring to the incivility on daily display inside the Capital Circle. An irony was that parliament, until 2012, banned footage from its chambers being used for comic purposes. Yet so self-satirising was Question Time that it did not require jokester middlemen.

More and more, the Senate, supposedly the deliberatively upper house, has taken on the character of the House of Representatives. It is the home to some of Canberra's sharpest partisans: Stephen Conroy, Doug Cameron and Penny Wong for the ALP; Cory Bernardi, Concetta Fierravanti-Wells and Eric Abetz for the Liberals; Barnaby Joyce for the Nationals; Christine Milne and Sarah Hanson-Young for the Greens. Rarely has debate in the upper chamber been so shrill or so infantile. Given her well-documented problems afterwards, it may seem cruel to single out Mary Jo Fisher's bizarre performance of the 'Hokey Pokey' and the 'Time Warp' during a debate on climate change. But with each pelvic thrust she diminished the standing of the Senate. Nor was there anything deliberative about her fellow South Australian Cory Bernardi's fevered assertion that same sex marriage would lead 'crazy people out there' to push for 'consensual sexual relations between humans and animals'.

A bitter and abusive parliament also lost much-needed voices of moderation. On the conservative side, small-l Liberals like Petro Georgiou, Judith Troeth and Bruce Baird, who had all clashed with John Howard over asylum seekers. On Labor's, Lindsay Tanner, Stephen Smith and Martin Ferguson, three grown-ups in the party. Politicians of talent and stature ended their careers prematurely: Peter Costello, Brendan Nelson, Greg Combet, and again Smith and Tanner. Their departure accelerated the country's political fall.

The world took note. In proclaiming Australia 'the next Golden State', *The Economist* was shocked nonetheless by its penurious politics. 'From this unpromising ground, little thoughtful activity emerges,' wrote its veteran correspondent John Grimond, echoing Patrick White's thoughts on the great Australian emptiness. 'Its current political leaders, with notable exceptions, are perhaps the least impressive feature of today's Australia.' During the 2010 election, *The Economist* assailed the country's 'desperately impoverished politics'.

After watching parliamentary question times, with its mix of Dorothy Dixer softballs from the government benches and angry onslaught from the opposition, Matthew Engel penned a savage critique for the *Financial Times*. From the Israeli Knesset to the Dáil in Dublin, Engel had witnessed a few 'crazy' parliaments. Overwhelmed by its weirdness, he deemed Canberra's House of Representatives to be the worst. Watching Question Time was an especially torrid experience. 'Theatre?' he asked in horror. 'Only of the absurd. Almost every single word is scripted, and Australia seems to have completely lost the plot. Mercifully, the Australian parliament sits for only about 80 days a year (the human brain – and bottom – could hardly tolerate much more).'

Like others, he was confused by how such an impressive country produced such a vicious politics. 'Since the Aussies are currently running the most successful economy of any western democracy,' wrote the former editor of *Wisden Cricketers' Almanack*, and a long-time visitor to this country, 'it might seem a sensible place from which to borrow ideas. But Australia's current prosperity is based on flogging its natural resources to the eager Chinese: it can't be anything to do with its politicians.' Engel ended with a flourish: 'The one thing the MPs can do is overthrow their leaders, which they do with great zest, in the manner of Roman slaves celebrating Saturnalia.'

Even one-time admirers of Australian politics were appalled at the behaviour on display. Iain Dale, the British conservative blogger, arrived a self-professed admirer of its confrontational parliamentary tradition. Then he observed two sessions of Question Time. 'I have never seen anything like the Australian parliament,' he wrote. 'It is an absolutely shameful, horrific spectacle.' He added: 'Australians take adversarial politics to ridiculous levels. The pure hatred and loathing on the faces of the Prime Minister and Leader of the Opposition have to be seen to be believed.'

Another long-time admirer, Kurt M. Campbell, the Obama administration's one-time point man on Asia, put it succinctly: 'The country's politics have often followed an unusual inverse relationship: the better the times, the nastier the politics.'

Nor was it just parliament that drew negative reviews. Campaigns were even worse. Niall Ferguson, the Harvard academic and author, happened to be in Australia during the 2010 campaign, and was appalled. 'It is true to say that there is a quality of Australian political debate very reminiscent of local politics in Glasgow when I was growing up,' he told Mark Colvin on ABC's *PM* programme. 'There is a parochialism combined with, I'm going to say, an edge of nastiness that is very familiar.' As well as being ugly, it seemed inward-looking. 'Now it may seem mean to use a term like parochialism but I think it is justified when you reflect on the magnitude of the changes that we are living through – massive shifts in the global economy, a radical transfer of economic power from the west to the east. And one listens to the contenders for the Australian premiership discussing in the most oblique and mealy-mouthed way issues about immigration and infrastructure that really, you know, sound more like Strathclyde Regional Council than a debate for the leadership of a major power in the Asia-Pacific.' He was right. The smallness of national politics gave it a municipal feel. It was as if Gillard and Abbott were competing to become the mayor of a medium-sized city, rather than contesting the leadership of an ever more thrusting nation.

Comical as well as nasty, Australian politics also became a global laughing stock. Canberra more than met the requirements of the viral age, serving up a steady stream of inadvertently hilarious videos that instantly became what these days we call an internet sensation or, on Twitter, a must-see. The showreel included Anthony Albanese ventriloquising Aaron Sorkin's script-lines from the movie *The American President* ('Tony Abbott is not the least bit interested in fixing anything,' he said, repeating lines first delivered by the actor Michael Douglas. 'He's only interested in two things – making Australians afraid of it and telling them who's to blame for it.'); Bill Shorten loyally echoing the words of the prime minister, even if he did not know what they were ('I don't know what the PM said,' he declared during an interview on Sky News, 'but I agree.'); Kevin Rudd munching on his ear wax; or Craig Emerson's peculiar decision to break into song with his 'Whyalla Wipeout', which was all the more side-splitting because of the time it took his hapless aide to press 'play' on the ghetto blaster providing the backing track. Emerson's singing was a reminder of how Canberra transforms the supposedly highly intelligent into clowns. Emerson was one of the few members of the Gillard ministry who held a PhD, in economics from the Australian National University.

On the Liberal side, there was Julie Bishop's 'death stare', the environment minister, Greg Hunt, quoting from Wikipedia on the BBC to dismiss any link between bushfires and climate change (Wikipedia 'opens up with the fact that bushfires in Australia are frequently occurring events during the hotter months of the year', he blathered), and Tony Abbott's mysteriously mute response to questioning from Channel Seven's chief political correspondent, Mark Riley, where he stood silent and motionless, aside from juddering nods of the head, as if he had just been set free, near hypothermic, after being trapped inside a butcher's cold room.

Abbott, though he deserved to be taken more seriously, was easy to lampoon. Commonly he was referred to as the 'Mad Monk' in the foreign press. His crude assessment that the argument behind global warming was 'absolute crap', though lauded by the growing band of climate-change sceptics, drew scorn from the international science community. In a lighter vein, his penchant for skimpy swimwear became a staple of overseas coverage. Once I had to argue with an editor in London to persuade him that British viewers should be introduced to the term 'budgie smugglers' and shown the pictures of him wading into the surf in his skimpy Speedos. Thereafter, London wanted those shots every time.

Even for a correspondent who tried to convince international audiences that Australia was not a country where a Crocodile Dundee-like character lurked behind every eucalypt, Bob Katter was irresistible. First, there was his campaign video during the 2010 election, where the 'Force from the North', resplendent in his ten-gallon hat, showed that he could rap and pump iron at the same time. Then there was his live interview with Kerry O'Brien in a special edition of *The 7.30 Report* on the Sunday evening after Saturday's inconclusive poll. 'There's a freedom issue here,' said Katter, in a soundbite that came dressed as a gift horse. 'You know we're not allowed to fish much at all, we're not allowed to go camping or shooting or even boiling the billy. We've got a terrible problem with the deadly flying foxes. They're going to kill many more people than taipan snakes do in Australia.' The only thing missing were corks dangling from his hat.

Parliament House seemed unusually highly populated by oddballs. Stranger still, some of them came to occupy the most senior parliamentary positions. Taking over the speakership of the House of Representatives, and mindful of the low regard in which parliament now was held, Peter Slipper set out to impose a stricter sense of discipline by ejecting people from the chamber in the manner of a London bobby dispersing a mob of East End urchins. But the Queenslander himself had no authority and was ridiculed as a figure of fun. Small wonder. First there were the dandyish sartorial trappings he brought to the job. The collarette of a Wiltshire curate. The white bow-tie of a Cunard steward. The creaseless gown of an Oxbridge vice-chancellor. Looking like a character from *Northanger Abbey*, it was almost as if he had disappeared down some Victorian-era wormhole only to see the light of day again on the banks of Lake Burley Griffin. Then came his newly instituted weekly procession, during which he edged towards the chamber behind the golden mace of parliament with such stiffness and precision that it looked as if he were clenching a crisp fifty-dollar note between his buttocks. Not since Shane Warne was snapped wearing a pair of Playboy undies and cavorting with an inflatable penis had an Australian male suffered such a lapse of judgement in clothing and prop selections.

Slipper, of course, ended up bringing even more dishonour on the House. In a curious affair which also had echoes of the 19th century, with its suppressed homosexuality, and also a 21st century twist, with the use of smart phone technology, he fired off a series of lewd text messages likening the female genitalia to shellfish. 'They look like mussel removed from its shell,' he wrote to his aide, James Ashby, the target of his affections. 'Look at the bottle of mussel meat.' In another, he was blunter still: 'Look at a bottle of mussel meat. Salty Cunts in brine!'

An effect of Slipper's bizarre behaviour was to grant an air of normalcy to figures like Bill 'Wild Bill' Heffernan, a long-time crackpot with a penchant for impersonating other people on the telephone, whether an ASIO agent, the devil or Barnaby Joyce. Similarly, the South Australian senator Nick Xenophon, who had entered parliament with a frivolous reputation because of his eye-catching antics, looked like a parliamentary colossus, a Capital Circle Cicero.

Even Slipper seemed compos mentis compared to the Family First senator Steve Fielding, who once dressed up as a giant beer bottle to advertise his campaign for a bottle return scheme and who pushed a mini-shopping cart around Parliament House to highlight cost of living pressures. Having flicked the switch to vaudeville, Fielding struggled to turn it off. As with Mary Jo Fisher, it seems cruel to dwell on his shortcomings because they hinted at more serious deficiencies. Among the cruellest things I have seen on Australian television was when Fielding, a 'Young Earth creationist', appeared on the same *Q&A* panel discussion as the evolutionary biologist Richard Dawkins. After realising he was up against a clown, the Oxford professor actually ended up showing more mercy than the show's producers, who had set him up to be ridiculed. But Fielding was impossible to ignore. For a time, he held the balance of power in the upper house. At the height of the global financial crisis, his support for the Rudd government's stimulus package was vital. In a sign of his goofiness, he demanded $4 billion to fund his own mini-stimulus package.

The 2013 federal election, more so than its ugly sister the 2010 campaign, was even easier to send up. For starters, it threw up Stephanie Banister, the One Nation candidate who thought Jews followed Jesus, and mistook Islam for a country. She had come to the attention of the Channel Seven interviewer because she had gone round her local Woolworths daubing stickers on Nestle products warning: 'Beware! Halal food funds terrorism.' *Politico*, the online daily of Beltway insiders in Washington, asked whether she was the 'dumbest candidate ever'.

On the Warhol scale of transitory fame, Banister had a rival in Peter Dowling, the head of the Queensland parliament's ethics committee, who sexted a selfie of his penis 'plonked in a glass of red wine'.

Jaymes Diaz, the Liberal candidate for Greenway, also made global waves, for his hapless response to the reporter from Channel Ten who requested that he outline the Coalition's six-point plan to stop the boats. 'Well, one of the points, the key point would be stopping the boats when it's safe to do so,' he yammered, as he struggled to come up with a single one. When I had visited the seat of Greenway in northwest Sydney a few months earlier, even diehard Labor activists, sitting forlornly in a sparsely attended Sunday morning branch meeting, were resigned to defeat. It was the ALP's most marginal seat in New South Wales, and its third most vulnerable in the country. But they had not reckoned on the haplessness of Diaz.

Mining this comic gold, *The Daily Show* put together one of its most hilarious riffs, which alongside Diaz and

Banister ran the footage of Tony Abbott upending the traditional campaign technique of kissing babies by smooching the back of a young mother's head. Had the comedy show waited another 24 hours, it could have included Abbott's more memorable gaffe, his admission that he would never claim to be 'the suppository of all wisdom'. Nor did Clive Palmer get a mention, though he could have been invented with the Comedy Central cable channel in mind.

Occasionally, Australian politics received a laudatory foreign press. Julia Gillard drew praise for the carbon tax, most notably from *The Atlantic* magazine, which placed her in its list of '50 brave thinkers'. Still, the magazine only got the politics behind this move half-right. It noted that she was '[n]udged out onto this limb by the politics of coalition-building', when truly the Greens had dragooned her. Michael Bloomberg, the then mayor of New York, praised the Gillard government's stringent new tobacco labelling laws, which opened up an important new front in the fight against Big Tobacco. Gillard's misogyny speech went down a storm internationally, where its domestic context, the defence of Peter Slipper, meant nothing. *Jezebel*, the feminist blog, called her 'one bad-ass motherfucker', no less.

Tellingly, however, it was politics of a different vintage that often caught the eye. In the aftermath of the Sandy Hook massacre in December 2012, where 20 children and six staff at a school in Connecticut were gunned down by a deranged 20-year-old, John Howard became an unlikely hero of the US comedy shows for his brave advocacy of gun control in response to Port Arthur. The iconic image of Howard fronting up to a hostile crowd of gun-owners, the bulky lines of his bullet-proof body armour easily visible through his suit jacket, flashed around the world. Overall, though, the global coverage of Australian domestic politics was almost universally negative.

Of course, it was not as if Australian commentators required haughty outsiders to point out what they could see for themselves. Alarmed by the rowdiness of parliament, *The Daily Telegraph* set up a meter to test the decibel level of the House of Representatives, and then compared it to the noise level in a daycare centre. Channel Nine's Laurie Oakes, the dean of the Canberra press gallery, also yearned for more grown-up politicians. 'The sad truth is we have a couple of political pygmies heading the two major parties,' he wrote during the 2010 campaign. 'Both have small ambitions for the country. Both are afraid to lead.' Thereafter, as the quality of politics plummeted further, the tone of his weekly columns became even more excoriating. After enduring yet another risible photo-opportunity, which saw a party leader donning the mandatory fluoro jacket, he could take it no more. 'During the week, Tony Abbott lavished praise on a company investing $50 million in a recycling plant "that will convert garbage into power". It was not a bad description of what the Opposition leader himself is up to.'

For Canberra watchers, Horne's well-worn dictum about the country being 'run by second-rate people who share its luck' came to be continually recycled. Had they delved deeper into the Horne canon, however, they would have found quotes from his autobiography, *An Interrupted Life*, that were even more pertinent. Savaging the quality of politicians in the immediate post-war period, he wrote that 'Canberra had the mentality of a small frontier settlement . . . that parliament provided a living exhibition of semi-literates; that the most serious distortion of newspaper reporting of parliament was to make politicians seem better than they were . . . that politics was marked by tedium, stupidity and vulgarity; that most politicians were too old; that too few were university graduates, too few had been abroad, and most showed narrow prejudices against the "un-Australian"; that many politicians were openly prejudiced against modern trends towards sex equality and saw women as wives and mothers but not as citizens; and not one of them could be described as liberal. They were all book-banners and intolerant bourgeois moralists.'

Outside of the Canberra press gallery, the public's aversion to Canberra politics intensified. Because of compulsory voting, Australians do not have the option of expressing their disengagement through low turnouts, the usual indicator of a sickly democracy. They do, however, get the chance to cast informal votes. In 2010, 5.5 per cent of the electorate chose that path, an unusually high proportion. In 2013, the figure was higher still, 5.9 per cent. That was the worst level since the 6.4 per cent informal vote in 1984, an anomalous election because it marked the introduction of above-the-line voting in the Senate which puzzled voters. Confusion, especially among non-English speaking voters, remained a factor. The constituencies of Watson, Fowler and Blaxland, the seats with the highest proportion of non-English speaking voters, returned the highest informal tallies in 2013, as they did in 2010. But the national trend surely had more to do with a sense of malaise than muddle.

In the last two federal elections, the commonplace refrain of shopping mall vox pops was that neither side deserved to win, and that the 'None of the above' party would have romped home to victory. In 2010, the leaders' debate even had to be rescheduled so as not to clash with *MasterChef*, a sign of how unappetising politics had become. The inconclusive result on polling day was a product of this broad feeling of discontent. There was unhappiness with the Labor government, but not enough enthusiasm for Tony Abbott to lift him to power.

Voter disdain towards Gillard and Abbott continued during the minority government phase, and was highlighted by the comparative popularity of Kevin Rudd and Malcolm Turnbull as preferred prime minister. In September 2012, after allegations surfaced about Abbott's boorish student antics, polls showed that Turnbull was twice as popular as the man who replaced him. Rudd, too, had a 32-point lead over Gillard in the preferred leader stakes. Voters seemed to favour 'Ruddbullism', a less destructive form of politics that occasionally produced bipartisanship on issues like the first stimulus package and reconciliation, rather than two party leaders who brought out the worst in each other.

The miscellany of fringe parties in the Senate, which according to the stock analogy made the upper house resemble the bar scene in *Star Wars* with its assortment of freakish characters, can be seen as but another symptom of this malaise. The 2013 election saw the return of two senators from the Palmer United Party, and one each from the Australian Sports Party, Family First, the Democratic Labour Party, the Liberal Democratic Party and the Australian Motoring Enthusiast Party. Hardly top gear.

There also seems to be a rising mood of anti-incumbency, certainly at the federal level, overturning the long-standing preference for stability. The 2007–2010 Labor government became the first since 1931 not to win outright a second term in office. Then, after Tony Abbott won in 2013, the new federal government almost instantly faced a barrage of negative polls.

Especially disdainful are the young. In 2013, for the second year running, the annual Lowy Institute poll found that less than half of 18–29 year olds agreed with the statement: 'Democracy is preferable to any other form of government.' One obvious explanation was the raucous tone of political discourse.

It all suggested that the cultural cringe had been supplanted by the political cringe: an overwhelming sense that Canberra had become embarrassingly second-rate. A study published in 2013 by the Scanlon Foundation and Monash University came up with the telling finding that the Australian public were concerned more by the quality of politicians and government than they were by asylum seekers.

Politicians have not been a complete turn-off. The ABC political panel show *Q&A* attracted a loyal viewership, even though it often brought the ugliness of parliament into the lounge room, and appeared to encourage heated confrontations which it could run as promos for next week's show. Still, the editions that appeared to draw plaudits, as well as the more appreciative audiences, were those excluding politicians altogether.

Annabel Crabb's *Kitchen Cabinet*, where she interviewed politicians at their cookers, barbeques and renovated white countertops, turned out to be an unexpected ratings winner, partly because of the winsomeness of its hostess. But it also demonstrated that Australians preferred their MPs away from everyday politics, when they conversed like normal human beings rather than regurgitating prefabricated messages of the day. When politicians were depoliticised, people tuned in.

The surge of popularity and instant revisionism that Julia Gillard came to enjoy after being ousted from office in 2013 was part of the same trend. During her years as prime minister, she sounded like a political automaton. On leaving The Lodge, she rediscovered her true voice, which sounded refreshingly natural, softer and less overtly political. In her appearances before sell-out audiences in Sydney and Melbourne, she also displayed a newfound magnanimity, a virtue rarely witnessed in parliament. Evidently, this is how

Australians would prefer their elected representatives to be. They warmed to their politicians when they did not act like politicians.

Australian politics changed abruptly on 9 July 2006, when an era of leadership stability quickly gave way to the era of leadership speculation. That morning, Sunday titles in the News Limited stable carried an exclusive report from press gallery veteran Glenn Milne, revealing the details of an arrangement between John Howard and his deputy Peter Costello on a timetable for the handover of the Liberal leadership, and with it the prime ministership. Milne's front-page story, published under the headline 'PM Broke His Secret Deal', came with a smoking gun – or, more accurately, a dog-eared scrap of paper that the former defence minister Ian McLachlan had carried in his wallet for more than a decade. With the diligence of a company secretary, McLachlan had recorded a meeting conducted in December 1994 at which Howard supposedly pledged to serve one and a half terms as prime minister. Costello, now entering his 11th year as treasurer, had come to regard it as a promissory note. With his tacit blessing, the private became public and ended up on the front page of 'The Tele'.

Over the years, the press gallery had grown used to Costello venting his frustration over his thwarted ambition and Howard's alleged treachery. What made this episode different was the growing feeling that Howard, who had now passed his 65th birthday, had done his dash. With the treasurer seen as a more potent threat, and with McLachlan's note providing documentary evidence backing his claim, Canberra witnessed a frenzy of leadership speculation. Unbeknown to us at the time, the rumpus that followed set the tone for the next six years.

Costello, as history now knows, did not have the numbers or 'the ticker' to roll his long-time boss and rival. Howard has also since admitted that, prior to Milne's story appearing, he was prepared to step aside, but decided after its publication to stay on. However, the uncertainty over whether he would contest the 2007 election as leader continued almost until polling day itself. Each new doom-laden poll only heightened the swirl of doubt encircling his leadership. So did each hike in interest rates. In a biography of John Howard written by Peter van Onselen and Wayne Errington, Costello questioned his boss's commitment to economic rationalism, a deliberately low blow which led to another burst of conjecture. It also emerged that Costello had informed three journalists over dinner at the Water's Edge restaurant in Canberra in June 2005 that he could win the forthcoming election but that Howard could not, which again produced another flurry.

As late as September's APEC summit, cabinet members gathered secretly at a hotel in Sydney's CBD, a meeting initiated by Howard, and reached the consensus that their elderly leader should go. The problem was that only Joe Hockey and Malcolm Turnbull had the courage to tell him directly. Howard insisted that there would have to be a putsch so as not to make him look like a coward running away from certain defeat, but no one was prepared to organise it.

Even after APEC's family photo had been taken, with just weeks to go before the 24 November polling day, there was conjecture that he might dramatically step aside, not only to save himself the disappointment of being evicted from Kirribilli House but the humiliation of losing Bennelong, his suburban Sydney seat. Instead, he came up with a fudge, 'a conditional retirement plan', as he called it, which would see him continuing on as prime minister in the unlikely event of victory but handing over to Costello relatively shortly afterwards.

The ALP, faced with a leadership dilemma of its own a year earlier, had acted more ruthlessly. When Kim Beazley confused Rove McManus with Karl Rove, the party room decided it was time for its gaffe-prone leader to go. The Rudd/Gillard ticket that emerged not only looked stable, but for those already looking over the political horizon it seemed orderly and predictable. If Rudd went on to win big in the federal election, as he did, he would presumably serve a couple of terms before handing over to his ambitious deputy, whose backing had been instrumental in lifting him to the leadership.

Such was his soaring popularity to begin with that Rudd had the demeanour of a prime minister who would one day have the word 'era' attached to his name. For the next three years, his relationship with Gillard was also workable. 'He could woo the electorate and she could pull the caucus in behind him,' wrote Bruce Hawker in his memoir of the 2013 campaign. 'They were the yin and the yang of the Labor Party.' Then, catastrophically, it fell apart. It was not unusual for opposition parties to change leader. But for a government to change prime minister after such a brief spell in office was unprecedented.

On the Liberal side, too, the presumed succession plan never eventuated. The morning after the 2007 election brought the surprise announcement from Peter Costello that he would not seek the vacant leadership. The problem was, of course, that no one truly believed him, so he immediately became a destabilising presence on the backbenches. A Costello leadership would have brought discipline and a measure of certainty to the party room. Without him, the party initially floundered.

Over the next three years, Brendan Nelson, who always looked like a caretaker leader, was rolled by Malcolm

Turnbull, who in turn was ousted by Tony Abbott. The member for Warringah, whose accident-prone campaign in 2007 suggested he was simply too erratic ever to reach the top, became the main beneficiary of this age of speculation. Liberal politics seemed to conform to chaos theory. The small note plucked from Ian McLachlan's wallet had helped end the career of the politician it was supposed to help and ultimately blown Tony Abbott into office.

What made this unsettled phase in politics all the more striking was the stability preceding it. Between them, Hawke and Keating kept Labor in power for 13 years. Between February 1967 and March 1996, the ALP only had four leaders, the others being Whitlam and Bill Hayden. Howard managed almost 12 in The Lodge, becoming the longest serving prime minister since Menzies. For the first time in Australian political history, not only had the prime minister served more than ten years in office, but also the two other most senior members of the government, Costello as treasurer and Alexander Downer as foreign affairs minister. By contrast, Labor, under Rudd and Gillard, sustained a majority government for just three years.

Without question, some of the turbulence has been the product of dysfunctional personal relationships at the top of both parties. The mutual distrust between Howard and Costello. Rudd's poisonous relations with Cabinet colleagues. Turnbull's aloofness from his party. Gillard and Rudd's seething hatred.

Between 2010 and 2013 minority government was also a factor, because the government's wafer-thin majority meant its survival was almost continually in doubt. Yet as the demise of Beazley, Nelson, Turnbull and Rudd demonstrated, it predates 2010's inconclusive election. Instability has become endemic, for behavioural and structural reasons.

Much of the blame lies with a myopic fixation with polling. In every capital city, public opinion surveys help keep a running score. For the Beltway commentariat, presidential approval ratings influence the balance of power between the White House and Capitol Hill. They contribute to the background mood music, but do not have the same make-or-break effect on leaders. As for Britain, a poll might provide a useful lead for a Sunday newspaper on an otherwise quiet weekend, but they rarely prompt leadership speculation, as they do here, or determine the outcome.

Nor do polls dominate the news agenda to anywhere near the same extent. In Australia, they have become major news events in their own right, the weekly highlight of often meagre newsroom diaries in a country short on breaking stories. For 24/7 news channels, newspapers online and the Twittersphere, they are manna from heaven. The breathlessness in the coverage of polls heightens their faux news value even further. Reducing the number of Newspoll and Nielsen surveys would for political reporters be akin to cancelling entire rounds of the NRL and AFL for sports writers.

This highlights a broader problem of how the modern-day media and politicians accentuate their worst traits. In the absence of bigger stories, Australian journalists often overly dramatise fairly undramatic events, and vest in them a sense of artificial urgency. The weight bestowed on polls offers a prime example, so, too, the headlines routinely generated by the arrival of boats carrying asylum seekers. The tendency is not just to reflect what is happening, but rather to view events through that fairground hall of mirrors beloved of foreign correspondents, with all its exaggerations and distortions. Because of the media's disproportionate response, politicians react disproportionately as well, creating ever more frenetic news and political cycles, a mad and ceaseless tumble. If there was more news in Australia, surely there would be less leadership speculation.

Thus, as the Rudd coup in June 2010 served to show, Canberra has reached the point where a relatively short run of lacklustre polls could ignite a full-blown leadership crisis. The trigger for the Gillard mutiny was the publication of a Nielsen poll suggesting that a Rudd government would lose that pollster staple 'the election held tomorrow'. Soon after she became prime minister, however, the polls started to show that Gillard was in trouble, and Rudd was more popular, which led to a continuous rumble of leadership speculation.

In other countries it is ordinarily policy failures, like Britain's poll tax, or scandals such as Watergate, that lead to the resignation or dismissal of leaders. In Australia bad polls, more so than the policy shortcomings that caused them, are career-enders. This over-reliance on Newspoll and Nielsen has made a mockery of the cliché that 'there's only one poll that matters'. In Canberra, every poll matters.

An additional reason why they are watched more closely than in Britain, America or elsewhere is because elections come around so quickly. The concertinaed cycles of three-year terms mean that politicians are in continual campaign mode, and focused perpetually on winning the next election. Just as short-termism is built into every policy decision, it dictates political thinking as well. Canberra is beset by a version of the fight-or-flight response, that state of hyper-arousal and combat readiness. Because an election is never far off, there is continuously the sense that blood is about to be spilt.

The abbreviated electoral timetable means, too, that leaders are not given much time to recover from a poor run of polls. Not for Canberra the sporting dictum form is temporary, class is permanent. Form is what counts. Had he not been rolled, my sense is that Rudd would have won the

2010 election comfortably enough. During his slump, he outclassed Tony Abbott in a healthcare debate at the National Press Club, and even John Howard thought he would have gone on to win a second term. The last two Newspolls of Rudd's abbreviated prime ministership showed that, after preferences, the ALP was still ahead of the Coalition. But the Labor caucus was restless and impatient. On the night before his downfall, he reached a tentative agreement with Julia Gillard that he would hand over the leadership later in the year if the government's poll numbers did not pick up. Then a few minutes later, after talking on the phone with her numbers men in an anteroom, she strode back into his office to inform him of the impending spill.

There is, of course, another explanation for Rudd's downfall. It was not that the faceless men feared he was going to lose. Rather, they feared he was going to win, and could not abide another three years of his tantrums, intellectual arrogance and disdain. Union leaders especially wanted a prime minister who did not give the impression of wanting to shampoo the carpet after they had visited.

Engineering his downfall was easy. By contrast, mounting a political coup in Britain is a cumbersome affair akin, in military terms, to manoeuvring an entire naval carrier group. With Australia, there is a litany of martial metaphors from which to choose: the stealth attack; the lightning strike; the quick assassination. All can be pulled off with considerable ease.

The hothouse effect of the bush capital, where politics is all consuming, adds to the trigger-happiness. Lacking much of a hinterland, palace gossip and poll-induced intrigue have become the highest form of entertainment. Serious policy work is obviously being done, and also being reported, but for politicians and journalists alike the sugar hit of leadership speculation trumps less calorific fare. The distractions of the big city, as the madness on Sydney's Macquarie Street proves, does not necessarily lead to a less fixated politics, but the claustrophobia of the Capital Circle, and the micro-culture it has nurtured, is harmful. The nexus between reporters and politicians is made all the more incestuous by the presence of news bureaux in the heart of the parliamentary complex. This differs from Westminster and Washington, where news organisations maintain a presence on Capitol Hill and the Houses of Parliament but also have separate offices outside. Even the architecture of Parliament House reinforces the sense of enclosure. Visitors bestriding the turf laid on its roof make it feel even more hermetically sealed, peering through glass as if looking into some parliamentary zoo. Rarely do its occupants get to breathe fresh, untainted air. There is not even a bar, where gossip and intrigue could vanish into a drunken haze. It is not a healthy ecosystem.

Parliamentary sessions are so short and strung out. The House of Representatives convened for just 66 days in 2013, and not at all in January, April, July or December. The House of Commons, by contrast, met for over 120 days, with a two-month summer recess in July and August. Because sitting weeks in Canberra are so infrequent, they inevitably become the focus of intense activity, which means that parliamentary politics is conducted at a hurtling and disorientating pace. The artificial deadlines imposed by Qantas flight schedules out of Canberra on a Thursday evening only add to the chaotic clatter of events. The timing of what became known as Rudd's non-challenge for the leadership early in 2013 was dictated by the parliamentary calendar. Rudd's lieutenants felt they had to move in March, even without lining up sufficient support, because the Labor caucus was not due to meet until the budget session in mid-May.

The fly-in and fly-out nature of Canberra life, along with its workaholic ways, adds to the sense of unreality. Insalubriously, MPs often end up sharing digs with other MPs. Living in such close proximity in these political frat houses, it is hardly surprising that parliamentarians end up being so completely immersed in politics.

The tribal effect of factional politics also goes a long way towards explaining the 'coup culture'. Factional politics is regarded as a zero sum game, where a victory for one side automatically means a defeat for the other. Consequently, politics is in a permanently antagonistic state, as these factional rivalries play out. The prominence of the 'faceless men' also means that an excessive amount of political power is vested in just a few hands. And when those conspiratorial hands have a smart phone in their grip, the effects can be fatal, as Bill Shorten demonstrated from his table at the Vietnamese restaurant Hong Hua on the eve of Rudd's removal in June 2010. That midwinter night, it took just four powerbrokers – Shorten, Mark Arbib, Don Farrell from South Australia and David Feeney of Victoria – to overthrow a first-term prime minister not yet a thousand days into his job. MPs who went against these powerbrokers, or their backers in the union movement, ran the risk of de-selection.

Britain, in contrast, has loosely assembled camps rather than disciplined factions, and no faceless men or women. Moreover, the only figure with powers equivalent to Canberra's political overlords is the prime minister or party leader. De-selection is rare in Britain. Westminster MPs have more to fear from their electorates than their local constituency organisations, which means they are less easily bullied and corralled.

The fear of de-selection among sitting members – the possibility that they themselves might face a coup in their own parliamentary constituencies – not only contributes to the instability but also fuels partisanship. Among the most noticeable trends in the increasingly unruly US House of Representatives is how the high re-election rate for incumbents – 90 per cent – acts as a bar to moderation, compromise and bipartisanship. Overwhelmingly for House members, the threat to their careers comes not from voters in the general election, but insurgent primary challengers from within their own parties. Moderate and pragmatic lawmakers are especially at risk, because the party can so easily punish them for straying from the partisan path by backing a challenger. In Canberra, where the incumbency rate is also close to 90 per cent, the same dynamic is at work. The politically deviant, which these days translates as the bipartisan-spirited and independent-minded, run the risk of de-selection. On the other hand, loyal partisanship, with all the faux aggressiveness and Dorothy Dixers that come with it, is rewarded with the promise of longevity.

In improving the quality of politics, the media should take some responsibility. To begin with, it needs to wean itself off polls. Perhaps it needs to wean itself off politics. With the hours now devoted to the Capital Circle on the continuous news channels, it is inevitable that the tittle-tattle of palace gossip and the latest round of leadership speculation consume so much airtime. For the print and online media, the problem with writing articles on leadership speculation is that the story arc does not end until there has been a leadership change. One anonymously sourced story spawns another, and they end up having a metastasising effect. In *The Stalking of Julia Gillard*, Kerry-Anne Walsh listed over 130 stories or columns from respected commentators and press gallery reporters between December 2010 and the prime minister's eventual fall in June 2013 essentially saying

'Time's up, Julia!' The drumbeat was ceaseless. Over a two-year period, Walsh's list, which was by no means exhaustive, revealed there were only two months when a 'Gillard is doomed' story did not appear in the press. Almost invariably, these reports accompanied bad polling data. Even after she survived what turned out to be a non-challenge from Kevin Rudd in March 2013, which was supposed to settle the matter definitively, a further run of grim polls did for her just three months later.

Getting political reporters to write about policy has been likened to getting children to eat greens – for the record, Aaron Sorkin came up with that line, and placed it in the mouth of *The West Wing*'s Josh Lyman. All of us enjoy political junk food, but a healthy diet should include Canberra's equivalent of broccoli and kale. For journalists operating in the unremitting atmosphere of the press gallery in an ever more wired age, overpoliticisation has become an occupational hazard.

Covering Australian politics for the BBC, I was often asked whether great ideological or philosophical questions lie at the heart of these leadership contests, a line of questioning laughable to Australian ears. Instead, it is more a case of hardened political professionals calculating how best to cling on to power, where governing capabilities are considered less important than vote-winning capabilities. Politics has essentially become a battle of approval ratings and electability rather than a contest of ideas.

Over the years, however, Canberra has taught us an ugly lesson: that it pays to be ruthless. Widespread is the belief that coups work, and blood is rarely shed in vain. Replacing Bill Hayden with Bob Hawke on the eve of the 1983 election helped secure Labor's victory – although Hayden was comfortably ahead in his last poll as leader. The ALP might not have won a fifth term in office had Paul Keating not rolled the 'Silver Bodgie' in December 1991. Kim Beazley would have struggled against Howard in 2007, whereas Rudd won in a canter. Spills may be an unedifying spectacle but they work.

The whiff of blood is by no means the only problem. Canberra is also giving off the stench of decay, as stagnant ponds are prone when they are not replenished. Politics is so septic because the talent pool is so small. Australia has come to be dominated by a new political class that knows little else but politics.

Consider the members of Julia Gillard's cabinet, whose biographies read like a mustardy *Who's Who* of union officials and former Labor staffers. Simon Crean was a former president of the ACTU, as was Martin Ferguson. Greg Combet was its secretary. Penny Wong was the legal officer for the Liquor, Hospitality and Miscellaneous Workers Union. Nicola Roxon was an organiser for the National Union of Workers. Tony Burke worked for the Shop, Distributive and Allied Employees' Association. Chris Evans was a state secretary of the Fire Brigade Union. Stephen Conroy was the superannuation officer at the Transport Workers' Union. Joe Ludwig was national president of the Australian Workers' Union. Bill Shorten was AWU's national secretary.

Those lacking a strong union pedigree could usually boast a long career in the party. Wayne Swan served as an adviser to leaders Bill Hayden and Kim Beazley. Stephen Smith worked as an adviser for Paul Keating. Craig Emerson served on Bob Hawke's staff. Chris Bowen was a Labor councillor and mayor. Anthony Albanese worked for Bob Carr, during his time as the premier of New South Wales. Julia Gillard herself served as chief of staff for the former Victorian premier John Brumby.

Just about the only exception was the former frontman of the band Midnight Oil, Peter Garrett, who was parachuted into the seat of Kingsford Smith ahead of the 2004 election with the secrecy of a midnight raid. His stealth candidacy was fiercely opposed by senior figures at the ALP headquarters in Sussex Street, precisely because they regarded him as an outsider and carpetbagger. Garrett, who was not even a party member when first he announced his candidacy, continued to be regarded as if a squatter in a caucus room. His treatment showed the hostility exhibited to newcomers deemed not to have served a lengthy apprenticeship in the party or union movement.

The new Abbott ministry is more diverse, partly because success in the private sector is still seen as an important prerequisite. George Brandis, Eric Abetz, Julie Bishop and Kevin Andrews came from the legal profession. Peter Dutton is a former policeman. Scott Morrison headed up Tourism Australia, though he worked previously as an apparatchik in New South Wales. Malcolm Turnbull, with his background in law, banking and high technology, has the sort of CV that reads like a composite of at least three high achievers. Still, the two most senior figures in the government worked as political staffers. Abbott was John Hewson's spin doctor, while Joe Hockey was a policy adviser for the former New South Wales Premier, John Fahey. Then there is Christopher Pyne. After graduating from university, he worked as a staffer for the former Howard government minister, Amanda Vanstone. Then, at the age of just 25, he became an MP. Intensely combative, his career bolsters the theory that the earlier a politician reaches Canberra the more chest-pumpingly partisan they become. Perhaps it should be called the 'Pyne rule'.

As for the young guns in the Liberal Party, two of the MPs spoken of as possible future leaders entered parliament steeped in Capital Circle politics. Take Kelly O'Dwyer. When she contested the Melbourne seat of Higgins, Peter Costello's old seat, she cast herself as 'a little Aussie battler with a strong lineage in small business'. But she had also been a political combatant in Canberra, where she served for four years on the political staff of the former treasurer. The Kooyong MP Josh Frydenberg, another high-flyer, worked for John Howard and Alexander Downer.

While it seems axiomatic that politics should come to be dominated by political lifers, it actually marks a break from the past. When in the late 1970s academics started paying closer attention to the make-up of the federal parliament, they found that while MPs in no way reflected the age, gender or educational profile of the general populace they were at least occupationally representative. Then, in the 1980s, a spate of studies discovered that farmers, shopkeepers, merchants and most professional groups, like lawyers, were over-represented. Ever since, the most striking trend has been the rise of political functionaries. In the parliaments between 1970 and 1990, union officials, political staffers and state legislators occupied 21 per cent of the seats. When Narelle Miragliotta of Monash University and Wayne Errington of ANU crunched the numbers for 1991 to 2007, they found that the figure had more than doubled to 44 per cent.

The latest research on the 43rd parliament shows that for the first time in Australian history more than half of MPs – 52 per cent – worked as full-time political advisers, electorate officers, union officials and organisers, or state legislators at some stage prior to entering parliament. Of these 78 MPs, two-thirds were from the ALP. The Liberals, however, were catching up. Of the new MPs who entered parliament in 2010 who previously held full-time political jobs, two-thirds were Liberals.

The march towards political professionalisation can be traced back to the Whitlam years, and the decision to appoint ministerial advisers drawn from the ALP. By 1983, the number of advisers spread across the ministries had swelled to 210. By 2006 it had more than doubled to 445. Over the same period, MPs heavily bolstered their constituency offices, creating even more full-time political operatives. In the 1970s, one employee – an electorate secretary – usually sufficed. By 1985, it was two or three. By the 2007 election, it was three or four. Among these political staffers a caste system has come into effect. Those who toiled away in electoral offices tend to end up on the backbenches, while those who worked in Canberra are earmarked for ministerial posts. Then there are the Brahmins among Brahmins – or careerists among careerists – the factional chieftains. The system is self-perpetuating. When vacancies arise, candidates tend to be plucked from the political pool. The caucus room has become a near closed shop.

Careerist politicians have embraced a quasi-corporate culture in which messages are market-tested, policies are packaged and sold, and arguments are reduced to slogans. The corollary is that leaders are subject to the same 'hire 'em and fire 'em' rules of the boardroom.

The isolation of Canberra exacerbates the talent deficit. A political dormitory town rather than a city to put down roots and live proper family lives, it has put off many wannabe politicians. I have spoken with some who envy the Westminster practice, where MPs usually live with their spouses and children in London during the week and return to their constituencies at weekends. In Australia, where parliament sits more infrequently, there is an expectation that MPs will live in their constituencies, and subject themselves to the arduous Canberra commute.

This has a doubly damaging upshot. It acts as a strong deterrent for middle-aged people with families – often precisely the individuals with the experience and life beyond politics who would make accomplished lawmakers. It has also brought promising careers to a premature end. Lindsay Tanner cited the time spent away from his family as one of the principal reasons for bringing his career to an abridged end.

Party elders have long voiced concerns about the paucity of political talent. 'Could Ben Chifley win a Labor pre-selection today?' asked the former New South Wales state minister Rodney Cavalier in a 2005 speech to the NSW Fabian Society. Answering his own question, Cavalier ruled out any possibility that a railwayman from Bathurst could enter parliament, still less become leader. Instead, he lamented the emergence of a political class populated by union officials, parliamentary staffers and party employees. The archetypal Labor parliamentarian, he said, was 'cased at university where she is achieving less than academic greatness. He will have demonstrated a willingness to follow a leader, not to step out of line . . . His first serious employment is with an MP. Or a minister where she will know naught of the subject area of the minister's portfolio. Or a union where he will not have worked in the industry covered by the union employing him.'

Senior conservatives have bemoaned the same trend. In 2003, John Howard complained about the shrinking political 'gene pool'. The year before, another senior Liberal delivered a speech in Melbourne warning that declining party membership rolls had given rise to a small political cadre. There were 'fewer, less representative candidates', he said, and 'fewer, less-mainstream ideas on which to draw for policy'. The speech was entitled 'Operators vs. Representatives', and its author was Tony Abbott.

The upshot of rising professionalism has been a sharp decline in the amateur wing of politics. The rank and file of both major parties has been decimated. So much so that just 1 per cent of Australians are now involved in political parties, compared with the 5 per cent who now participate in environmental and animal welfare groups. The ALP's membership is half what it was at the end of World War II, and in recent years has gone into something nearing free-fall. Between 2002 and 2010, its membership slumped from 50,000 to 37,000. A decade ago, the party had 1140 branches. Now it is close to dipping below 1000. Concerns about branch-stacking, the tactic used by factional leaders to ensure favoured candidates win pre-selection, have given way to worries about 'branch stripping', the dwindling membership.

Like Labor, the Liberal Party is facing a membership crisis. In Victoria, the party's traditional stronghold, it could boast 49,000 members at the end of the war. By 2008, it was just 13,373. Almost 90 per cent of members were over 60 years old, while just 6 per cent were under 30. This had led to the closure of 84 branches, almost a fifth of the total, and the party's efforts at recruiting new members had not been hugely successful. Less than half of the recruits who had joined the party since 2000 were still members.

Nor have the major political parties ever faced such stiff competition for talent. The online activist group GetUp! claims to have more active members – 650,000 – than all the political parties combined. Its founders are two Australian Harvard graduates, Jeremy Heimans and David Madden, who saw in online activism more potential than conventional political careers. Starved of new members, the parties are bereft of new talent.

History shows that the party apparatus and union movement can produce leaders of high calibre, like Bob Hawke and Paul Keating. Nor is the pool entirely dry. Along with O'Dwyer and Frydenberg, who studied at both Oxford and Harvard, much is also expected on the Liberal side from Paul Fletcher, the MP for Bradfield in Sydney, who holds an MBA from New York's Columbia University and enjoyed a successful career in the communications sector. Yet he also served as chief of staff for the former communications minister Richard Alston during the Howard government.

Labor insiders point to promising young politicians including Jason Clare, the former home affairs minister, who represents Keating's former seat of Blaxland; Ed Husic, who is also from the western suburbs of Sydney; Melissa Parke, the MP for Fremantle who worked as an international lawyer in a string of trouble-spots from Kosovo to Gaza; and the impressive Andrew Leigh, a Harvard graduate who is like a one-man intellectual blood-bank. But Clare worked as an adviser to Bob Carr, Husic was both a political staffer and national president of the Communications, Electrical and Plumbing Union. Tellingly, Leigh, the member for the capital seat of Fraser, beat a factional fix to win pre-selection, something perhaps possible only in Canberra where local factions are nowhere near as strong. In a seat elsewhere, a union stooge or political functionary would presumably have beaten him.

Traditionally in Australia, the diversity debate has focused on getting more women into politics. Perhaps the focus should shift towards hunting down that more elusive of species: the talented outsider for whom politics is a calling rather than a career.

Among Peter Slipper's many mistakes was to think he could raise standards in Canberra merely by imitating the ceremonial trappings of Westminster. Instead, he could have looked more closely at the reforms British lawmakers have introduced over the years to elevate parliamentary life – the procedural rather than the processional. A few wardrobe adjustments were nowhere near enough. Canberra needed an extreme makeover.

Westminster Question Time, though still raucous, has become less unruly than its Australian equivalent, largely because of moves to limit the involvement of the prime minister of the day. Time was when the likes of Gladstone and Disraeli, and their ministers, would face questions from Monday to Thursday, the basis of the Australian model. In the 1950s, however, lawmakers decided, out of courtesy to Sir Winston Churchill, then an ailing septuagenarian, to spare the prime minister this ordeal. In what came to be known as Prime Minister's Questions, Churchill faced a 15-minute cross-examination on a Tuesday and Thursday afternoon, paving the way for the bi-weekly sessions that survived until New Labour took office in 1997.

Tony Blair, who believed that his Downing Street staff could occupy their time more profitably than briefing him for PMQs, decided unilaterally to hold them once a week – though, to avoid accusations he was hiding from parliament, extended the session to 30 minutes. Blair also altered the scheduling, appearing at the stroke of noon rather than after lunch, another move intended to make PMQs more business-like and orderly. The tradition continued, meanwhile, of questioning ministers on a fortnightly rota, with each session devoted to a single portfolio, which again is more orderly than the ministerial free-for-all in Canberra.

The Blair-era reforms succeeded in taking some of the heat and rancour out of PMQs. The knock-about was short and sharp, like a good boxing match that lasts just a few rounds, unlike the pavement brawl that resumes each afternoon in

Canberra and continues unabated throughout the week. It was not good for the press gallery. It starved the continuous news channels of their parliamentary showtime. But it improved the quality of debate by reducing the level of hostility.

Following the 2010 federal election, largely at the urging of the independents holding the balance of power, the 43rd parliament instituted reforms aimed at lowering the temperature. Question Time is now meant to finish by 3.30 pm. Answers are supposed to be directly relevant to the question asked. Limits have been placed on the number of points of order. Alas, the advent of minority government made the mood even more adversarial, and brought Question Time into more disrepute.

Were Question Time reformed, the prime minister would not be exposed to the same degree of parliamentary scrutiny and not have as much time to explain the government's policies to the House. When Paul Keating limited his appearances, the then opposition leader John Howard accused him of being a part-timer. But scrutiny long gave way to the sport of prime minister-baiting, just as elucidation from the government benches has been replaced by cheap point-scoring. For those in the Canberra village, who seem to greet Question Time much like the inhabitants of a remote hamlet welcome a visiting circus, life might become drearier. Twitter would be denied its post-lunch #qt fun. But would not #auspol ultimately benefit? Surely it would raise the standard. After all, Question Time has rarely, if ever, seemed so irrelevant to the daily lives of average Australians. Canberra talking to Canberra – or, as is more often now the case, Canberra yelling at Canberra.

Westminster is far from perfect. Nor is the debate particularly high-pitched. When David Cameron became the

Conservative leader he was determined to end the Punch and Judy style of PMQs, but has been disappointed by his inability to usher in a 'quieter tone'. The Speaker, John Bercow, has likened the noise of PMQs to the howl of the South African vuvuzela, and complained of its 'yobbery and public school twittishness'. Further reforms are being mooted, including ending the practice of referring to fellow lawmakers as the 'Honourable Member for . . .'. Were MPs required to use each other's real names, they might be less insulting. Despite Westminster's shortcomings, many Australians who tuned in to important parliamentary events in recent years, like the phone-hacking debate, were struck by the quality of the discussion. It heightened the sense of political cringe.

Reforming the Senate should also be a priority, with consideration given to tightening party registration rules to make it harder for fringe parties to prosper. Here it is worth remembering that Steve Fielding, who wielded such enormous power during Rudd's first term, won election to the upper house on less than 2 per cent of the primary vote in Victoria. Faced with the problem of ballots the size of tablecloths, and a party list that included the Three Day Weekend Party, the Four Wheel Drive Party and the What's Doing? Party, New South Wales ruled that more than 2000 people were needed to register a new party. The federal limit remains at 500.

In urgent need of reinvigoration, the major parties are experimenting with broader reforms. US-style primaries are especially in vogue, the thinking being that public interest will be stirred if members of the community, as well as members of the party, pick candidates. When Bob Carr, the former Victorian state premier Steve Bracks and John Faulkner conducted a review of the ALP after its near defeat at the 2010 election, primaries were a key recommendation. But these contests are principally seen as a recruitment tool to entice new party members rather than attracting outside candidates. In Labor's mayoral primary in Sydney, the refugee advocate Linda Scott, who worked as a staffer for Senator Faulkner, was the winner. The Sussex Street favourite, critics complained that she would also have come out on top in a conventional pre-selection battle.

Attracting people of a higher calibre into politics, with an assortment of backgrounds, is a recurring problem. Senior Labor figures like Bruce Hawker believe that Senate vacancies should be used to recruit outsiders, much as modern-day British prime ministers have made use of the reformed House of Lords to bring in clean-skins from the business community. A bolder reform might see non-elected members of the cabinet, again as a means of fast-tracking the talented and capable. But it is hard to see this American model being transplanted here.

As for curbing Canberra's coup culture, the ALP, at Kevin Rudd's insistence, has already made a significant structural change. In 2013, an electoral college, with a 50–50 weighting split between the parliamentary party and rank-and-file membership, decided the leader. When Bill Shorten beat Anthony Albanese, he became the first to be elected under these new rules. Never before had the party membership been granted such influence.

Defenders of the Canberra system argue, rightly, it is not quite 'Fucknutsville', the term used by Barack Obama's one-time chief of staff Rahm Emanuel to describe Washington DC and its crazed dysfunction – although there are shades of the same partisan excess and obstructionism. They also point out that Australian politics is largely corruption free, at least at the federal level, if not the state.

Yet Canberra has also had its own expenses scandal, even if not on the Westminster scale. Australian MPs, unlike their

British counterparts, did not claim for ornamental duck-house garden features or for the cost of cleaning 13th-century moats. Still, voters wondered why parliamentarians were charging taxpayers to attend weddings, sporting grand finals, and, in Tony Abbott's case, an ironman triathlon. Again, it widened the rift that has opened up between voters and their MPs. It also showed the extent to which politicians see themselves as full-time political operatives. In their minds, attending grand finals with their families is a political activity. For George Brandis, so too was celebrating the wedding of the right-wing former shock jock Michael Smith. Abbott thought nothing of claiming $9400 in 2010 so that he could promote his book *Battlelines*, which underscored once more the problem of partisan overkill.

But there is also a more serious indictment to be made. It is the extent to which policy is now dictated by the primacy of politics.

Chapter 4

THE PRIMACY OF POLITICS

AUSTRALIA'S OFFSHORE DETENTION CENTRE on the faraway Pacific island of Nauru shares a road with a rubbish dump. The gravel track weaves through the scarred and unwelcoming terrain of the island's mining fields, where the industrial removal of high-grade phosphate deposits has created a craggy and unnerving landscape. The jungle surrounding the facility is so thick and hostile that no fence is required to prevent the detainees from escaping. The vegetation also camouflages it from the outside world. A less hospitable setting is hard to imagine.

Despite Nauru's tropical weather and swaying palms, new arrivals learn quickly that the world's smallest republic is far from paradise. Dotted with razor-sharp coral, its seas are not only unenticing but repellent. Wading into the ocean is a self-lacerating act of recklessness. If the jagged coastline accentuates the sense of enclosure, the four-and-a-half-hour flight from Brisbane, which operates only a few times a week, reinforces the sense of isolation. The road encircling the island, which takes little more than 20 minutes to drive, is lined with dilapidated dwellings and half-derelict buildings. Many local residents live in squalor, but at least they have the option of leaving.

In the heyday of Nauru's mining boom in the 1970s and 1980s, this microstate, with a population of just 10,000 people, was per capita one of the richest nations in the world. Nowadays, it is one of the poorest. Poverty is a central reason why successive Nauru governments have agreed to host Australia's offshore processing of asylum seekers. It helps guarantee a line of Australian aid, and boosts local employment. Evidently, the Australian government needs Nauru as much as Nauru needs Australia. It offers a fix for the problem of boat people heading to Australian shores, the country's most paranoiac political issue. A Pacific Solution.

In June 2013, my cameraman and I became the first journalists to be allowed into the newly renovated camp. Beforehand, we had been shown secretly filmed footage from inside the detention centre, where boat people had been living in overcrowded army tents. We had seen smuggled-out photographs of asylum seekers who had sewn their lips together with unsterile needles, in silent protest at their indefinite detention. We had been told about the regular suicide attempts and acts of self-harm. One man tried to hang himself using the rope holding up one of the makeshift tents. Another had to be talked down from a nearby cliff edge. We had listened to the harrowing testimony of Australians working inside the camp, who have been shocked by the conditions. The 45 degree heat. The smothering humidity. When Amnesty International managed to gain access six months before, it delivered a withering assessment. The detention centre was 'a toxic mix of uncertainty, unlawful detention and inhumane conditions that are creating an increasingly volatile situation'. The conditions were, if anything, worse in Australia's detention centre on Manus Island, because young children were among the detainees.

Up until our arrival, the journey for reporters assigned to the Pacific Solution beat stopped at the gatehouse. They were thwarted by the strict media ban imposed by the Australian government. We had been granted access because the Department of Immigration had replaced the army tents with permanent accommodation, and believed that the conditions had been transformed. Their one final reservation before signing the paperwork allowing us inside was that we would broadcast around the world images of the polished new buildings, negating the deterrent effect of the detention centre. The need to demonstrate that Australia wasn't operating a tropical gulag, after a welter of negative press and damning reports, finally clinched it in our favour. But only just.

The facility had been designed not with comfort in mind but at least a measure of civility. The rooms, housing two 'clients', as the Department of Immigration then called the asylum seekers, had a bunk-bed, desk, lockers and two personal safes. Though there was still no air conditioning, each room had a large fan and natural ventilation. On the landing outside each room, there was a communal area so the asylum seekers could mingle. The central courtyard, where the men tended to spend most of their days, was protected from the harsh sunlight by a playground-style canopy, though there was no natural shelter.

Mindful of religious and cultural sensibilities, the old olive green army tents, which had housed the detainees, had been turned into places of worship – a Hindu temple for the Tamil refugees from Sri Lanka, a mosque for those from Iraq and Afghanistan. The menu, prepared in state-of-the-art kitchens still with the sheen of brand-new stainless steel, offered a taste of home. Plasma screens showed television channels from their countries of origin, at least one for each language. Banks of computers granted access to email and the internet. There was a purpose-built recreation centre, with games consoles and exercise equipment. Asylum seekers were given phone cards so they could make calls home. If they signed up to English language classes and other educational activities, they could earn extra phone card credits.

Despite a noticeable security presence, the approach stopped short of being penal. Many of the Australians running the camp were also compassionate, the type in previous postings whom I often ran into running NGOs in conflict zones or dispensing aid in the aftermath of disasters. The detainees were allowed to leave the camp on supervised excursions to play volleyball and go on walks, or to swim in one of the few places along the coast that was not too treacherous. Teams of Salvation Army counsellors, contracted in by the Australian government, had struck up friendships with some of the people in their care. The Salvos, as one would expect, were especially well meaning.

Still, many asylum seekers felt like prisoners. They could never leave the camp without supervision, a change from the laxer rules under the Howard government, when they were allowed to walk around the tiny island and mix more freely with the locals. That four-and-a-half-hour flight to Brisbane might as well have taken 100. They were not going to be able to board a flight out any time soon, which was precisely what made Nauru so unbearable. Held indefinitely, the 545 detainees had no inkling when they might leave. It could be anything up to five years. The average length of time boat people spend in detention is two to three years.

Under the strict conditions of our entry, modelled on the media restrictions imposed by the Pentagon at Guantanamo

Bay, we were not allowed to show the faces of the men or reveal their names in case their asylum claims were rejected, and they were sent home. But over 90 per cent of boat people turn out to be bona fide refugees.

Compared to the tent city, the physical conditions had vastly improved. That was apparent immediately. Because we were not allowed to speak to the men themselves, however, it was hard to assess the psychological conditions: the torment of being kept on such a remote island, separated from their loved ones, day after day, month after month, year after year.

Told beforehand that a film crew would be on site, we expected the detainees to mount some form of demonstration. When a few months earlier a crew from the ABC had scrambled to the top of a hill overlooking the centre, the asylum seekers tried to form a giant protest sign. With a camera in their midst, we expected something more dramatic. As we made our way through the detention centre, accompanied everywhere by a media handler flown in especially from Canberra, the mood was unexpectedly calm. Not a single asylum seeker approached us, or tried to communicate in any way. Our visit passed without incident.

Soon after, the politics of asylum seekers took another ugly turn. Back again as prime minister, and determined to demonstrate his toughness, Kevin Rudd announced that boat people who paid smugglers to ferry them across the Indian Ocean would no longer be allowed to settle in Australia. Never. Instead, if their asylum claims withstood scrutiny, they would be settled in Papua New Guinea, a country not far from being the kind of failed state they had tried to flee. 'YOU WON'T BE SETTLED IN AUSTRALIA,' read the hurriedly produced posters, advertising the government's hardline new approach. While it did not apply to those already in detention, the rumour mill on Nauru went into overdrive.

With manic suddenness, the detention centre was engulfed in flames, as about 150 detainees unleashed their fury on the newly constructed buildings. An accommodation block was burned down, so, too, the dining room and health centre. Much of the new detention centre, which had cost almost $100 million to build and a further $100 million to operate, lay in ruins. None of the staff were injured, which suggested that the detainees were rebelling against the system rather than the people implementing it. In the midst of the riot, a Nauruan politician went on television to call for the island's strongmen to converge on the detention centre to help police. They heeded the call, brandishing iron bars and machetes. Australia's asylum-seeker policy had come to this: the charred remains of a Pacific Solution detention centre, a macabre blackened shell, its perimeter patrolled by vigilantes.

Rudd, in announcing the Papua New Guinea Solution as it inevitably came to be dubbed, had not primarily been seeking a workable policy. Prime minister only a few days, there had not been enough time to address the problem in a deliberative manner. Rather, with the election about to be called, he was looking for a vote-saving fix. Labor had long given up hope of winning votes on this issue. Instead, he was desperate to neutralise it. In doing so, he was competing headlong in 'the race to the bottom', which, on the eve of his dethronement in 2010, he vowed sanctimoniously to avoid. Trying to inoculate himself from the opposition's catchcry 'Stop the Boats' overrode his humanitarian impulses. Addressing the asylum-seeker issue before becoming Labor leader in 2006, Rudd had recalled the parable of the Good Samaritan: 'The biblical injunction to care for the stranger in our midst is clear,' he wrote in *The Monthly*. Now a political injunction held sway.

No policy area in Australian public life defies speedy remedies or easy solutions so much as the boat people dilemma, partly because of the ruthlessness of the Indonesian people-smuggling rings, and partly because of the readiness of asylum seekers to risk their lives on rickety boats that often sink. Since 2001, some 1400 asylum seekers have drowned trying to reach Australia. Still, no issue has become so riven with petty and ugly partisanship. Nothing speaks more piercingly of the primacy of politics.

Over the four decades that boats have been coming, the debate has changed beyond all recognition. When the first vessel arrived in 1975, carrying Vietnamese asylum seekers fleeing the communist victory, they were broadly welcomed by the Fraser government and Labor opposition, who displayed none of the cynical politicking evident now. 'The right supported the refugees as escapees from communism,' noted Robert Manne, 'the left as part of the project of burying White Australia.'

Mandatory detention, which was intended as a temporary deterrent, only came in during the Keating government, in response to the arrival of mainly Cambodian boat people. But the politics of boat people changed more radically in the late 1990s under the Howard government, following a surge in Middle Eastern asylum seekers from Afghanistan, Iraq and Iran. Terms like 'illegal immigrants' entered the political lexicon, even though asylum seekers are not 'illegals' however they arrive. Under the 1948 Universal Declaration of Human Rights, which Australia helped draft, everyone has the right to seek asylum in a territory that they have reached. The use of the word illegal is presumably intended to imply, wrongly, that boat people have committed an offence in coming. 'Queue jumpers' was another demonising term. Asylum seekers were denigrated and criminalised. Even the term 'boat people' has become debased, an abstraction shorn of human meaning.

Myths have also been allowed to fester. It is misleading to suggest that boat people add to the congestion of the suburbs. If a boat person is granted asylum, the annual refugee intake is adjusted accordingly. The overall number remains the same. To imply that a boat person adds to traffic jams on overclogged roads, or to allow that view to go unchallenged, is not just scapegoating of the most cynical kind but a reckless abrogation of political leadership.

The 2001 election saw another threshold crossed, when John Howard refused to allow a Norwegian freighter, the MV *Tampa*, that had rescued hundreds of Afghan asylum seekers to land in Australia. Oft-told is the story first revealed by Peter van Onselen and Wayne Errington in their biography of Howard of how he had been approached by Jackie Kelly, the then member for Lindsay in the western suburbs of Sydney, as he made his way to Question Time on 27 August. At that time, the captain of the *Tampa* was pleading for permission to come ashore, not least because the vessel had 460 people on board but only 40 life vests. 'One Nation is chewing us up,' said Kelly, to which Howard reportedly replied: 'Don't worry, Jackie. That's all about to change.' In parliament that afternoon, he announced that the *Tampa* had been denied permission to land in Australia, a country that would 'decide who comes here, and in what circumstances'. By the time of the Liberal campaign launch in October, he had honed that phrase, and it became the mantra of his campaign: 'We will decide who comes to this country, and the circumstances in which they come.' The unyielding policy also had a name: the Pacific Solution.

As the 2001 Tampa election showed, a hard-hitting stance against boat people had mainstream electoral appeal, and also allowed the Liberal Party to tap into the xenophobic and racist fringe that had flocked to One Nation in the late

1990s. Even more handily for the Coalition, it exposed tensions in Labor's bifurcated base between working-class voters and more affluent progressives – the suburban battlers and the inner-city elites. The 2001 election taught both sides an ugly lesson. It set the scene for the cruelty auction that has followed.

Judged by the crude measure of stopping the boats, the Pacific Solution proved effective. Between 1999 and 2001, 180 boats reached Australia, carrying 12,000 asylum seekers. Between 2002 and 2007, the period during which the Pacific Solution was in effect, just 18 boats carrying fewer than 300 boat people arrived. But the cost of the harsh policy, in terms of the psychological damage inflicted on those held in indefinite detention, was incalculable. Then there was the reputational cost to Australia, which repeatedly came in for criticism from the United Nations and international human rights groups that regarded it as a pariah state. Repeatedly, UNHCR, the United Nations' refugee agency, slammed the policy for its tough physical environment, restricted legal regime, and slow processing of claims that did not meet minimum international protection standards. Patrick McGorry, the mental health expert who in 2010 was made Australian of the Year, described the offshore detention centres as 'factories for mental illness'. The Pacific Solution was also staggeringly expensive. An Oxfam report in 2007 found that it cost more than $500,000 per person to process asylum seekers on Manus Island, Christmas Island and Nauru.

As prime minister, Rudd ended the Pacific Solution, closing down the detention centres at Nauru and Manus Island in Papua New Guinea and dispensed with temporary protection visas, another Howard government tool. Even so, the detention centre on Christmas Island in the Indian Ocean remained open. Soon, however, the boats started to return. The figure reached a hundred by March 2010. Rudd responded by getting tough.

'I make absolutely no apology whatsoever for taking a hard line on illegal immigration to Australia,' he said in October 2009, when he requested that the Indonesians deploy warships to block boats carrying Sri Lankan asylum seekers. He also started to use the language of 'illegal immigration', even though Rudd would have been fluent in the international conventions in which asylum seekers were deemed unauthorised but not unlawful. What made Rudd's nervous response even more pusillanimous was that his approval at that time was 71 per cent – that endless honeymoon phase when he looked invincible. 'A leader with that kind of stratospheric standing might choose to start a different conversation with the Australian people,' observed the ABC's Chris Uhlmann at the time, 'and not assume that the old arguments always prevail.' It was more a case of the old politics prevailing. The lingering trauma for Labor of the Tampa election acted like a clamp on Rudd's mind.

As a result, his rhetoric towards asylum seekers became harder and harsher, and he engaged with Malcolm Turnbull in what the political reporter Phillip Coorey described as a 'he-man contest'. In truth, it felt more like a professional wrestling match, because both leaders appeared to be faking it in order to win cheers from the cheap seats at the back.

Soon both of them were gone, and under Julia Gillard and Tony Abbott the debate became even more rancorous and contemptible. 'Stop the Boats' was the new conservative leader's favourite catchcry. Gillard, faced with both a rhetorical onslaught and an uptick in the number of unauthorised arrivals, lurched desperately from one policy fix to the next. The fruitless search for a Malaysian Solution was followed by the pursuit of an East Timor Solution. When that also failed, the Labor government eventually reverted back to the Pacific Solution, with the reopening of the detention centres on Nauru and Manus Island. Labor had returned to a policy caustically described by its first immigration minister Senator Chris Evans as 'a cynical, costly and ultimately unsuccessful exercise'.

The commonplace has it that good policy makes for good politics. Here was the inverse: ugly politics made for ugly policies. The incessant politicisation of the question made it all the more difficult to conduct a reasonable debate, and to carry out a considered policy-making process.

The inaptly named East Timor Solution had been especially risible. Announced in the midst of the 2010 federal election campaign, Gillard said the plan was to open a regional offshore detention centre in East Timor, an approach which had support from some refugee advocates. But although she had proposed the idea to East Timor's president, Jose Ramos-Horta, she had not entered into talks with the prime minister, Xanana Gusmao, who said his country was 'very unlikely' to accept the idea. Again, it was policy on the hoof – the political hoof.

Delivered at the Lowy Institute in Sydney, a non-partisan foreign policy think-tank which politicians sometimes descend on to give the impression of rising above the political fray, the speech in which she announced the new policy showed how cynical were the politics of boat people. It was framed as a response to Julian Burnside, the barrister and well-known refugee advocate, who had challenged her 'to point out to the public that at the current rate of arrivals it would take about 20 years to fill the MCG with boat people'. Burnside had also complained that the boat people policy was designed to appease 'rednecks in marginal seats'.

On the first point, she said, Burnside was 'very, very right'. In the context of Australia's migration programme, boat people made up less than 1.5 per cent of permanent immigrants each year. It would, indeed, take at least 20 years to fill 'the 'G'. On the second issue, she argued, Burnside was 'very, very wrong'. It was misleading, she said, 'to label people who have concerns about unauthorised arrivals as "'rednecks"'. These people should be free to express their concerns in whatever manner they chose. The immigration debate, she said, 'must not be constrained by self-censorship or political correctness'. It read like an invitation to let racist rip, or, at the very least, a continuation of Labor's policy of appeasement towards the redneck fringe.

Days earlier, she had been even more explicit. 'I'd like to sweep away any sense that people should close down any debate, including this debate, through a sense of self-censorship or political correctness,' she had said. 'People should feel free to say what they feel. For people to say they're anxious about border security doesn't make them intolerant. It certainly doesn't make them a racist – it means they're expressing a genuine view.' That was true. Not everyone concerned by the influx of boat people was racist or xenophobic. Yet, as with her speech at Lowy, she displayed more concern for the feelings of 'rednecks' and xenophobes than the plight of asylum seekers.

Eventually, the Gillard government outsourced policy-making to a panel headed by the former defence chief Angus Houston. Framing its proposals as 'hard-headed but not hard-hearted', it suggested the reopening of the Nauru and Manus Island detention centres, but urged also a major leap in Australia's annual humanitarian intake of refugees from 13,750 to 20,000 in the hope of offering alternatives to the treacherous maritime routes. In a sign of the hurtling pace at which asylum-seeker policy was patched together, the government adopted all 22 recommendations that very day and pledged to have a bill before parliament codifying them into law within 48 hours. Little more than a month afterwards, the first boat people landed in Nauru, even though government ministers on the island warned against that hurried timeframe because the detention centre was nowhere near ready.

On both sides, the political opportunism has been craven. Australia's immigration minister, Scott Morrison, built his pre-parliamentary business career as the head of Tourism Australia by enticing visitors to these shores. He has built his political rise on deterring and demonising asylum seekers, the most vulnerable of travellers. The man behind the 'Where the Bloody Hell Are You?' campaign was also the most prominent Liberal barracker for 'Stop the Boats'. The more publicity came his way, the more hardline he became. So much so that in February 2011, on the morning when victims of a boat people tragedy off Christmas Island were due to be buried in Sydney, he launched an ill-tempered attack on the Labor government for paying for family members to make the long journey for the funeral. Among those grieving relatives was Madian El Ibrahimy, a detainee at the Indian Ocean detention centre, whose wife Zman, four-year-old son, Nzar, and eight-month-old daughter, Zahra, had all died at sea. 'Do you think you run the risk of being seen as heartless on the day of these funerals to be saying – to be bickering over this money?' asked Barbara Miller, whose report that morning was broadcast on ABC's AM programme. Morrison replied, 'When it comes to the question of do I think this is a reasonable cost then my honest answer is "No". I don't think it is reasonable.'

Seasoned commentators struggled to recall a nastier instance of gutter politics from a prominent politician since the heyday of Pauline Hanson. Labor accused him of 'stealing soundbites from One Nation'. John Hewson called his comments 'inhumane'. Malcolm Fraser was scornful: 'I hope Scott Morrison is just a fringe element in the party.' But it was being allowed to become a mainstream view.

Morrison also enraged certain members of the shadow cabinet, some of whom thought he was trying to demagogue his way to greater seniority, and then the leadership. At least one exacted revenge by supplying damaging leaks from a shadow cabinet meeting the previous December, discussing strategy for the forthcoming year. 'What are we going to do about multiculturalism?' Morrison was reported as saying. 'What are we going to do about concerns about the number of Muslims?' Morrison, a born-again Christian who attends a Hillsong-style Pentecostal mega-church in the Shire, evidently did not think the parable of the Good Samaritan applied to boat people.

What made Morrison's behaviour all the more brazen was that it stood in such marked contrast to his political persona at the outset of his parliamentary career. During his maiden speech to parliament in February 2008, Morrison quoted Bono as he made an impassioned appeal for more aid to Africa – hardly a hot-button issue for his constituents in Cronulla – and voiced admiration for William Wilberforce and Desmond Tutu. Yet as the party moved to the right, following the election of Tony Abbott as leader, so, too, did he. Abbott quickly came to regard him as his most effective frontbench performer.

Morrison, while still shadow immigration minister, received a torrid time when he appeared before the Foreign Correspondents' Association in Sydney, whose members bemoaned the cruelty of offshore processing, and the xenophobia that politicians like him seemed happy to unleash. Morrison was not only unapologetic, but left in good spirits. Though he had failed to win over the room that lunchtime, his primary focus was the presence at the back of cameras from the Australian networks who had dutifully recorded his soundbite of the day – a vapidity about Labor aping the policies of the last conservative government and trying to build 'a stairway to Howard'. Morrison did not care about the international opprobrium. His message of the day was aimed squarely at Australian lounge rooms.

Perversely, Australian politicians seemed almost to revel in the international criticism of their boat-people policies, because it validated their tough stance. This unrepentant approach brought to mind the terrace chant of fans of Millwall, British football's most unfashionable club: 'No one likes us, we don't care.' Australian politicians were prepared to incur negative coverage in *The Economist*, *The Guardian*, the *Financial Times* or on the BBC so long as they were receiving a good press from *The Daily Telegraph* or *Herald Sun*. Sometimes, as when the United Nations Human Rights Commissioner Navi Pillay lambasted Australia on its mandatory detention of asylum seekers, the Malaysia Solution and the harshness of its detention regimes, outside criticism was regarded as a plus. For the Labor government, her damning critique showed its policies were not the soft touch that the Liberals claimed.

As with the polling fixation, the media is implicated – even its most responsible outlets. The arrival of each new boat, along with the eye-catching imagery of floating shanties captured on a long lens and set against the azure seas, always makes for an easy lead story. More often than not, these reports follow the same dreary formula: those ocean shots; the transfer of refugees to the dock at Christmas Island; the doorstep fuming of opposition politicians, followed by defensive assurances from the government. The excessive coverage helps explain the discrepancy between the public perception of boat people and unauthorised 'plane people', who land in their thousands with temporary visas and who then seek asylum. Plane people are twice as likely to have their asylum bids rejected, but their entry into the country goes largely unnoticed by the media, and thus they escape political and public censure.

Boat arrivals, by contrast, are ripe for tabloid sensationalism. 'INVASION' was *The Daily Telegraph*'s front-page banner in July 2010. 'Up to 800 asylum seekers could arrive during the election campaign,' it reported, 'with the navy bracing itself for an influx of up to 12 illegal boats.' Twelve boats. And they had not even yet arrived. That did not deter *The Daily Telegraph* from mounting another scare campaign. 'OPEN THE FLOODGATES – Exclusive: Thousands of boat people to invade NSW' was its front-page splash little more than a year later. When brought before the Press Council, the *Tele* did not even try to justify the word 'invade'. It was indefensible.

For international news organisations at this time, the boat people issue was never a 'numbers' story. Ringing up the newsdesk in London to report that a boat had been intercepted carrying 30 or so Sri Lankan asylum seekers, when other countries faced dramatically larger numbers, elicited a mystified response. Why are you calling? What made this a story, however, was the paranoiac reaction: how a comparatively small problem could generate such a disproportionately high-pitched outcry and such a low-pitched political response.

With the reopening of the offshore detention centres, the inhumane treatment of asylum seekers again became an international story. By then, the bitter debate and posturing embroidered the narrative of Australia's waning politics. To visit Nauru was also to report on Canberra.

*

When Kevin Rudd became prime minister he offered a series of correctives to the excesses and omissions of the Howard era rather than proposing a galvanising programme of his own. The first act of his government was to ratify the Kyoto treaty, a shift which seemed to indicate a definitive break from the past and that also drew a standing ovation from delegates to the UN Climate Change Conference in Bali. Yet the main plank of his policy, the proposal for an emissions trading scheme contingent on a global agreement from the major international polluters to curb emissions, was not dissimilar to the approach advocated by Howard in his final months as prime minister. Moreover, environmental groups were derisive about his paltry emissions targets and his refusal to curb coal exports, which created so much pollution elsewhere. Rudd's first parliamentary act was to issue the long-overdue national apology to members of the Stolen Generations. Again, however, the main rudiments of the Howard government's much-hated Northern Territory intervention remained in place. The rougher edges of WorkChoices were smoothed away, but parts of the Coalition's controversial labour laws remained unadulterated in the new Fair Work Act. Rudd withdrew Australian diggers from Iraq, the second front of the Bush administration's 'War on Terror', but bolstered the Australian presence in Afghanistan, the first post-9/11 battleground.

Frequently assailed for 'me-tooism' during the 2007 campaign, Rudd's main departure from Howard came at Labor's campaign launch over extravagant spending commitments. 'Today I am saying loud and clear that this sort of reckless spending must stop,' he declared. His intention, though, was to underscore his conservative fiscal credentials. He uttered the words 'economic conservative' almost as much as he parroted the phrase 'working families'.

Though Rudd achieved a resounding victory, and was given a personal mandate by the electorate, his policies were Howard-lite as much as Kevin 07. A lifelong republican, Rudd had promised to accelerate the debate, but he had no desire to get too far ahead of public opinion on the question. Thus it remained in neutral. His boldest move on the foreign stage, to announce plans for an Asian Union modelled on the European Union, were not even half-baked. Not only did they catch the country's foreign policy establishment by surprise but also Australia's closest neighbours.

In government, Rudd seemed to exhibit a prime ministerial form of attention deficit disorder, flitting with careering speed from one policy idea to the next without adequately developing any of them. For a party that had spent 11 years out of office, the Labor Party was strangely bereft of a reform programme.

For a leader who prided himself on being a policy wonk, Rudd also seemed short of big policies. In long essays for *The Monthly* prior to taking over from Kim Beazley, which doubled as pitches for the leadership, Rudd presented himself as a heavyweight political thinker. His November 2006 essay, 'Howard Brutopia: The Battle for Ideas in Australian Politics', sought to frame the forthcoming federal election as an ideological contest between social democracy and the 'market fundamentalism' of neo-Liberalism. 'The time has come to forge a new coalition of political forces across the Australian community,' he said, 'uniting those who are disturbed by market fundamentalism in all its dimensions and who believe that this country is entitled to a greater vision than one which merely aggregates individual greed and self-interest.' Once in office, however, he made little attempt to enunciate that great vision.

Nor had his first *Monthly* essay on the German theologian Dietrich Bonhoeffer offered much in the way of programmatic specificity. It promised changes on WorkChoices and Kyoto, and hinted at a softening of the policies towards asylum seekers, but little else. In advertising his religious convictions, he was essentially trying to convey a political message, that he understood the conservative character of the Australian populace and was a softer version of Howard. Both essays were primarily about politics rather than policy, what spin doctors call framing and messaging.

The fabled 2020 summit was intended to display the intellectual restlessness of the new prime minister, along with his transformative intent. Instead, it exposed the paucity of the new government's thinking. Of the 962 ideas put forward during that weekend of whiteboards and marker pens, only nine were adopted. To the most daring ideas, like a bill of rights, a reconstitution of an indigenous peak body modelled on ATSIC, or the loosening of ties to the United Kingdom, Rudd applied the sponge. Only piecemeal proposals made it from the whiteboard into policy: the creation of a new children's television channel, a national workplace mentoring programme, bionic eye research, an indigenous cultural centre and a business and school roundtable. The efforts of a thousand of the country's brightest and best thinkers ended up looking like the work of a children's parliament. But Rudd and his fellow summiteers were misaligned. Participants had flown to Canberra ready to propose ideas that were good for the country. The prime minister's focus was on what would boost the Labor Party and government. Civilians, many of them, in the partisan struggle, they had not applied the all-important test: would their ideas be politically advantageous?

Throughout the Rudd years, initiatives advertised as ground-breaking policies truly were populist gestures. The ill-conceived Grocery Choice website, the government's response to mounting cost of living pressures, was quickly abandoned when ministers realised it was unworkable. Likewise, the FuelWatch scheme was scratched. Political window-dressing had rarely been so blatant.

Some of the policies were rushed out, without due care, because of the media requirement to be seen to be taking action, and to come up with what modern-day apparatchiks call 'announceables'. The prime minister's office had received warnings from the minister in charge, Peter Garrett, about pressing too quickly ahead with the pink batts insulation scheme, but they were ignored with fatal consequences. It fitted a pattern. As Tanner opined: 'All political behaviour is now governed by the need to look like you're doing something' – 'the illusion of action'.

When Rudd briefed his new speechwriter James Button, he demanded that every speech contain 'a detachable module of announceables'. They were intended to feed the media beast. 'Rudd had run government the way he had run for office, on the principle of continuous campaigning,' George Megalogenis later complained. 'Each day was devoted to winning more favourable mentions in the media than his opponent.'

Often, this meant accentuating the trivial. At the beginning of 2010, Rudd's aides believed he would kick off the new year by outlining his plans for a carbon emissions scheme, so central to the greening of Australia. Instead, he decided to launch a children's book co-authored with the actor Rhys Muldoon about the prime ministerial pets, *Jasper & Abby and the Great Australia Day Kerfuffle*. Rudd has been described as 'Australia's first post-modern prime minister' because, in the words of the conservative historian Greg Melleuish: 'We have moved from an era of principle to an era of appearances.'

Rudd's botched approach to climate change revealed how quickly his first prime ministership descended into political myopia. In 2009, when Malcolm Turnbull signalled his willingness to hatch a bipartisan deal on the ETS, despite the rising discontent within Coalition ranks, Rudd preferred to make political hay. Penny Wong, the then climate change minister, urged her leader to 'cuddle' Turnbull. Yet as Peter Hartcher notes: 'Rudd told his staff to maximise Turnbull's pain.' 'Kevin prioritised politics over events,' his then press secretary Sean Kelly later reflected. 'It meant we didn't get the ETS over the line.'

His later backtracking from the ETS also demonstrated a broader failure of Australia's more recent leaders to shape the debate. In 2009, Rudd 'scarcely said a word on the subject', according to James Button, even though 'the emissions trading scheme was crying out for a speech explaining it'. Politicians seemed to regard public opinion as immutable, thus nullifying one of the prime assets of power: a platform from which to persuade – what the Americans call the bully pulpit.

Rudd eventually became a victim both of his own political vindictiveness towards Turnbull and timidity in the face of the growing chorus, post-Copenhagen, of climate change sceptics. Just as Turnbull was felled by Abbott, running on an anti-ETS platform, Rudd floundered when he was forced to retreat from the ETS. Having championed climate change as 'the greatest moral, economic and environmental challenge of our generation', he ditched his signature policy as soon as his personal popularity began to evaporate. Rather than explain his climb-down in a reasoned manner, he did it on the fly at a hurriedly convened press conference on the fringes of a hospital visit. That morning Lenore Taylor, then of *The Sydney Morning Herald*, published a story that Labor's so-called 'Gang of Four' – Rudd, Gillard, Wayne Swan and Lindsay Tanner – had decided to delay the implementation of the ETS for at least three years. Rudd's chief of staff, Alister Jordan, drafted the makeshift announcement in the front seat of the prime ministerial Holden, as his boss toured the hospital. Green Kevin had become Yellow Kevin.

Following the coup in June 2010, Julia Gillard opted for knee-jerk correctives rather than anything more coherent. First, she announced a withdrawal from the mining tax, which the resources sector had attacked in an advertising blitz targeted in marginal constituencies. Then, in the pages of the Murdoch Sunday tabloids, via a strategically placed front-page splash, she revealed her preference for a 'Small Australia' immigration policy rather than the 'Big Australia' alternative that would have seen the population reach 36 million by 2050. Her public disclosure to Kerry O'Brien during her first foreign visit that she preferred to be a 'stay at home' prime minister rather than a globetrotter was also political. Rather than to remain closer to her homeland, she wanted to distance herself from Kevin '747' Rudd.

As for what she believed, it was hard to tell, other than some generalised commitment to education – the kind of banality upon which it was hard to disagree. Each new week seemed to bring an unveiling of the 'real Julia'. Yet these exercises in reinvention and rebranding underscored how she was struggling not only to find her voice but even to locate herself. That was why the Rudd camp's leaks against her during the 2010 campaign proved so damaging: they revealed she was proposing policies as prime minister, a rise in pensions and parental leave, that she argued against as deputy prime minister. Exacerbating her problems, she stood at the bridge of a party that had lost both anchor and compass. Labor had approached the campaign, as Laura Tingle of the *Australian Financial Review* put it, 'a shallow, timid outfit that doesn't seem to know what it wants to do, except win'.

Her approach during the 2010 campaign to climate change was to issue a definitive pledge not to introduce a carbon tax – 'There will be no carbon tax under the government I lead,' she said. Instead, she planned to turn environmental policy over to a Citizens Assembly, made up of 150 voters. Focus groups had long helped mould policies, but this marked the apotheosis of this method. The policy was a focus group.

After the 2010 election, when her priority was the survival of her precarious minority government, policies were dictated by the terms of political deals. The carbon tax, which she had lobbied against in cabinet and ruled out during the campaign, was the price of Greens' support (a hefty price, too, given that Bob Brown was never going to throw in his lot with the Liberals). Her ongoing support for the National Broadband Network partly stemmed from the rural MP Tony Windsor's enthusiasm for the project, because of its impact on rural Australia. Her commitment to 'pokies' reform secured the backing of the Tasmanian independent MP Andrew Wilkie.

Her public opposition to same-sex marriage was portrayed as being principled. 'I feel that I got on this tram at a different spot,' she explained after leaving office. Yet when she considered softening her position, she was evidently hamstrung by an assurance given to Joe de Bruyn, the socially conservative leader of the Shop, Distributive and Allied Employees' Association, who demanded that she hold firm. (When Kevin Rudd reversed his own stance on the issue, he claimed that the turnaround followed a discussion with a gay member of his staff. But the timing of his announcement, coming just months before he ousted Gillard, seemed part of a calculated effort to isolate his nemesis.)

Education was the area of special interest for Gillard, but the proposals that emerged from her government bore the name of David Gonski, the businessman who put them together. They could hardly be called Gillard's signature reform. Rightly, she was lauded for bringing in a National Disability Insurance Scheme and for introducing plain packaging for cigarettes, but these reforms were hardly difficult sells to the public. Taking on Big Tobacco was popular. Giving assistance to the parents of children suffering from chronic disabilities was never going to cause a stir. Neither involved any political cost. Nor did either policy bear her personal stamp. Bill Shorten was the driving force behind the disability scheme. The Attorney-General Nicola Roxon was the flag-bearer on cigarettes.

The emptiness of Labor's agenda was neatly summarised by the fabulously gruff former resources minister, Martin Ferguson: 'The problem was we had two people who went into parliament with one ambition and one ambition alone – to be prime minister.' Lindsay Tanner, without naming names, lamented that Australian politics was 'drowning in vacuous narcissism'. As a result, 'the battle for ideas is at an all-time low in Australian political life'.

Tony Abbott followed the trend of his two predecessors in trying to undo the faults of the previous governments rather than offering much in the way of an animating programme of his own. His political rise had been based on unremitting negativity, and his two clearest promises were to get rid of the carbon tax and to stop the boats. On Twitter, Rupert Murdoch lauded Abbott for his strong-held beliefs. 'Conviction politicians hard to find anywhere,' he punched out. 'Australia's Tony Abbott rare exception.' But those convictions did not easily translate into policies. Because of his confrontational 'junkyard dog' style, he seemed better suited to being leader of the opposition than prime minister.

At least Abbott had collected his thoughts together in

his 2009 book *Battlelines*. From the broken federation to 'better dental health', from Australia in the Asian century to the problems of indigenous communities, he covered a fair amount of intellectual terrain. But readers of this largely lifeless tract were left with little sense of his overarching vision for Australia.

The shallowness of the Liberal agenda became apparent from the start. Rather than announcing a bold reform, the government demonstrated on its first day in office pettiness by blocking the appointment of the former Labor premier of Victoria, Steve Bracks, who was due to become Australia's consul-general in New York – he was replaced by the former Liberal senator and Howard-era stalwart Nick Minchin. It even forced the ABC broadcaster and former Hawke aide Barrie Cassidy to resign from the council of the Museum of Australian Democracy, and packed the board instead with conservatives, such as the daughter of Robert Menzies, and even Sir David Smith, who was famed for reading from the steps of the Old Parliament House the proclamation from Sir John Kerr sacking Gough Whitlam. Vindictiveness rather than vision appeared to be the new government's driving force.

Even the pro-Liberal *Spectator Australia* complained after three months of the Abbott government that 'a worrying perception has crept in that there is no grand plan with no philosophical backbone'. The same accusation could have been made of the Rudd and the Gillard governments. Of ideologues Australians have always been mistrustful, but not of ideas – the dearth of which was evident on both sides of politics.

For Labor, the recent crossflow of talent between Britain and Australia highlighted the triumph of the political over the philosophical. Within the British Labour Party, there has been keen interest in the work of Tim Soutphommasane, the Australian philosopher who has theorised on how the left can reclaim patriotism, and not surrender it to the right. His thinking has influenced the Labour leader Ed Miliband, and been featured prominently in the *New Statesman*, the organ of the British left. When the Australian Labor Party looked to Westminster, however, it hired John McTernan, a sweary spin-doctor happy to perpetuate the myth in Canberra that he was the inspiration for Malcolm Tucker, the potty-mouthed star of the satirical drama *The Thick of It*. His appointment as Gillard's abrasive communications director showed the preference was for brawn over brains, for aggressiveness over intellectual ambition.

But then Australian politics had reached the point where slogans obviated the need for thoughts, and polls and focus groups substituted for convictions. It was 'government of the people, for the people, by the weekly opinion polls', according to the cartoonist Alan Moir. 'Focus group hell' was how Neil Lawrence, the advertising man who had worked at the heart of the Labor machine, described it. 'Focus groups turn into "fishing expeditions",' he complained. 'Fears, prejudices and concerns are uncovered. "Messaging" is developed and tested to best exploit these . . . The message is delivered as holy writ to the party. Message becomes policy. The aggregate of such policies is "leadership".'

The mightiest focus group of all is the western suburbs of Sydney, that battler bellwether. Policies are expected to pass what is called 'the *Tele* test', an ability to win the approbation of the Murdoch tabloids. But 'the *Tele* test' is truly the western suburbs of Sydney test, because the *Telegraph* is seen as their parish pump. This particularly irked Lindsay Tanner, a proud Melburnian. 'Labor politicians speak of "the *Tele* test" as if there is no other political reality in Australia outside the pages of *The Daily Telegraph*. The fact that it sells a lot fewer papers than the Melbourne *Herald Sun*, and that only a small proportion of marginal seats are located in the paper's heartland in western Sydney, doesn't seem to matter.'

In America, the Republican ascendancy in presidential politics, from the civil rights era to the election of Barack Obama, was based on what was called 'the southern strategy'. It targeted disgruntled white voters, who were socially conservative and frightened about the pace of racial change. During this 40-year phase, all the Democrats who won presidential elections – Lyndon Johnson, Jimmy Carter, Bill Clinton and, diehards would still argue, Al Gore – hailed from the south. They pursued milder versions of 'the southern strategy'. Australian politics has now come to be dominated by a 'western strategy', targeted at the suburbs. In America, the touchstone election was 1968, when Richard Nixon won by exploiting white fears about the speed of racial advance, a breakdown in law and order and the psychedelia of the sixties counter-culture. In Australia, it was the Tampa election in 2001, with all its dark overtones, because it showed how the west supposedly was won.

Consequently, the battlers of this western mortgage belt receive an inordinate amount of attention and consideration. When Julia Gillard wanted to demonstrate her toughness on the boat people issue, a 'community concern' in the west, her media handlers manufactured a photo opportunity on a navy patrol boat in Darwin harbour at which they made sure David Bradbury, the member for Lindsay, the key western suburbs battleground seat, stood alongside her on board.

A climactic moment of the 2010 campaign came when Gillard took on Abbott at the RSL club in Rooty Hill, another western suburb. Why, for long stretches of the campaign, the entire federal election felt like a battle for Rooty Hill.

Making one of her recurrent attempts to relaunch her prime ministership, Gillard spent a week touring the western suburbs, much like an emperor might visit one of the restless outposts of his empire. While there, she pandered to battler bigotry with a blast of the dog whistle, by pledging to 'stop foreign workers being put at the front of the queue with Australian workers at the back'. Labor advisers described her comments as 'economic patriotism', but they sounded blatantly xenophobic. She even went as far as to stay in a local hotel, her choice inevitably the Novotel in Rooty Hill.

When she retreated from pokie reform, it was not just that she no longer needed the support of Andrew Wilkie to keep her in office. She feared the mutinous western suburbs, the unofficial home of electronic gaming. Clubs NSW, modelling its campaign on the mining sector's ad blitz – which, ironically, was masterminded by Neil 'Kevin 07' Lawrence – had launched a television air war.

On the Liberal side, too, the west has come to wield something akin to a veto. Malcolm Turnbull was hobbled from the beginning of his leadership because while progressive-minded voters at eastern suburbs supper parties feted him, he struggled to connect with battlers in the west. The Liberal Party's centre of gravity had shifted from the big end of town in Sydney and Melbourne to the western suburbs, even if its past three leaders have come from three of Sydney's most affluent constituencies. Turnbull, who lived in the richest enclave of the country's richest parliamentary constituency, was a victim of this geographic and demographic realignment.

Ironies abound. The home to two million people, the western suburbs is the country's most ethnically diverse region. New immigrants outnumber battlers. Routinely, the region is erroneously pigeonholed. 'Western Sydney can be whatever you want it to be,' the psephologist Peter Brent has argued, 'a white underclass, "aspirational", falafel-land, McMansion-land, Ugg boots and flannelette shirts, cashed-up bogans.' Moreover, 'Westie' resentment has traditionally arisen from grumbles that they were being ignored, when the opposite is now true.

The presumed political decisiveness of the western suburbs is also mythic. Even at the height of the Howard government's battler popularity, Labor held a vast majority of parliamentary western suburbs seats. The few that went Liberal were the kind of outer-suburban swing seats, like Lindsay, that the government of the day would ordinarily expect to win. Besides, it is always worth remembering that 90 per cent of the Australian electorate lives in northern, eastern and southern suburbs, not to mention the western enclaves of other cities, along with the bush and outback.

The tunnel-vision focus on the western suburbs is also a product of the chronic parochialism that has come to infect political life, even though external events have regularly changed the course of history. In the run-up to the 2001 election, it was the attacks of September 11, which heightened fears about Islamic terrorism and outsiders, and gave the issue of border protection such sinister resonance. Ahead of the 2007 election, it was the unpopularity of the war in Iraq and also the detention of David Hicks without trial at Guantanamo Bay that violated Australia's sense of fair play and due process. In contrast to 2001, where it provided a much-needed boost, Howard's support for the Bush administration's War on Terror hammered him.

The failure of the Copenhagen climate change conference in December 2009 had a profound impact on domestic politics. So much so that it was possible to talk of a BC phase – Before Copenhagen – and its aftermath. Ahead of the summit, where he was appointed to serve as a 'friend of the chairman', Rudd looked invincible. After its failure, almost instantly he looked vulnerable. Copenhagen also gifted Tony Abbott, the newly installed Liberal leader, with a galvanising issue. It was easier to prosecute the argument that Australia should delay the implementation of an emissions trading scheme when the major polluters, America and China, had made such timid commitments.

An environmental catastrophe also played a part in Rudd's ouster six months after Copenhagen. This time it was an oil spill in the Gulf of Mexico, which led Barack Obama, for the second time, to postpone his long-awaited visit to Australia. Air Force One had been scheduled to touch down in Canberra on 18 June 2010. Kevin Rudd was culled on 24 June. Given the improbability of the ALP knife-wielders moving against their leader so soon after such a high-profile visit from the US president who was such a cheerleader, Rudd became almost as much a victim of Deepwater Horizon as those poor pelicans mired in thick black gunge.

Similarly for Tony Abbott, the biggest crisis during his first hundred days came from an external event: Edward Snowden's exposure of sensitive National Security Agency documents detailing Australia's electronic eavesdropping on the Indonesian president that ended up in the *Guardian Australia* and on the ABC. The boat people debate is often conducted in ridiculously provincial terms, as if there had been no civil war in Sri Lanka, no human displacement in Iraq and no persecution of the Shia Hazara people in Afghanistan.

The very idea in this ever more interdependent world that domestic and foreign policies can exist separately is a ludicrous false dichotomy. Julia Gillard may have lamented being taken away from Australian classrooms by the demands of summiteering, but those two prime ministerial activities are actually part of the same goal: maintaining Australia's position in the world. Post-Copenhagen, however, pretty much all politics became local.

If Australian politics is so bad, then why has the country done so well? At first glance, it seems to be modern-day Australia's greatest paradox. In the aftermath of the global financial crisis, the question became even more pertinent, since the recession-free run continued. In the first quarter after the collapse of Lehman Brothers, the economy contracted by 0.5 per cent, the first negative growth in eight years. But in the following quarter it rebounded by 0.4 per cent, thus avoiding two successive quarters of negative growth, the standard definition of a recession. 'Fuck' was the relieved response from Wayne Swan, who suddenly found himself shunted up the running order when speaking at international summits and conferences. Naturally, everyone wanted to know how he and Australia had done it.

The most obvious explanation is that the mining boom, and the attendant export bonanza, bailed out the present crop of leaders. According to Glenn Stevens, the governor of the Reserve Bank, the 'terms of trade boom is potentially the greatest gift the global economy has handed Australia since the gold rush'. The Treasury went even further, describing the rise of resource-hungry China as 'the most profound and beneficial transforming force in our history'. The terms of trade between 2003 and 2013 have been the strongest in 150 years.

Yet just as the mining boom did not save Australia from the 1997 Asian financial crisis or the 2000 recession, it was not solely responsible for inoculating Australia from the contagion of the global financial crisis. As the Rudd government responded with a massive stimulus package, it helped that the nation had such a healthy balance sheet, which was partly down to the tax revenues from the resources sector. But that by no means offers the only explanation why Australia continued to grow.

Above all, the financial crisis showed the strength of the reform legacy, and the sturdiness of the Australian model. As Peter Hartcher has written: 'The new Australian model, more than two decades in the making, had been put through a brutal stress test and emerged, unscathed and untroubled.' Unlike in America and Britain, there were no bank failures or government-sponsored bailouts. Here, Australia was indebted to Paul Keating's 'Four Pillars' banking reforms and also Peter Costello's 'Twin Peaks' regulatory framework.

The anti-merger Four Pillars policy had long been criticised, not least by the banks themselves, for limiting their ability to compete internationally, but this was the very thing that limited their global exposure to the banking crisis. In praising Australia's banking sector, the International Monetary Fund also noted that the Four Pillars policy had limited the presence of international banks, and built up a strong domestic deposit base, which helped too.

Nor did Australia suffer from a sub-prime mortgage crisis, partly because the banks operated under tighter regulations than in the US. The IMF had praised the banking watchdog, the Australian Prudential Regulation Authority, for its 'intense supervisory approach'. Costello's monetary management had also bestowed Australia with a fortress balance sheet, and with it the highest credit rating imaginable – useful defences.

The Reserve Bank of Australia, whose independence was another key reform from the Hawke/Keating era, also proved up to the challenge. Australia had managed to avoid the 1997 Asian financial crisis – what Ross Garnaut has called the 'defining event in the economic history of East Asia' – because of the sure-handed fiscal management of Ian Macfarlane, who decided against raising interest rates to shore up the dollar. In response to the global financial crisis, his successor, Glenn Stevens, and his board cut interest rates to emergency levels, from 7.25 per cent in March 2008 to 3 per cent in April 2009, which helped stave off recession.

Like the RBA, the Treasury did not panic. The advice from the Treasury secretary Ken Henry has already entered the annals of Australian economic history. 'If you really want to make a difference,' he said in the immediate aftermath of the collapse of Lehman Brothers, 'go early, go hard and go households.' That provided the frame for the stimulus package announced two days later by the government. 'The institutional heroes of the GFC were undoubtedly the Reserve Bank and Treasury,' according to George Megalogenis. 'Monetary and fiscal policy moved in tandem for the first time.'

Readers will note the absence so far of political leaders from this narrative, but they deserve significant mention. For the global financial crisis showed what could be achieved when politics was put on hold. On a VIP flight to Perth, on which Rudd brought together his key economic advisers, he announced that he was prepared to take decisions that would risk the wrath of the tabloids. 'Forget about what is going to win us the news [cycle] or lose us the news [cycle],' an aide recalled him saying. 'What is the most responsible thing to do?'

Nor did Malcolm Turnbull, the then Liberal leader, attempt to politicise the crisis. Acting in the national interest, he threw his support behind the first stimulus package. In the immediate aftermath of the crisis, bipartisanship reigned, the political temperature in Canberra dropped and Rudd's decision-making benefited as a result. Whereas Henry had advised the prime minister to go hard and go early, it was Rudd who decided on the size of the stimulus, which at $10 billion was almost double the figure recommended by the Treasury. Rudd and Swan had also acted quickly to forestall a run on the banks, by announcing on a Sunday that the government would guarantee all bank deposits. It staved off a Monday morning panic.

Proof was offered of that hoary old adage that Australia thrives in adversity, but struggles to manage prosperity. However, it also demonstrated what politicians could achieve when they temporarily suspended the partisan game. With prosperity at risk, they could act together in the national interest.

This spirit of bipartisanship did not last long. For his personal role in navigating Australia through the global financial crisis, Swan was honoured with an international award, from the magazine *Euromoney*, of Finance Minister of the Year, much to the merriment of his then shadow, Joe Hockey. To uproarious laughs from the opposition benches, who did not seem at all perturbed by the racial prejudice upon which the joke relied, Hockey pointed out that in 2001 the Pakistan finance minister had also been a recipient. 'That is quite an extraordinary one, that one,' guffawed Hockey. What Hockey was too uninformed to know was that the Pakistan finance minister in question was Shaukat Aziz, who was credited with the reforms that led the country's economy to double in size. To do so, he had given up a highly remunerated career on Wall Street, where he was earmarked as a possible future CEO of Citibank. Aziz was also brave. After becoming prime minister, he was regularly targeted for assassination by the Taliban, who killed his chauffeur and eight others in one close but unsuccessful attempt in 2004 when a suicide bomber detonated explosives adjacent to his car. Compared to Aziz's achievements, Hockey's seemed rather slender. One can easily imagine him running a branch of the ANZ in Neutral Bay but not a global bank. Yet this was also another example of Canberra turning the good into the bad. Hockey, the son of an Armenian-Palestinian, is widely regarded as one of the most big-hearted parliamentarians, and known for his unsung acts of kindness.

Australia's ongoing success can be explained by an updated version of Horne's Lucky Country argument. In the sixties, it was 'the luck of our historical origins', the fact that the British model provided an institutional framework in which the country could prosper. Nowadays, politicians benefit from the policy inheritance from Hawke, Keating and Howard that created the Australian model, with its blend of free market reforms tempered by judicious regulation, which continues to serve the country so well. It has offered much-needed protection from the poison of present-day politics.

Thus, what seems like a paradox is actually two sides of the same coin. The very reforms that made the Australian economy so strong contributed to Australian politics becoming so weak. Success has bred complacency, intellectual laziness and pettiness. Canberra was bankrupt, but its impoverishment was a consequence of a politics of prosperity.

When there is no policy inheritance to fall back on, contemporary politicians have tended to struggle. It explains why global warming has become the third rail of Australian politics, at once hazardous and lethal. Three prime ministers and two party leaders lost their jobs partly because they could not come up with a sustainable policy and political strategy to back it up. John Howard's refusal to ratify Kyoto, after initially signing up to it, showed him to be too out of touch, too set in his ways and too closely aligned with George W.

Bush. Howard's successor, Brendan Nelson, trying to straddle divisions within the party over the issue, first adopted a sceptical line on Kevin Rudd's proposal for an emissions trading scheme, only to reverse himself under pressure from Malcolm Turnbull. Yet he ended up alienating both sides, which cost him the leadership. Turnbull, convinced of the science and also keen to 'green' the Coalition in the same way David Cameron had refashioned the British Conservatives, broadly supported Rudd's push to enact the ETS ahead of the Copenhagen climate change summit. But his environmentalism and high-minded disdain for climate change sceptics within his party room proved to be his undoing. On the Labor side, too, Kevin Rudd and Julia Gillard struggled to come up with a policy that was politically viable, and ended up losing their jobs.

When Ross Garnaut launched his landmark report on global warming in 2008, he characterised climate change as 'a diabolical policy problem . . . harder than any other issue of high importance that has come before our polity in living memory'. It has been so hard for this crop of leaders to cope with, because the reform era did not offer them an answer or a model. Instead, climate change became an issue where the deficiencies of Canberra politics, on both sides, intersected: the failure to educate the public and the unwillingness to defend unpopular policies requiring prime ministerial illumination (which explained Rudd's difficulties, and also some of Gillard's); of how major policy decisions were now dictated by political deals (as with Gillard's carbon tax pact with the Greens); the extent to which policy was governed by narrow, internal party politics rather than guiding principles (which proved Nelson's undoing, and was also evident in Rudd and Gillard's approach), and how glibness and sloganeering often stood in the way of evidence-based policy-making (which was apparent in Abbott's 'tax on everything' jibes about the carbon tax and his appraisal of man-made climate change as 'absolute crap').

With asylum seekers, politicians run into the same problem: that the reform era had not left them a template. Tony Abbott is fond of saying that John Howard handed Labor a solution, which they turned into a problem. It's a neat one-liner, but the Pacific Solution offered the most Pyrrhic of political victories.

In most other areas, especially the economy, second-rate Australian leaders no longer require luck. Instead, they can fall back on the Australian model built by their predecessors. Even this generation of leaders has not yet managed to squander that inheritance.

Chapter 5
REDNECK NATION?

FOR A COUNTRY HABITUALLY maligned as an outpost of male chauvinism and racial prejudice, the opening of its 43rd parliament in 2010 presented a tableau of tolerance. Not only did it feature the country's first female prime minister but also its first female governor-general. Looking more regal than the monarch she represented, Quentin Bryce cut an especially trailblazing figure. A former federal sex discrimination commissioner, she had served as the first female governor of Queensland, Australia's most illiberal state, and also been the first woman admitted to the state bar.

Julia Gillard's cabinet included a record-equalling four women. Among them was the finance minister, Penelope Ying-Yen Wong, whose biographical details spoke of the changes overtaking Australia. Born in Malaysia, she was the first Asian-Australian member of the cabinet. She also happened to be a lesbian, who was about to become the parent, with her gay partner, of a beautiful little girl.

The opposition front bench still looked like a boys' club,

membership of which seemingly stipulated that blue ties be worn at all times. Yet the Liberals' deputy leader, Julie Bishop, had become the first female to scale that high in conservative politics.

Compared to the previous intake, the number of women in the 43rd parliament had declined slightly from 68 to 67. Still, 30 per cent of its membership was female, a substantially higher figure than in Britain (22 per cent) or America (18 per cent).

For Bob Brown, the first openly gay leader of an Australian political party, this would be his last opening ceremony. But his departure paved the way for his fellow Tasmanian, Christine Milne. Never before had two parliamentary parties wielding meaningful power been led by women.

Most of the political editors who peered down from the press gallery – and especially the correspondents who got top billing on the evening news – were men. Nonetheless, women were heavily represented, too. There was the veteran correspondent Michelle Grattan, who, like the legendary Helen Thomas in the White House press corps, had endured decades of sexist jibes, and even the sight, according to Canberra lore, of a flaccid penis dangled before her when she was up against deadline ('Put it away, cobber,' was reportedly her unflustered response). Alongside her were some of the country's most influential reporters and commentators: Laura Tingle, Lenore Taylor, Sabra Lane, Katharine Murphy, Lyndal Curtis, Heather Ewart, Samantha Maiden and Annabel Crabb. Kerry O'Brien at that time still presented the ABC flagship, *The 7.30 Report*, but it would not be long before a woman, Leigh Sales, took over the anchor's chair. Kate Torney, the ABC executive who made the appointment, was also the first woman to become director of news at the national broadcaster.

For the first time in its 109-year history, during which 1093 people had served as members, the House of Representatives also welcomed its first indigenous MP. Ken Wyatt, a Liberal from Western Australia, celebrated by wearing a kangaroo skin adorned with feathers from a red-tailed black cockatoo. In the foyer of Parliament House, he was also greeted by a traditional smoking and Welcome to Country ceremony, a ritual first instituted by Kevin Rudd in 2008 to make indigenous culture more central in public life. In that spirit, many MPs accepted the invitation of the Ngambri elder Matilda House to be cleansed on the forecourt of Parliament House, where eucalypt leaves smouldered in the spring sunshine.

Along with this racial first came a religious first. The Labor MP, Ed Husic, the son of Bosnian immigrants, became the chamber's first Muslim. He took his oath of office on the Koran.

At the state level, too, there were signs of greater tolerance. Two years earlier, Anna Bligh had become the first Australian woman to win election as a premier. In the Queensland state legislature, 30 out of 89 members were women, the third highest level of female representation of any legislative body in the world. South of the border in New South Wales, Kristina Keneally became the state's first female premier. In the country's oldest state, the premier, the deputy premier and the state governor were all women. In 2011, Lara Giddings became Tasmania's first female premier. It meant that South Australia was now the only state or territory not to have been led by a woman.

As is so often the case in Australia, however, appearances could be deceptive, and the picture was not as positive as it seemed. Julia Gillard owed her rise to the so-called 'faceless men' who continued to dominate the ALP's macho politics. There were no faceless women. During her short spell in office, Gillard had also started to experience a torrent of sexism, which raised the question asked intermittently over the years of whether Australia was ready for a female prime minister. 'Strewth, there's a Sheila running Oz,' was the *Daily Mail*'s cheeky take from London, a headline that served as a reminder of how Australia continued to be regarded globally as a near-impregnable bastion of male chauvinism with a ceiling made of exceptionally resilient glass.

In New South Wales, Kristina Keneally appeared to be a marionette controlled by shady Labor chieftains, all of them men. 'I am nobody's puppet, I am nobody's protégé, I am nobody's girl,' she protested on the floor of the state legislature. But few believed her. Her promotion could never be portrayed as a feminist triumph. Rather, the thinking behind it was to put a telegenic face on an unsightly political machine.

Anna Bligh's popularity had also nose-dived, despite her sure-footed response to the 2011 floods, when some international viewers mistakenly thought they were watching the country's new female prime minister. Dumped by Queensland voters at the 2012 election, her defeat meant that no female premier had ever won re-election.

After his election, Ken Wyatt had found himself the victim of racist hate mail when some voters realised that they had voted for an Aboriginal, something that was not immediately apparent from his appearance. His constituency office received at least 50 abusive emails and telephone calls.

Ed Husic had also been the victim of prejudice. Blasting the dog whistle, his one-time Liberal opponent, David Barker, criticised him for being a 'strong Muslim' – although, to its credit, the Liberal Party dumped Barker as a candidate. As for Julie Bishop, she would soon be called a 'bimbo' by the Labor backbencher Steve Gibbons.

The experience of Gillard, Bligh, Wyatt and Husic, as well as offering such a visible sign of progress, also spoke of how far Australia still had to go before it could bury its reputation as a redneck nation.

It has always been easy to cast Australia as unusually xenophobic, racist and intolerant, and to agree with Barry Humphries' zinging one-liner: 'Xenophobia is love of Australia!' Following Federation, the first legislative acts of the new parliament were to mint the 'White Australia' policy into law, with the Immigration Restriction Act and the Pacific Islander Labourers Act. This was no accident. Racial purity was the new nation's crucible idea, born of what Alfred Deakin, the country's second prime minister, described during his speech on the immigration bill as 'the instinct for self-preservation'. It would protect the people of Australia from 'the coloured races which surround us, and are inclined to invade our shores'. Fully in support, Edmund Barton, Australia's first prime minister and the leader of the Protectionist Party, declared: 'I do not think that the doctrine of equality of man was ever really intended to include racial equality.' The Labor Party was in furious agreement. The first clause of its 1905 manifesto upheld 'the cultivation of an Australian sentiment based on the maintenance of racial purity'.

Jack Lang, the famed Labor premier of New South Wales, called the White Australia policy 'Australia's Magna Carta', and praised it for stopping Australia being 'engulfed in an Asian tidal wave' – language that would find an echo decades later. It was a Labor immigration minister, Arthur Calwell, who joked in parliament in 1947 that 'two Wongs don't make a White', which entered the annals as the ugliest of racist slurs.

During World War II, black American GIs arriving to defend Australia were blocked from entering the country by officious officials enforcing the letter of the White Australia policy. When they were finally let in, the troops were deployed in the north, a safe distance from the major cities.

Even after the war, when Australia adopted a mass immigration policy, it was the product of nativist thinking. Primarily it was 'a defence against a renewed threat from the north', according to the historian John Hirst. 'Better the dark-skinned Greek than the Japanese.' Remarkably, the White Australia policy was not killed off until the early 1970s, a full decade after a young preacher from Montgomery, Alabama, had stood in front of the brooding statue of Abraham Lincoln and delivered the 'I Have a Dream' speech.

The condition of indigenous Australians points not only to a malignant legacy of racism, but also an ongoing breach between black and white Australia. The first Australians were not granted a full menu of constitutional rights until the 1967 referendum, and to this day are not mentioned in the preamble to the constitution. The forthcoming Recognition Referendum, which enjoys bipartisan support, aims to rectify this. Worryingly, however, the vote, planned for 2013, was postponed because of the widespread feeling that the country was not ready, and the necessary preparatory work had not been done. Understandably, the authors of the constitutional amendment wanted to be deliberative, in order to get the language absolutely right – the words they originally came up with were deemed too strong by the Gillard government. But the idea that educational work was still required to prepare white Australia for the change was dispiriting nonetheless. At least the parliamentary committee overseeing the drafting process includes two Aboriginal lawmakers, Ken Wyatt and the former athlete Nova Peris, now a Labor senator.

Even the national apology to members of the Stolen Generations had faced bitter opposition, not least from

John Howard, even though uttering a two-syllable word came at such little cost to white Australians. After all, there was never any question of it being accompanied by reparations or compensation.

The rise of Pauline Hanson in the mid-1990s gave the redneck nation of lore a figurehead – a flame-haired bogan Boadicea, who ran a fish and chip shop. 'I and most Australians want our immigration policy radically reviewed and that of multiculturalism abolished,' she said during her maiden speech to parliament in September 1996, following her election as the member for Oxley. 'I believe we are in danger of being swamped by Asians.' Her words, which resonated for so many lower income Australians who felt their livelihoods were threatened by mass immigration, lit up the switchboard at Parliament House. 'Love at first sight,' was how the columnist Paul Sheehan described the reaction from a significant portion of the population.

From the prime minister of the day John Howard came the sound of silence. Retrospectively, in his memoir, he argued that he condemned Hanson in two interviews on Channel Nine with Ray Martin. Yet his failure to come out emphatically against her infuriated even Liberal loyalists. Rather, in a speech to the Queensland Liberal Party following Hanson's incendiary remarks in parliament, he seemed almost to welcome her presence on the political scene. The events of the past six months, he said in an oblique reference to Hanson, lifted the 'pall of political correctness' and allowed Australians to 'speak a little more freely and a little more openly about what they feel'. Howard now claims he was misunderstood. The problem was that he himself had called for a curb on Asian immigration in 1988, saying during a radio interview that it needed to be 'slowed down a little' – an admission for which he later apologised.

Howard stoked racial fears during the 2001 election when he refused to grant the *Tampa* entry, and lied about asylum seekers tossing children overboard so the Australian navy would have no choice but to rescue them. Liberal Party commercials featuring the prime minister's pithy declaration, 'We will decide who comes here, and in what circumstances,' were replayed ad nauseum. 'The race card has been introduced into this election,' complained Neville Wran, the former Labor premier of New South Wales. 'It's a card and an introduction which we and our children will live to regret.' The former Liberal leader, John Hewson, assailed Howard for unleashing the 'latent racial prejudice in significant sections of the Australian community'. Perhaps most damning of all was the veteran diplomat Richard Woolcott, the former head of Australia's Department of Foreign Affairs and Trade: 'We are witnessing a recrudescence of those old barbarisms: racism, religious intolerance and jingoism.'

The Cronulla riot in December 2005 appeared to show again how racism lurking so close to the surface of national life could burst into the violent open. But Howard did not see it that way. There was 'no underlying racism in Australia', he said afterwards, which seemed an extraordinarily blinkered view, and denied the evidence of the ugly footage from the Shire showing young white men baring their chests, flexing their pumped-up muscles, brandishing their Southern Cross tattoos, waving their Aussie flags and hurling punches and racist abuse. 'Fuck the wogs,' slurred one young man who was part of the 'we grew here you flew here' flash mob.

The spate of violent attacks against Indian students in Melbourne and Sydney brought another rash of unfavourable headlines, not least from South Asia where the country's histrionic media went into overdrive. Not all the attacks were racially motivated. Primarily they were street crimes rather than hate crimes, according to the Victoria Police, who believed Indian students were especially vulnerable because of their anti-social working hours. But I heard first-hand from enough victims who described how the hail of punches was usually accompanied by a hail of racist abuse.

In the Australian workplace, it is easy to uncover evidence of racial discrimination. When a group of economists fired off 4000 fake job applications, it revealed that an applicant with a Chinese name had to make 68 per cent more approaches to secure an interview than a candidate with an Anglo-Saxon name. In the Australian Defence Force, a 2007 study found that 94 per cent of its permanent members were born in Australia, New Zealand, the UK or Ireland. Only 1 per cent were Asian-born. In the 43rd parliament, just 1.3 per cent of lawmakers were of a non-European background – Ken Wyatt, Penny Wong and Senator Lisa Singh, the country's first parliamentarian of Indian origin.

Regularly I found myself covering stories, like the attacks on Indian students, which reinforced the prejudiced worldwide view of this supposedly prejudiced country. Just as US-based reporters end up spending a disproportionate amount of time on guns and God, Australian-based correspondents served up a steady stream of bigotry stories. Communities like Camden in New South Wales continued to resist attempts to build Islamic schools in their bucolic midst. 'I don't want my kids learning Islamic,' said a leading light in the local community group, who wore a cowboy hat adorned with the Australian flag and who seemed to be auditioning for the role of the next Pauline Hanson.

Other small towns, like Woodside in the Adelaide Hills, bitterly resisted the opening of onshore processing centres. A sign had gone up on the approach to town, 'No refugees, honk if you agree,' which got 65 honks in the space of

45 minutes. At least, the sign did not read: 'Fuck off, we're full.'

During the 2007 campaign, there was the infamous Lindsay pamphlet scandal. A flyer distributed by the husband of the Liberal MP Jackie Kelly purported to come from a made-up group called the Islamic Australia Federation. It thanked the ALP for its support of the Bali bombers. Muslims had overtaken Asians as the main target of discrimination.

As victims of prejudice took to social media to publicise their attacks, or uploaded onto YouTube videos of ugly incidents, Australian racism went viral. There was an instant digital outcry when the ABC presenter Jeremy Fernandez described in almost real-time on Twitter how he had been subjected to a vicious racist rant in front of his two-year-old daughter while taking her on the bus to day care. 'Anyone who says racism is dying is well and truly mistaken,' he wrote, in a stream of tweets. 'It's a sad thing when a coloured man in 2013 has to show his kid how to hold their nerve in the face of racist taunts.' Fernandez broke down and cried when he had dropped his daughter off at day care. What made his story all the more powerful was that Fernandez could easily be the face of the new Australia, a poster-boy of immigrant success. Born in Malaysia, of southern Indian heritage, he came here with his family 22 years ago, aged 13, and is one of the national broadcaster's rising stars.

Commercial television threw up a rogues' gallery of miscreants, who spoke of a more endemic problem. When Channel Ten cast around for a host to front its new breakfast programme, it thought it had found the ideal candidate over the Ditch in Auckland. Paul Henry's career was on the skids in New Zealand, following his resignation from the broadcaster TVNZ for lampooning the surname of one of India's senior politicians Sheila Dikshit, during a segment on the Commonwealth Games. 'The dip shit woman', and 'Dick Shit', he called her, dissolving into a cackle of hyena-like laughter with each mention of her name. 'It's so appropriate, because she's Indian,' he added, 'so she'd be dick-in-shit wouldn't she, do you know what I mean?' Henry, who had tried unsuccessfully to win a seat in parliament with the conservative National Party, had form. Homosexuals, he said on air in 2009, were 'unnatural'. Susan Boyle, the Scottish singer, was 'retarded'. When a Greenpeace campaigner appeared on his programme that same year, he poked fun at her facial hair. In another infamous episode, he questioned whether the country's governor-general, Sir Anand Satyanand, who was of Indian descent, was 'even a New Zealander'.

His controversy-punctuated career had not escaped the attention of Channel Ten. Far from it: that was precisely why they wanted him. Rather than reworking his on-screen persona, they wanted him raw. Alas, Australian commercial television is a place where the racist, the sexist and the homophobic can find a richly remunerated home.

Henry did not disappoint. The boat people debate gave him the perfect platform, and he was quick to seize upon the comic potential of a plan from the Gillard government to give families the opportunity to house asylum seekers. 'Why not criminals?' he asked. 'Not murderers, but low level criminals. You could – the jails could be smaller and you could put them in homestay situations. The mentally ill.' When his co-host, Andrew Rochford, who acted as Henry's minder, said it was not as if they would end up living in the linen cupboard, Henry spotted another opening. 'Oh, that's a good idea. That's a good idea, 300 bucks a week for the linen cupboard,' he said, manically. 'You'd want to get the linen out, wouldn't you?' Now, he was hitting his rhythm. 'Oh, these shirts are dirty. Ergh,' he said. Then he pretended to hold up towels, and sniffed them, as if he had just noticed dog shit on his shoe. 'Oh no, don't ask.' And still he went on. 'We've got someone living in the linen cupboard, kids, just don't go in there.' Unbeknown to Henry, thousands of Australians supported the scheme, and volunteered to billet boat people in their homes.

In New Zealand, Henry's departure from TVNZ stirred debate over whether he had fallen victim to political correctness gone mad. To give him such a high-profile role in Australia, given his long track record of polluting the airwaves, was political incorrectness run amok. Quickly, the ratings for the breakfast show slumped. It was pulled after 281 days.

When it comes to chasing ratings with bigots and xenophobes, Channel Ten is by no means the worst culprit. Channel Nine is more of a serial offender. Not many reputable broadcasters would allow onto its airwaves Sam Newman, the presenter of the AFL version of *The Footy Show*. Channel Nine regard him as a prized asset. Delving into 'Sam's Mailbag' during the show in 2009, he plucked out the story of a 107-year-old woman in Malaysia, who had just married a new husband. 'What sort of monkey would be marrying that woman?' he asked, brandishing a photo of the groom. 'Ah, that monkey right there,' he added. The footballer Brendan Fevola, not a figure one would normally expect to play the grown-up in the room, interjected. 'You can't call him a monkey.' But Newman was undeterred. 'This doesn't go to Malaysia, this programme, does it?' he said. 'That man is not long out of the forest.' Remarkably, the network defended Newman, describing the monkey gibe as 'irreverent' satire rather than a racist insult.

Nine evidently had few qualms about Newman's bigoted on-screen persona. In 1999, he had 'blacked up' to impersonate the indigenous footballer Nicky Winmar, a player who had allegedly been the victim of racial vilification from fellow players and who had once raised his guernsey to brandish his black skin in protest at the abuse he was getting from the crowd. Newman had also provoked an outcry when he made fun of the sports journalist Caroline Wilson's dress sense by carrying a lingerie-clad model onto set, upon which he stapled a cut-out of her face. Calls for his sacking also followed another segment, a pre-recorded interview with the Tasmanian MP Paula Wriedt, whom he deemed 'worth coming on'. Once again Nine backed its controversial host, claiming that his comment was misconstrued and that he was merely extending an invitation to appear on the programme.

In some respects, the sins of Channel Nine's tabloid news show, *A Current Affair*, are even more egregious, because they come from the news division. What became known as 'The Asian Mall' story was particularly heinous, because it was presented as journalism, and must have passed through some kind of editing process. It claimed, wrongly, that Asian businesses were 'kicking out' white shop owners at a shopping mall in Castle Hill, a suburb in northwest Sydney, so that they could target the area's growing Asian population. 'Concerned citizens' spoke of an 'Asian invasion'. To spice the pot even further, the reporter interviewed Pauline Hanson, for whom the eviction of white shopkeepers proved that Asians were swamping Australia. Gladly playing on her own idiocy, Hanson asked the government to 'please explain'.

Following complaints from residents of Castle Hill, upset at being portrayed as racists, the media watchdog, the Australian Communications and Media Authority, weighed in. It found that the report contained 'inaccurate factual material' and had a 'gratuitous emphasis on ethnic origin', not an inaccurate description of *A Current Affair*'s in-house style. The programme is, after all, a repeat offender. In February 2012 it ran a story headlined 'Asian bride invasion'.

Its Channel Seven rival, *Today Tonight*, ploughs the same xenophobic furrow. In May 2012, it sent Pauline Hanson on an undercover mission to expose a black market in passports that was supposedly placing Australia's borders in peril. According to Tim Soutphommasane, 'all that was on display was a tabloid reprisal of old fears about Australia being invaded by yellow hordes from Asia'. For Channel Seven, its fly-on-the-wall documentary show, *Border Security: Australia's Front Line*, has also been a ratings hit. In my first week in Australia, it was the highest ranked show, beating even the tribute programmes broadcast for Steve Irwin.

As well as the transgressions of the tabloid news shows, discrimination works in subtler ways, too. Until recently, Channel Ten's *Neighbours* had not included an Asian cast member who lasted on the show more than a year. Instead, it featured transient characters, like the Korean exchange student, Sunny Lee, who could be extricated quickly.

Compared to Sam Newman and *A Current Affair*'s horrors, Channel Nine's other controversies look like relatively minor misdemeanours. But that is not how the *Hey Hey It's Saturday* 'blackface skit' appeared to the visiting star, Harry Connick Jr. A staple of Australian viewing in the 1970s, the variety show spooled back to that unreconstructed era when it aired a talent segment in which five men appeared in frizzy, gollywog wigs with their faces daubed in black make-up and impersonated the Jackson Five. Halfway through the song they were joined by another person pretending to be Michael Jackson, whose face was painted white. Connick Jr, a guest judge on the show, signalled his immediate displeasure by scoring the performance '0'. 'Man, if they turned up looking like that in the United States . . .' said the singer, 'it'd be hey hey there's no more show.'

Later, as the final credits were about to roll, he was invited back onto the set of the live broadcast so that host Daryl Somers could issue a grovelling apology. The singer, a native of New Orleans, explained that the skit would have been unacceptable in his homeland where 'black minstrels' evoked the era of Jim Crow, when the races were separated in the American south from the cradle to the grave.

During the blackface controversy, Bill O'Reilly of Fox News came to the country's defence. The skit 'is not representative of Australia', he said. 'This is just a bad decision by stupid producers.' Unquestionably that was true. But it was broadcast here, and probably would have stirred little controversy had not the judging panel included an American. In the UK or US, I suspect, the idea for the skit would not have made it past the first production meeting, but in Australia it was deemed well within the parameters of the funny and acceptable. Perhaps nobody sounded the alarm through fears of being seen as a prude or wowser, arguably a more serious offence in Australia than some old-fashioned racial stereotyping.

The Australian arm of Kentucky Fried Chicken, when it launched a new advertising campaign to go with its sponsorship of Twenty20 cricket, mined similar negative stereotypes. In one of the adverts, a lone white cricket fan, dressed in the green and gold of the national team, kept on having his view obstructed by a group of West Indian fans, dancing and swaying to a calypso beat. Seeking to pacify the black folks in front, he pulled out a bucket of fried chicken. Immediately, they were subdued. Again, on Madison Avenue or in London's Soho, the idea for the slot surely would not have made it past a brainstorming session. In Australia, the concept took an untroubled journey all the way to air, where it found a happy home on Channel Nine in commercial breaks between overs.

What made the controversies all the more arresting was the discrepancy in responses between Australia and America. In the US, Kentucky Fried Chicken came close to provoking a boycott from civil rights groups angry over the use of such a derogatory stereotype. Harry Connick's star power also meant the *Hey Hey* skit generated a wave of negative American coverage (even though it later emerged that the singer had himself once blacked up for a comedy sketch). By strange coincidence, Julia Gillard, the then deputy prime minister, happened to be in Washington at the time, a capital still aglow from the election of Barack Obama. Faced with questions on the controversy back home, she opted for the stock response: that it was only meant as a joke. 'Obviously, I think whatever happened was meant to be humorous and would be taken in that spirit by most Australians,' she said. With that brief explanation, Gillard revealed the racial sensibility gap between Australia and America. When it comes to acceptable racial behaviour, most other developed countries have adopted a higher standard than Australia. In other countries, the blackface skit would have been deemed socially unacceptable, commercially damaging and plain insulting. In Australia, it was commonly brushed away with a laugh or teasing punch to the upper arm.

The flippancy of Australian racism came to the fore again after a young Collingwood fan racially vilified Adam Goodes, the indigenous star of the Sydney Swans, at the MCG in 2013. Towards the end of the game, part of the AFL's Indigenous Round of fixtures, the 13-year-old girl called him 'an ape'. Goodes, one of the code's model players, was appalled. 'It's not the first time on the footy field I've been referred to as a monkey or an ape. It was shattering,' he said afterwards. 'I just thought how could that happen? And all this week, you know, this week is a celebration of our people and our culture.' After the game, Eddie McGuire, the president of Collingwood, had personally sought out Goodes to apologise. But only a few days later, he reignited the racism row during his breakfast radio programme. To promote the opening of the new stage show *King Kong* an inflatable gorilla was to be paraded in Melbourne. 'Get Adam Goodes down for it, d'you reckon?' McGuire wisecracked. Rather than opting for the traditional 'it was only meant as a joke' defence, afterwards he claimed it was 'a slip of the tongue' and that he did not have a racist bone in his body. But it felt like a return to the bad old days of *The Bulletin* in the early 1960s when 'Abo' jokes were a staple of the cartoon page.

The easy embrace of racially insensitive language is part of the same problem. After arriving in Australia, I was shocked at how often I heard the word 'Abo', even from well-remunerated and supposedly well-educated Australians who should have known better, and doubtless did. They used it even in polite company. The word 'Lebo' was also modish, and spoke of the creeping Islamaphobia that followed the attacks of 9/11 and the Bali bombings. But again this vocabulary pointed towards low-level racism and racial insensitivity rather than deep-rooted malevolence. It was primarily a patronising ignorance.

While I quickly learned that 'wog' had a wholly different meaning in Australia – to utter it in the UK is immediately to identify yourself as a hardcore racist – I thought it dispiriting nonetheless that newly arrived immigrants adopted a slur as an ethnic badge of honour partly to accelerate their assimilation. Bringing with them good ethnic food helped win greater acceptance – the route to the Australian heart is often through the stomach. But new arrivals also sought favour by making fun of their own ethnicity, which they knew would appeal to the piss-taking side of the Australian character.

Not insignificantly, the group of doctors who performed the blackface skit on *Hey Hey It's Saturday* were testament to the changing face of modern Australia. It included a Sri Lankan-Australian, an Indian-Australian, a Greek-Australian, an Irish-Italian-Australian and a Lebanese-Australian.

On assignment in Australia for *The Daily Show*, the British comedian John Oliver was struck by the prevalence of racism. 'Australia turns out to be a sensational place, albeit one of the most comfortably racist places I've ever been in,' he said on returning to America. 'They've really settled into their intolerance like an old resentful slipper.'

Covering Australia, however, I was constantly struck by a more powerful counter-story that often went unreported: a story of multicultural success. Few countries have experienced such massive and rapid demographic change in so short a space of time with such little violent backlash or ethnic unrest. Since the war, when over 90 per cent of its population was Anglo-Celtic, seven million immigrants from more than 230 countries arrived in what was to become a largely harmonious multi-ethnic nation. Australia's proportion of people born overseas – 26 per cent – is the highest of any OECD nation with a population of over ten million people, but other countries with smaller immigrant communities confront more serious problems with racism. The latest research suggests that one in eight Australians is avowedly racist, which sounds high. But in the US, the figure is one in five, while in the EU it is one in three. An explanation of why Australia has a less severe racism problem than Britain or France is that the country harbours so many ethnicities that it has diffused negative feelings against one particular group.

For a country where the 'White Australia' policy endured with mainstream and bipartisan support for so long, multiculturalism took hold with remarkable speed and relative ease. 'Australia today is a collection of minorities,' wrote the influential journalist Craig McGregor in 1980, less than a decade after the policy had been consigned to history. The old idea about 'a single-ethnic nation, unified in everything from colour (white) to race (Anglo-Saxon) to culture (European) to ideals (everyone the same) has just about been abandoned'. That same year, the Special Broadcasting Service, or SBS as it is better known, went on air, with a documentary fittingly enough entitled *Who Are We?*. A major milestone not only for Australian broadcasting but also for society as a whole, its creation meant that multiculturalism had its own publicly funded television channel.

The 1967 referendum may have been a long time coming, but it won overwhelming support. Ninety per cent wanted to improve the lot of indigenous people, which suggested strongly that Australians were moving away from the White Australia model. Never before had a Yes vote in a referendum drawn such broad support. This spirit of greater inclusiveness had been evident, too, during the 1956 Olympics, when Melburnians welcomed the world to their city, and also invited foreign Olympians into their homes. With the game's organisers unable to accommodate all the competitors, local people were asked to help billet them. This open-home policy produced a surprising degree of open-mindedness, with Melburnians showing a preference for non-Anglo guests. Melbourne came to be dubbed the 'Friendly Games', partly because of the city's hospitality. Ironically, Dame Edna Everage, a creation intended to savage narrow-minded monoculturalism, was modelled on an Olympic hostess. The discrimination shown by Dame Edna's fellow hostesses, however, was positive: they wanted athletes of colour in their homes. 'After that,' observed Clive James, 'the White Australia policy had no chance of survival.'

The Melbourne Games had another nice multi-ethnic touch. For the first time at the closing ceremony, the competing national teams mingled together as they marched around the MCG's athletics track. The idea came from a Chinese-Australian, 17-year-old John Ian Wing, who wrote anonymously to the organising committee with his suggestion, acted upon at every Olympics since.

Hansonism proved a shorter-lived phenomenon. One Nation received 22 per cent of the vote in the 1998 Queensland state elections, giving it the largest share of the vote among conservative parties in the state and 11 of 89 seats in parliament. At that year's federal election, in which Hanson lost her seat, the party's support peaked nationally at 9 per cent. Thereafter it dwindled. When Hanson ran for the New South Wales Legislative Council in 2011, she received just 2 per cent of the vote. One Nation's one-time figurehead is now a figure of fun. Nothing spoke more of her has-been status than her appearance on *Dancing with the Stars*. One Nation is no longer a serious force.

Cronulla was an aberration, so shocking because these kinds of incidents are so rare. It was an ugly snapshot that did not reflect the broader picture. There has been no repeat, and from a distance Cronulla looks like a relatively minor disturbance compared to racial conflagrations seen in France, Germany and Britain. Glen Steele, the former Cronulla Sharks player whose bare-chested inflammatory speech that hot afternoon whipped up some of the hatred, even wrote a letter the day afterwards to the Lebanese community blaming his racist rant on drunkenness. 'I am deeply embarrassed and ashamed,' he wrote, discomfited, rather than proud, at being portrayed as the tattooed embodiment of Australian racism.

When in September 2012 a group of Islamic extremists protesting an anti-Muslim film produced in America clashed with police on the streets of Sydney's CBD and carried placards reading 'Behead all those who insult the prophet', the columnist Greg Sheridan described it as 'a crisis for Australian multiculturalism'. ABC's *7.30* even called it a 'Muslim uprising', showing that even a reputable news programme could be prone to the risible excesses of tabloid TV. But if a relatively small disturbance that resulted in the arrest of only nine people can truly be described as a 'crisis' then Australian multiculturalism must be in good shape. Muslim community groups were quick to condemn the violence, in which six police officers were hurt, and placed the demonstrators in their rightful context, as members of a small extremist fringe.

The attacks on Indian students badly dented Melbourne's international reputation. An Indian newspaper, the *Mail Today*, even went as far as to publish a cartoon depicting a police officer in the white robes and conical helmet of the Ku Klux Klan – much to the annoyance of Julia Gillard, who was quick to condemn the cartoon and its wider insinuation. But much of the international coverage overlooked the fact that Melbourne can actually lay claim, as its civic website proclaims, to being 'the home, workplace and leisure centre of one of the world's most harmonious and culturally diverse communities'. As early as the mid-1970s, 20 per cent of the city's population spoke a non-English first language, without any vicious backlash. Nowadays residents from 140 nations coexist happily side by side. One of the city's most popular recent politicians was Mayor John So, who was born in Hong Kong. When the Australian Institute of Criminology conducted a study of the attacks it found that international students were less likely to be assaulted than the average person in Australia.

Doubtless there have been racist overtones in the boat people furore. For many, visceral feelings are aroused by the sight of boats heading to Australian shores, even though so few reach the mainland. Australia can come across as 'The Frightened Country' described by Manning Clark. The debate would be altogether different, as Robert Manne has argued, if it were white farmers fleeing the Mugabe regime in Zimbabwe held in indefinite detention instead of Sri Lankans, Afghanis or Iraqis. But public antipathy is more complex. For a start, boat people are deemed to violate Australia's fairness code. As Manne writes: 'For many Australians the spontaneous arrival of asylum-seeker boats offends the central political virtue of the nation – the idea of the "fair go".'

Chris Bowen, the former Labor treasurer who grew up in the western suburbs of Sydney and represents an electorate there, says that the voters most concerned about unauthorised immigrants are authorised immigrants. 'The people who raise this most regularly and most passionately with me are recent migrants, and often refugees themselves, who had to wait in a camp for years, and still have brothers and sisters waiting to come out,' he observed. 'It's also about fair play: they don't think it's a fair or orderly system.' That last point is well made. The arrival of the boats flies in the face of the Australian preference for order and regulation.

Even Calwell's infamous parliamentary slur, ill-judged though it was, has been taken out of context. He was making a ham-fisted joke at the expense of a fellow parliamentarian, Sir Thomas White, which is why the word 'White' was capitalised in Hansard. That said, he continued to be a staunch defender of the White Australia policy. 'I reject, in conscience, the idea that Australia should or ever can become a multiracial society and survive,' he wrote in his 1972 memoir.

Calwell got it badly wrong. Not only has the nation become a multi-racial society, Australians have overwhelmingly embraced its diversity. 'Australians are largely tolerant people who are accepting and welcoming of other cultures,' was the conclusion of a 12-year study conducted by researchers at the University of Western Sydney, who interviewed more than 12,000 people. Overall, 86.8 per cent agreed with the statement: 'It is a good thing for a society to be made up of people from different cultures.' Only 6.5 per cent disagreed. Nearly 80 per cent also felt comfortable around people of different ethnic backgrounds. But the study also revealed problems. Many Australians – 41 per cent – had a narrow view of who belonged in Australia. One in ten had 'very problematic views on diversity and on ethnic differences'. Unsurprisingly, older white Australian men, without a formal education, tended to be the most racist.

Yet the main findings were positive, and broadly in line with other surveys. The 2013 Mapping Social Cohesion Report from the Scanlon Foundation and Monash University also found that 84 per cent agreed with the proposition 'multiculturalism is good for Australia'. When the National Australia Day Council commissioned a survey it found 89 per cent agreed that it was important to recognise cultural diversity, while 90 per cent thought it was important to recognise Australian indigenous culture as part of Australia Day celebrations. When in 2011 the OECD brought out a report studying racial tolerance around the world, Australia ranked at the very top alongside Canada.

Sports teams are starting to look more like Australia. The Mervs, Marks and Shanes have been joined by a Moises (Henriques, a Portuguese-Australian), an Ashton (Agar, of Sri Lankan descent) and a Fawad (Ahmed, a Pakistan-born cricketer, whose citizenship was conferred by a hastily arranged vote in parliament so that he was eligible for the 2013 Ashes series). In January 2011, Usman Khawaja became the first Muslim to don the Baggy Green, a player who struggles to cement his place not because of his religion but his dearth of runs. Cricket Australia is also trying hard to shed its Anglo image. To bolster a grass-roots effort aimed at attracting new immigrants to the game, it appointed a former Iraqi refugee, Sam Almaliki, as a development officer. His introduction to cricket came from watching fellow detainees at Sydney's Villawood detention centre.

The new occasionally clashes with the old. Fawad Ahmed came in for criticism from the former Test star Doug Walters after deciding not to wear the Victoria Bitter logo on his Australian shirt (Cricket Australia had asked if he felt uncomfortable doing so). 'If he doesn't want to wear the team gear,' said Walters, lapsing into the bigotry of old Australia, 'he should not be part of the team.' 'Well said, Doug,' said the ever-quotable David Campese, the epitome of the ugly Australian. 'Tell him to go home.' Overwhelmingly, though, non-Anglo players have been accepted. When Ashton Agar came close to scoring a century on debut against England in the 2013 Ashes, he became an overnight national hero.

The Socceroos, by far the most demographically representative team, is packed with the sons of immigrants: Schwarzers, Aloisis, Ognenovskis, Brescianos. Its star player, Tim Cahill, was born in Sydney of a Samoan mother and an English father of Irish descent. In a nation of immigrants, it is the migrant game. Successfully multi-ethnic A-League teams, like the newly formed Western Sydney Wanderers, have also brought harmony to a code which in the days of the now-defunct National Soccer League was occasionally a battleground for rival ethnic groups.

In an uplifting postscript to the Adam Goodes controversy, he was a deserved winner of Australian of the Year in 2014, and set as his goal raising awareness of racism. It was not the first time that the award had been used to right a racial wrong.

Just as Australia's economic model has proven unusually robust, the same is true of its multicultural model. 'Australian governments have always balanced the endorsement of cultural diversity with affirmations of national unity,' writes Tim Soutphommasane. 'The freedom to express one's cultural identity and heritage has been formalised as a right . . . but this has been balanced by civic responsibilities.' Robert Hughes, in a speech in New York in the early 1990s, said that Australia was 'no Utopia but a less truculent immigrant society' than America. 'Intelligent multiculturalism works to everyone's social advantage,' he said, 'and the conservative crisis-talk about creating "a cultural tower of Babel" and so forth is seen as obsolete alarmism of a fairly low order.' Bill Clinton, visiting Sydney in 1996, also gave Australian multiculturalism a presidential endorsement. Of his host city, he noted: 'I cannot think of a better place in the entire world, a more shining example of how people can come together as one nation and one community.'

Many on the right reject the notion of Australian multicultural success because they reject multiculturalism outright. 'I am always reluctant to use the term multiculturalism,' says Scott Morrison. Many on the left downplay this national achievement because it does not fit their critique of Australia as an intolerant society. Rather, each new racial row brings on a fresh bout of self-flagellation, underscoring their tendency to define Australia by its worst aspects rather than its best. In Britain, organisations like the English Defence League are not allowed to tarnish the country's entire reputation. In America, the Ku Klux Klan and other far-right groups have never killed off a belief in the American Dream. In Australia, by contrast, often all it takes is a boofhead on a bus shouting a stream of racist abuse for progressives to issue a blanket condemnation of their country.

There is no question that racism exists. But it is important to accurately describe its character. I find myself in agreement with the Melbourne academic Waleed Aly who has noted that the country has 'a fairly high level of low-level racism'.

The corollary is that there is a low level of high-level racism. The UK and US have much graver problems with organised racism. Australia does not have an equivalent of the National Front, the British National Party or the English Defence League. Few have probably even heard of Jack van Tongeren's far-right Australian Nationalist Movement, which was behind a series of fire-bombings against Chinese restaurants in the 1980s. When Van Tongeren, a proud white supremacist, ran for the Senate in Western Australia, he attracted just 0.13 per cent of the vote. Racially motivated hate crimes thankfully remain rare. In America and Europe they are routine. Likewise, ethnic violence is not a major problem.

What Australia does suffer from is a failure of leadership from politicians who rarely challenge their compatriots to be better, and who pander to baser instincts. 'Perhaps what gives Australian politics its flavour,' wrote David Marr in his book *Panic*, 'is the willingness of both Labor and the Coalition to indulge fears they haven't the courage or will to contest.' Here, Hansonism had a chain-reaction effect. It drew both the main parties further to the right. Even if its main protagonist is now a joke, 'soft Hansonism' is still in evidence both in the Coalition and ALP, especially in their approach to asylum seekers.

Of course, the Tampa episode, more so than Hanson's election, is seen as the turning point in Australian politics. It emboldened the Coalition to adopt even harsher policies against boat people, and spooked Labor into following suit. Yet the tough stance during Tampa was hardly the product of public clamour. 'The truth here is that leadership dictated the national response, not the other way around,' notes George Megalogenis. 'Howard set the tone and the electorate followed him.' The commentator Paul Kelly, after studying the Tampa election during a stint at Harvard, reached the same conclusion. 'Before Howard acted there had been little demand in Australia to halt the boats completely,' he noted. 'So, Howard led rather than followed public opinion.'

Howard also set the tone for future politicians, and they have followed him. Paul Keating later complained that in 'a nation of immigrants, John Howard let the racism genie out of the bottle' and accused his successor of 'high political irresponsibility'. Yet Keating hardly has an unblemished record, having been the first prime minister to bring in mandatory detention, unbottling a different kind of genie.

The most recent study from the Scanlon Foundation and Monash University shows that negative sentiment towards boat people and also Muslims is on the rise. Since Tampa, politicians on both sides have allowed the public to conflate these two groups. Australians hostile towards people of colour or multiculturalism use boat people as a proxy, with the tacit approval of the nation's leaders. Here again, a corrosive bipartisanship is in play.

Once, when compiling a report on the boat-people question, I spent the day in Penrith, a suburb commonly seen as being especially hostile to asylum seekers. Yet it was hard to find anyone who delivered the racist soundbites I had gone expecting. Even ute-driving young men, with the Southern Cross inked into their torsos – a cohort so often cast as racists – would not oblige. When asked to list their concerns, surprisingly few people in Penrith mentioned asylum seekers, the supposed hot-button issue. When they did, the most common complaint was that they jumped that imaginary queue. I had been guilty of the kind of political stereotyping that passes for mastermind strategising in both main parties.

I wrapped up the day in Penrith by interviewing David Bradbury, the then sitting MP, who was fighting hard to retain his seat. Of all the people with whom I spoke, Bradbury was the only one who regarded boat people as the number one 'community concern'. In thinking his constituents were more xenophobic than my vox pops suggested, he inadvertently highlighted a recurring problem: politicians on both sides see Australia as more racist than the evidence suggests it truly is.

Yet another example came when Labor chieftains blocked Anoulack Chanthivong, a Laos-born graduate of Sydney University whose parents arrived here in the mid-eighties as refugees, from running for a state seat in Sydney's south-west. Evidently, they did not think the Westie electorate was ready for an Asian candidate, despite the fact that Chanthivong, a highly articulate young politician, had already served nine years as a councillor, including a term as mayor.

Politics and society would both immeasurably benefit were more leaders to acknowledge the success of the multicultural model. Alas, they remain caged by the 2001 Tampa election.

On 13 February 2008, thousands of indigenous Australians were drawn to the nation's capital by the promise of a single word – one that no Australian prime minister had ever publicly uttered in regret at the injustices endured by Aborigines and Torres Strait Islanders. Inside the chamber of the House of Representatives, the business at hand started with the cold grammar of parliamentary protocol. 'Motion offering an apology to Australia's indigenous peoples,' announced the clerk. Then, with great solemnity, Kevin Rudd stepped forward to deliver his speech. It was 3875 words long, but only one truly mattered: 'Sorry.' And he repeated it three times.

On the lawn in front of Parliament House, where a big screen relayed the apology to those who the chamber could not accommodate, loud and happy cheers rang out with every 'Sorry'. Then, as the speech ended, came the rare sight of a parliamentary standing ovation from virtually everyone in the chamber – the floor as well as the galleries. Only one MP, the Victorian Liberal Chris Pearce, who did not believe that the Stolen Generations exist, remained seated.

Clearly it was a moment of enormous cathartic power. Sally Pierce, a member of the Stolen Generations who had travelled up from Tasmania, arrived wearing a black t-shirt emblazoned with the word 'Sorry'. After Rudd had finished speaking, she replaced it with a new shirt inscribed with the word 'Thanks'.

For sorry-sceptics, too, this communal reckoning turned out to be unexpectedly emotional. After the speech, we had lined up Barnaby Joyce to explain his opposition to the apology to the global audience on BBC News. But when he stepped before the cameras his eyes were still red with emotion, and I found myself interviewing not a critic but a late convert.

As well as being a day of national atonement, it was also a moment of national awakening. Hitherto, how many Australians were aware, I wonder, of the grim inventory of statistics underscoring the breach between black and white Australia. An indigenous baby born on Sorry Day had a life expectancy 17 years shorter than a white baby. The overall death rate for Aboriginal people was three times higher. The unemployment rate was also three times higher. The incarceration rate was 14 times higher. Indigenous Australians were more likely than whites to consume alcohol at risky or high-risk levels (27.4 per cent to 20.1 per cent), but they were also more likely to abstain completely from booze – contradicting the lazy stereotype that all Aborigines have a grog problem. A sorry could never be mistaken for a solution, but at least it righted a longstanding wrong, what Rudd described in his speech as 'a stony and stubborn and deafening silence' when it came to delivering a national apology.

In the main, indigenous Australia has been a fly-over problem for white Australians. The closest many get to indigenous communities in the red centre is 30,000 feet as they jet off to Bali or Europe. Venturing into the outback, to visit rundown townships that were not quite Third World but definitely not First, itself felt like visiting a different land. It was the only time in Australia when I felt like a bona fide foreign correspondent.

While there was no physical border, there were the invisible barriers created by the permit system, which prevented unwelcome visitors from encroaching. By those with something to hide, journalists were often viewed suspiciously as unwelcome visitors. Unfortunately, these people often doubled as the gatekeepers. Sympathetic though we were to the idea that indigenous communities wanted privacy and the diluted version of sovereignty conferred by the permit system, it meant Aboriginal Australia was often harder to penetrate than Burma, at that time a closed society. The irony was inescapable. Indigenous communities suffered not from intrusion but neglect.

At least Aborigines were more visible now in mainstream Australian culture. Geoffrey Gurrumul Yunupingu was hardly an overnight success – he played for years with the Yothu Yindi band – but he made a powerful impact when he burst onto the national scene in 2008. Fortunate enough to be at one of his 'debut' concerts at the Sydney Opera House, I, like everyone else, was left spellbound by the transcendence of his voice. Within months, he had scaled the heights of the music charts. Growing up on Elcho Island off the coast of Arnhem Land, Gurrumul learned a handful of words in English, but the beauty of his music was universal.

Though films like *Ten Canoes* had attracted predominantly art-house audiences, *Samson and Delilah*, *Bran Nue Dae* and *The Sapphires* proved that indigenous movies could have mass appeal. Indigenous film-makers were also making a conscious effort to increase their accessibility. The musical comedy *Bran Nue Dae*, which was set in the Kimberleys two years after the landmark 1967 referendum, did not focus solely on the negative aspects of the indigenous experience, as Philip Noyce's masterpiece *Rabbit-Proof Fence* had done. Rather, it showcased the love of song, the love of land and the love of humour. 'This film is about laughter and fun, so hopefully people will feel okay about that,' its director Rachel Perkins told me at the time. 'It's almost as if they need a cue – "it's okay to laugh about Aboriginal stuff" – because previously they have never been able to. There's not going to be an angry Aborigine saying, "Don't you laugh at that, it's very serious stuff."' The trick has been to make cinema-goers feel good rather than feel guilty.

Likewise, *The Sapphires*, the story of a sisterly Aboriginal singing troupe whose quest for stardom took them from a Murray River mission to the frontlines of Vietnam, touched on the Stolen Generations but not in an accusatory way. It ended up grossing more than $10 million at the box office, one of just a handful of homegrown movies to reach that high watermark in the past five years. It was an unprecedented commercial return for a film from an indigenous director, Wayne Blair, with a mainly indigenous cast. On television, there has been the success of *Redfern Now*, produced by Rachel Perkins' production company, Blackfella Films, and *Mabo*, ABC's dramatisation of the life of the indigenous campaigner, Eddie. Perkins, who also produced the SBS documentary series *First Australians*, is a force of nature.

A common thread in all of these movies and television dramas has been the actress Deborah Mailman, who has emerged as one of the country's most-loved leading ladies. Blessed with a Julia Roberts smile and a face that, bulb-like, appears to light up, she has notched up a string of hits, from her debut movie *Radiance*, for which she won her first Australian Film Institute award, to her role as nurse Cherie Butterfield in the popular series *Offspring*. She can also claim some notable Aboriginal firsts. In her breakthrough role on commercial television, in the Channel Ten drama *The Secret Life of Us*, which focused on a group of twenty-somethings sharing a flat in St Kilda, she played the first indigenous character to have girl-next-door appeal. As with her role in *Offspring*, her on-screen character, Kelly, had not been written with an indigenous actress in mind. She also took part in what her co-star, the actor Rhys Muldoon, described as Australia's first on-screen 'white bloke–black chick fuck'. Prior to this, Aboriginal actresses had only taken part in sex scenes in which they were raped.

Her most overtly political role came in the telemovie *Mabo*, where she played Bonita Mabo, the wife of Eddie, the land rights hero. In it, she delivered perhaps her most complete performance yet, following the arc of Bonita's life from the inauspicious moment she first met Eddie on the street outside a pub through their ten-year legal struggle to the day in 1992 when the High Court ruled in her (by then deceased) husband's favour. Bonita, grey and wizened, heard the news on an ABC Radio bulletin and Mailman's rendition of her disbelieving joy at that instant is pitch-perfect – a statement as reverberant as any political slogan. Mailman's success, however, has been built on charming white audiences rather than confronting them. 'Don't load her up with indigenous stuff,' was the advice from a friend, when I interviewed her once after her success with *The Sapphires*. In some ways, she has adopted the same approach with white audiences. Like Geoffrey Gurrumul Yunupingu she does not press upon them a political agenda.

It is tempting to view Mailman as a Cathy Freeman of the arts, a torchbearer for others. But hers, like Cathy Freeman's, was a solo success. Only one other indigenous actor, Aaron Pedersen, features regularly on commercial television, and has achieved nowhere near the same prominence. Even *Offspring*, which does a better job at portraying polyglot Australia than the usual white-bread commercial dramas, only goes so far. Her character, nurse Butterfield, exists in isolation from her mob.

At the 2000 Olympics, Freeman may have sprinted '400 metres of reconciliation' but for many that became a figurative measure of the short distance indigenous Australians had come. For every Cathy Freeman, there were always thousands of young indigenous girls who would never make it out of their townships. For every Deborah Mailman, there are dozens of aspiring actresses who will never force their way into decent parts. Both may give a false impression of progress, but at least they are helping to close the mental gap between black and white Australia.

I recall once being in the BBC's Seoul bureau during one of the Korean peninsula's sporadic nuclear crises, and eavesdropping on a conversation between our resident correspondent and a programme team in London. A producer on the other end of the phone was insistent that Kim Jong-il should be described as a 'crazed dictator'. The correspondent, a highly respected Korea expert, refused because he adjudged North

Korea's then leader to be despotic but far from mad. Rather, he was a wily old bird, who regularly demonstrated his strategic smarts.

On the night that Julia Gillard was ousted as prime minister, I found myself having a similar conversation with London. Television news favours straightforward narratives, and the simplest one that explained her fall was that Australia could not cope with a female prime minister. Gillard's famed misogyny speech, which became a viral hit abroad, helped compose that storyline. With over a million hits on YouTube, her invective had reverberated around the world, and most obviously amongst women. 'I will not be lectured on sexism and misogyny by this man, I will not. Because if he wants to know what misogyny looks like in modern Australia, he doesn't need a motion in the House of Representatives, he needs a mirror.' The assumption, naturally, was that her sexist tormentors had finally felled her. Yet, as I insisted to that editor in London, she had also been the author of her own demise.

Fortunately, that night I could summon as my first witness one Julia Gillard, who had addressed the misogyny question during a valedictory press conference. 'There's been a lot of analysis about the so-called gender wars,' she wryly reflected. 'The reaction to being the first female prime minister does not explain everything about my prime ministership, nor does it explain nothing about my prime ministership. What I am absolutely confident of is it will be easier for the next woman and the woman after that and the woman after that and I'm proud of that.'

Without question, Gillard was the victim of ugly sexism, from Larry Pickering's pornographic cartoons depicting her with a phallus dangling between her legs to the vicious tirades from Alan Jones, who said her father must have 'died of shame' (afterwards, the broadcaster said it was right to 'man up' and apologise). The signs declaring 'Ditch the Witch' and 'Juliar . . . Bob Brown's bitch', which formed the backdrop for Tony Abbott's speech at an anti-carbon tax rally in 2011, were similar in some ways to the racist placards directed against Barack Obama at Tea Party rallies in Washington. As Gillard herself commented, had she been the first indigenous prime minister and Abbott had stood next to a sign reading 'Ditch the black bastard', it would have been the end of his career. Sexism, though, was not considered a cardinal offence.

For the three years and three days that she served as prime minister, as Julia Baird has written, 'we debated the fit of her jackets, the size of her bottom, the exposure of her cleavage, the cut of her hair, the tone of her voice, the legitimacy of her rule and whether she had chosen, as one member of parliament from the opposition Liberal Party put it, to be "deliberately barren"'. In her final months in office, there was that menu for the Liberal Party fundraiser, circulated privately rather than placed on tables, that ridiculed her 'small breasts, big thighs and "big red box"'. A radio presenter in Perth also asked if her partner Tim Mathieson was gay, a line of questioning to which a male prime minister would surely never be subjected.

Though Julia Gillard is now regularly cast as the embattled heroine, an Australian Joan of Arc, much of her record in office stands at odds with that reputation. On first taking up the job, she seemed almost to deny her femininity, and to downplay her gender in much the same way that Barack Obama had sought to minimise his race. 'I never conceptualise my prime ministership around being the first woman to do this job,' she said when delivering the first Emily's List oration in 2011. Instead, during that speech she emphasised her hardness, a trait shared with other female parliamentarians: 'They are tough women, resilient women. They are necessarily tough because politics is tough.'

At other times, she stressed her blokey affectations, decorating her office with a Sherrin football, her Western Bulldogs scarf, a Melbourne Storm scarf, some gumboots and an Akubra hat. It was almost as if she had deliberately set out to turn the prime ministerial suite of offices into a man cave. She seemed to be sending a deliberate message that blokes had nothing to fear.

Some of her personal attitudes also seemed to be surprisingly old-fashioned. During a soft soap profile of the First Bloke, Tim Mathieson, on Channel Nine's *Sixty Minutes* which involved a tour of The Lodge, she told the reporter Charles Wooley that she would never encroach upon his shed in the backyard. 'No girls allowed,' she said. 'No girls allowed.' While happy to knit clothes for Penny Wong's new daughter, she would not lend her support to growing calls for the legislation of same sex marriage. In media appearances, she seemed happy to conform to old-fashioned stereotypes, most notably the cover shot for *Australian Women's Weekly* which showed her knitting a toy kangaroo for the new royal baby – hardly the portrait of a 'bad-ass motherfucker'.

Were not her comments about preferring the classroom to international summits also self-demeaning? An inference easily drawn was that summitry was for men and schools were the more rightful place of women. Just imagine if Kerry O'Brien had posited it as a question rather than Gillard giving it as an answer.

Nor did she balk at posing with well-known sexists, such as Kyle Sandilands. The shock jock, adding to an already long list of bigoted misdemeanours, had only recently described a journalist who had written unfavourably of him as a 'fat slag', adding: 'You haven't got that much titty to be having that low-cut blouse.' But that did not stop the prime minister from inviting him to a charity event at Kirribilli House, to which the country's most infamous sexist pig came dressed as a fluffy bunny. Because presumably Sandilands was the conduit to a youthful, and blokeish, constituency, she was happy to embrace him while snapping selfies. It provided an awkward postscript for her misogyny speech.

Gillard at times was also the beneficiary of tolerant attitudes. American voters would not countenance an unmarried couple living in the White House. Still to this day in Britain it would cause a furore. But her relationship with Tim Mathieson was never a big deal for Australians, and certainly not a vote-loser. Nor was her atheism ever a serious issue, other than to Kevin Rudd who during a night on the lagers at the Adelaide Festival in 2012 reportedly called her 'a childless, atheist ex-communist'. But his comments spoke more about the viciousness of Australian politics than the prevalence of sexism.

The misogyny speech started out as a defence of Peter Slipper. That is why, as the essayist Anna Goldsworthy has shrewdly observed, two addresses were heard that day: one by the members of the press gallery, who instantly identified the crack of heavy political gunfire, and the rest of the world, unaware of the backstory, who pressed play on their computers and listened to an embattled woman giving voice to frustrations long felt by millions of others. 'Gillard is not quite the champion we would like her to be,' Goldsworthy observed, 'nor is Tony Abbott quite the villain.'

The pity is that Australia's first female prime minister got the job in such controversial circumstances, a putsch on a once-popular colleague not yet at the end of his first term in office. Then she clung on to it only after an election when the result was not clear-cut. In retrospect, it was probably a mistake for her to declare that she would not move into The Lodge until she had a mandate of her own, because the voters never delivered one. She was not an illegitimate prime minister, as the opposition claimed. But nor did she ever achieve a personal electoral triumph, as had Margaret Thatcher, Angela Merkel, Helen Clark, Kim Campbell, Edith Cresson or Benazir Bhutto.

Also it was her misfortune to gain power during such a vicious and destructive phase in Australian political life, when every character seemed ripe for assassination. But here again, her aggressive political style contributed to that savagery. Gillard had shattered the glass ceiling. The trouble was it felt like a smash and grab.

That is why it is mistaken to centre the sexism debate in Australia solely on her. As Gillard herself stressed, the focus should also be on the 200 ASX companies of which 3 per cent have female CEOs and in which just 9 per cent of key management are women. It should be on the relatively low female participation in the economy, at 60 per cent ranked only the 44th in the world, and the need for what she called 'economic emancipation'.

On the night she became prime minister, in a breezy interview with Kerry O'Brien on *The 7.30 Report*, Gillard declared it to be a 'good day for redheads'. Her departure was a good day for rednecks. But, tempting though it was for international news organisations to use a simple narrative to stereotype Australia, it was not a redneck triumph.

Chapter 6

THE SLOW DEATH OF BRITISH AUSTRALIA

QUEEN ELIZABETH II MADE what was billed as her final visit to her southern realm in October 2011, less than a month after the country marked the 60th anniversary of the ANZUS Treaty signed with America and the Gillard government commissioned its 'Australia in the Asian Century' white paper. During her reign the strategic relationship with America had become the basis of Australian security, with the US Seventh Fleet today performing much the same role as that undertaken by the Royal Navy up until the fall of Singapore. As for its economic security, Australia now looked predominantly to China, a reorientation that could be traced back to Britain's decision in the 1960s to turn its back on the trading partnerships with its former colonies and to look instead to the Common Market, or the European Union as it is now known. Coming at a moment in the national story when Canberra was celebrating its ties with Washington and also embarking on a closer relationship with Asia, the Queen's visit highlighted how Australia continues to be tugged in different directions – diplomatically speaking, the pull has long been as important as its much-vaunted global punch. Yet the biggest single clue to making sense of the country's national identity remains its British heritage.

The Queen of Australia, the guest of honour at a summit of Commonwealth heads of government in Perth, returned to a country that retained her youthful profile on its coinage and her portrait on the five dollar note. Public prosecutors are crown prosecutors. Some of those found guilty end up in Her Majesty's prisons. Public inquiries are called Royal Commissions. State lands are truly crown lands. In the outback and bush, royal flying doctors treat the sick and infirm. The country's naval fleet still bears the regal prefix. The prime minister jets around the world flying the flag for Australia in a VIP plane emblazoned with the insignia of the Royal Australian Air Force. A quarter of that flag features the Union Jack in its starry firmament. 'Britain at night', as the comedian Jerry Seinfeld has labelled it, or 'a sort of postcard addressed to Buckingham Palace', in the words of the broadcaster Phillip Adams.

Much of this country marks the monarch's birthday with a public holiday, a courtesy not even observed in my homeland. Australia Day celebrates the arrival of the First Fleet. There are still some 160,000 Britons who can cast a vote in Australian federal elections, a fancy franchise shared with other residents from the British Commonwealth but with no other non-citizens.

The opening line of the Australian constitution still states: 'Whereas the people of New South Wales, Victoria, South Australia, Queensland, and Tasmania, humbly relying on the blessing of Almighty God, have agreed to unite in one indissoluble Federal Commonwealth under the Crown of the United Kingdom of Great Britain and Ireland, and under the

Constitution hereby established.' As the historian John Hirst has observed: 'If for any reason there ceased to be a monarch in Britain, our constitution would seize up.'

Canberra, with its House of Representatives and Senate, may have borrowed the nomenclature of Washington, but the hybrid 'Washminster' model is a more loyal recreation of the Palace of Westminster. Parliament House has its own Usher of the Black Rod, who until 1996 wore a sword on ceremonial occasions, and golden mace, bearing the royal crown, coat of arms and cipher. At the commencement of each day's sitting, it is borne by the Sergeant of Arms, who precedes the Speaker into the chamber. Canberra also maintains the tradition of the new Speaker being 'dragged' to his chair, a ritual reaching back to the days when prospective speakers at Westminster were understandably reluctant to take up the role because they risked being beheaded by the monarch. At Question Time, politicians stand behind rosewood dispatch boxes that were a gift from George V. Hansard records their words, as it does those uttered at Westminster.

'In pinpointing what makes us distinctly Australian, we acknowledge the enormous debt we owe to Britain,' said Bob Hawke, that dinky-di Aussie, at a citizenship ceremony in 1988. 'Britain has given us the basis of many of the institutions of our free society: our system of parliamentary democracy, the principles of rule by law and the protection of the rights of the individual under the law, our system of liberal education.' The following year, Hawke suggested that immigrants to Australia 'have been attracted by our British heritage and institutions'.

Again, it is not an identical reproduction. Australians, like the Kiwis, were trailblazers when it came to female suffrage, and Australian women could vote long before Emily Davison threw herself in front of the King's horse at the Derby (an irony here is that the Australian group lobbying for greater female representation in parliament, Emily's List, takes the name of its American and British sister organisations). Compulsory voting would be an anathema to the British. Poms always go to the polls on Thursday rather than the more sensible turnout-boosting option of a Saturday. The Australian Labor Party adopted the American spelling. Tory moderates in Britain, evoking Disraeli, are known as 'One Nation conservatives', a description that clearly would not work here. Overwhelmingly, however, the trappings of Australian politics are British.

Up until the turn of the century, Britons with dual citizenship were allowed to grace parliament's red and green leather benches, which looked like hand-me-downs from the Palace of Westminster. The High Court ruling in 1999 which barred One Nation's Heather Hill from sitting in the Senate was particularly momentous, since it was the first time in Australian law that the United Kingdom had officially been declared a 'foreign power'.

To this day, Australians seemingly harbour no worries about being governed by politicians who were born in the Old Country, as the rise of the Welsh-born Julia Gillard and the London-born Tony Abbott attests. Abbott also reminds us that a Rhodes scholarship at Oxford remains the acme of Australian academic achievement. And, fittingly enough, he attended Queen's College.

As recently as 1949, when the Nationality and Citizenship Act came into force, Australians remained British subjects. The word 'British' survived on the front cover of an Australian passport until the Whitlam era. Until 1987, people here remained both Australian citizens and British subjects. It was not until the mid-1980s, with the passage of the Australia Act, that Australians lost their right of legal appeal to the

Privy Council in the UK. 'God Save the Queen' survived as the country's national anthem until 1984, seven years after a plebiscite decided to replace it with 'Advance Australia Fair'. Even more remarkably, it took until 1993 to remove the references to the Queen from the oath of Australian citizenship.

A common thread of Australian history has been its sluggishness in casting off these imperial accoutrements. Even though the Statute of Westminster was passed in 1931, removing the right of the British parliament to legislate for its dominions, Australia waited a further 11 years to finalise this constitutional piece of housekeeping. The Canadians, who were in much more of a rush to assert themselves, ratified it immediately. Among constitutional historians, there is still debate about when precisely Australia gained its independence. Was it 1931 or 1942? As John Hirst has noted, even when Garfield Barwick, the chief justice of the High Court, declared in 1969 that Australia was an independent nation, he could not isolate precisely when it achieved independence.

Britain provided the frame for Australian education. The tradition still persists of some of the top schools in the country being run by headmasters and headmistresses from the UK. The architecture of Sydney and Melbourne universities apes the Gothic revivalism of Oxford and Cambridge. Both are based on the collegiate system, with gowns still worn in some colleges at High Table. Sydney University's coat of arms features the lion of Cambridge and the open book of Oxford. Its motto is *Sidere mens eadem mutato* – 'The same mind under changed skies'. 'Our education would prepare us to be little Englishmen and Englishwomen,' said Robert Hughes, an alumnus, 'though with nasal accents.'

An inordinate amount of Australia's cultural space has been surrendered to the British-made or British-influenced, whether it be *Antiques Roadshow*, the latest Jane Austen dramatisation or *Downton Abbey*. The ABC is modelled on another 'Auntie', the BBC, and puts to air a surprising amount of British content. When I arrived, it was possible with some judicious channel hopping to watch British programming from the first thing in the morning to the last thing at night. Now the BBC channel UKTV, with its 24/7 menu of British shows, obviates the need for the remote control. Perhaps the next move is to create a Stephen Fry channel, although there are times when the ABC feels like that already. He has become as much an Australian national treasure as a British one.

Mainly British sports continue to dominate, where players compete still for trophies named after British aristocrats, the first Viscount of Bledisloe and the Earl of Sheffield. Frank Packer's post-war prediction that baseball would become the national sport now seems laughable. Basketball has also struggled to find a foothold. Results from the English Premier League regularly top the sports bulletins. Channel Nine claims to be the most 'Proudly Australian' network, but ever since the semi-retirement of Richie Benaud its cricket coverage has been fronted by an upper-class Englishman, Mark Nicholas.

So rich is the British flavour of Australian culture, low and high, that the idea of having an English-born head of state has never been that incongruous. It helps explain why the mental stepping stones to the Old Country are still so solid, sturdy and immutable.

The demographic make-up of the country is also still strongly British. At the 2006 census, when people were asked to describe their ancestry, almost a third – 31.6 per cent – responded English, compared to 9 per cent Irish, 7.6 per cent Scottish, 4.3 per cent Italian, 4.1 per cent German, 3.4 per cent Chinese and 1.8 per cent Greek. This is not to deny the transformational impact of other European and Asian influences, which have grown in recent times as the proportion of UK immigrants has declined. Even so, British arrivals continue to be surprised – startled even – by the resilience of Australia's Anglocentrism and how 'the British way' retains its permeating influence in so many realms of national life.

Perversely, Australians have often sought to become more British. Federation was never intended to mark a definitive break from Britain. Moreover, the celebrations on 1 January 1901 had a distinctly Anglo feel. 'The make-up of the parade was overwhelmingly British,' notes the historian Martin Crotty. 'British Empire troops dominated proceedings, along with the British gentry and religious representatives.' *The Bulletin*, in its first issue after the federation ceremony in 1901, enjoined readers to declare 'Australia for Australians' and to turn their back on 'Queen Victoria's nigger empire'. The following year, however, it declared: 'Britain is our natural ally, our best ally, and we will cleave to her as long as we may.'

From the outset, then, there was no great tension between Australian nationalism and imperial loyalty, and the two sat happily in tandem. As Alfred Deakin, the country's second prime minister, explained in 1905: 'The same ties of blood, sympathy and tradition which make us one Commonwealth here make the British of today one people everywhere.' Deakin used the word 'nation' seven times during that speech, as the historian James Curran has noted, but only once did it refer to Australia. The notion of dual allegiance, federation under the crown, quickly became deeply entrenched, which was hardly surprising in a new country where all but 2 per cent of its 3.8 million subjects could trace their bloodline back to the British Isles.

Nor did World War I and Gallipoli lead to a split, despite the appalling treatment of Australian diggers at the hands of British commanders and Winston Churchill. As Martin Crotty observed, 'there are many ways in which World War I made Australia more British, not less.' The internment and deportation of Australians of German birth, combined with the wariness towards Irish Catholics suspected of harbouring Fenian sympathies, reinforced the Anglocentric monoculture.

For the first 40 years of federation, British foreign policy doubled as Australian foreign policy. When Deakin complained about the French deportation of convicts to New Caledonia, the message was conveyed by the British ambassador in Paris. When he wanted America's Great White Fleet to visit Australia, the official invitation was sent via Whitehall to Washington. 'Even when these colonies federated,' noted Horne, 'it was believed that Australia was still not a true nation. Economically, strategically and culturally Australia was defined as part of the British Empire.'

Remarkably, it was not until 1944, when Australia signed a security treaty with New Zealand, the Canberra Pact, that the country forged its own, independent foreign policy – Curtin received a telling off from America as a result. Similarly, it was not until World War II that Australia established full, independent diplomatic relations with America, with the opening of an Australian embassy in Washington. In confronting Australia's conservative tradition, the long-held national mistrust of change, opponents of the status quo are unable to harness much of a countervailing republican tradition.

Supposed moments of national reorientation are by no means clear-cut. Prime Minister John Curtin's New Year's message in 1941, in which he boldly stated that 'Australia looks to America, free of any pangs as to our traditional links or kinship with the United Kingdom,' may have been, as Horne claimed, 'the single most significant statement ever made by an Australian Prime Minister'. However, the message was nowhere near as US-centric as is commonly supposed. Curtin also spoke of seeking Russian aid and of coming up with a Pacific strategy that included British, Chinese and Dutch forces. Gareth Evans, the former foreign affairs minister, aptly called it a 'half-turning point'.

Curtin didn't shun Britain. Only three years later, he delivered a speech at the Australian Club in London riven with subservience. 'We are a British community in the South Seas, and we regard ourselves as the trustees for the British way of life,' declared Curtin, 'corresponding in purpose and in outlook and in race to the Motherland itself.' Even as he engineered an historic strategic realignment, Curtin was reasserting the principle of dual allegiance with Britain. In so doing, he was simply giving voice to the dominant theme of the first 70 years of Australian federation: the country's ongoing attachment to Britain, constitutionally, diplomatically, economically and, above all, mentally.

That mindset, as the author David Malouf observed in his seminal essay *Made in England*, is Anglocentric. Australia inherited its sense of fair play, Protestant work ethic, low church puritanism, drunkenism, and 'British pragmatism and distrust of theory'. Australian philistinism was essentially 'British philistinism', a 'dislike of anything showy, theatrical, arty or "too serious"'. Then there is the 'British good sense and the British sense of humour'. The personalities are not identical. But the fact that Australians have inherited so many British ways of thinking has inhibited the development of intense nationalism. Again, it was a case of *Sidere mens eadem mutato*.

What makes Australia's loyalty to Britain and the monarchy all the more anomalous is that the national story has continually been punctuated by imperial slights and colonial condescension. Had successive British governments set out to concoct a strategy to alienate their Australian cousins, they could not have done much better than the disaster of Gallipoli, the Melbourne Agreement reached with the Bank of England during the Great Depression, with its crippling high interest rates, the great betrayal during World War II, the British nuclear tests in the outback and entry into the Common Market. And that list does not even include Douglas Jardine's unsporting leg theory or Harold Larwood's Body-line bouncers. The absence of any great anti-British backlash, save for the occasional sledge on the cricket field or some playful Pom-bashing on talkback radio, comes as something of a surprise to outsiders brought up to believe that Australia is one of the world's most fiercely patriotic nations.

The survival of the monarchy, in particular, throws up one of the great Australian anomalies: of how an increasingly patriotic country which has always prided itself on its laconic informality, irreverence, anti-authoritarianism, lack of snobbery and egalitarianism, continues to countenance an institution which stands in defiance of so many national maxims. Logically, these traits should have militated against the idea of hereditary privilege and an institution at the apex of a still sturdy British class system. So, too, should have Australia's soft sectarianism: Catholics outnumber Protestants, but their British co-religionists are blocked from the throne. Instead, the death of British Australia has been astonishingly slow, and the country continues to live in the shadow of 19th-century England. The story of Australia's Elizabethan age helps explain why.

Queen Elizabeth first visited in 1954, just three years after the government of Robert Menzies had codified its new affiliation with Washington with the signing of the ANZUS

Treaty. Nonetheless, she came ashore in what was still an enthusiastically British-orientated country, headed by a prime minister for whom the term Anglophile seemed wholly inadequate. Two days before she alighted at Farm Cove in Sydney, dressed in champagne chiffon with a delicate but unmistakable hint of green – the royal take on the garish national colours – 200,000 Sydneysiders choked the CBD merely to marvel at the royal decorations. So many thronged to see her attend the Lord Mayor's Ball at the Town Hall that 2000 people reportedly collapsed. By the time she was waved off from the quayside in Fremantle 57 days later, it was estimated that 75 per cent of the population had caught a glimpse of her at least once.

Much of this excitement stemmed from the simple fact that Elizabeth had become the first reigning British monarch to feel Australian soil beneath her feet. There was the novelty of seeing the Queen in the pale flesh. Australians also demonstrated their gratitude towards British visitors who had travelled so far to visit. No doubt there was also admiration for her stamina on a visit that took in every capital, with the sole exception of Darwin, and 70 country towns. By its end, the tally of tour statistics seemed positively Bradmanesque: she travelled 10,000 miles by air, racking up 57 flight hours, drove 2000 miles by car, which equated to 130 road hours, and notched up a century of speeches. During her visit to Canberra, she even unveiled a monument topped by the American eagle that honoured the United States for its defence of Australia.

Menzies wrote afterwards that the Queen had unleashed 'the most profound and passionate feelings of loyalty and devotion' and remarked on their strongly adhesive powers. 'The common devotion to the Throne,' he said, approvingly, 'is a part of the very cement of the whole social structure.'

In a man-on-the-street interview with the ABC, a war veteran went even further: 'The sight of our young Queen makes you realise that everything you've ever fought for is worthwhile.'

Long before the Queen's spin doctors and image-makers came to think in such cynical terms, she left Australia having pulled off the most stunning of publicity coups. The royal entourage was an early forerunner of what today would be called a public relations juggernaut. And that visit, the first of 16, firmly established the strong personal bond that survives until this day.

Waving her goodbye on the quayside in Fremantle, Menzies' chief concern was that the trip had been so arduous, and logistically complicated, that it might deter more frequent visits. His fears were borne out, since almost a decade elapsed before she visited again. When it came to opening the Melbourne Olympics in 1956, her husband, the Duke of Edinburgh, had to deputise, presumably since no Australian was considered worthy.

For Menzies, and many of his compatriots, absence evidently made the heart grow fonder. On the Queen's return visit in 1963, he scaled new rhetorical heights and plumbed new sycophantic depths. At a dinner at Parliament House in Canberra, he called Her Majesty 'the living and lovely centre of our enduring alliance', and echoed the misty-eyed words of the 17th-century poet Thomas Ford: 'I did but see her passing by / And yet I love her till I die.'

By the early sixties, however, there were signs that a growing number of Australians did not share Menzies' toadying deference. The Queen's 1963 tour coincided with the lead-up to the change in currency from the imperial to the decimal system, and the national debate over what to call the new money. Both Menzies and his treasurer, Harold Holt, lobbied hard for the 'royal', expecting it to be a popular choice.

But the public would not have a bar of it. As Holt informed the cabinet four months after the Queen's visit: 'None of us . . . judged that there would be so widespread and hostile reaction to the name as has occurred.'

Australians also took note of Britain's announcement in 1961 that it intended to join the European Common Market, which weakened the economic relationship. By the end of the decade, America had replaced Britain as the major source of foreign investment. Between the mid-forties and mid-sixties, the UK share of Australian exports declined from 37 per cent to 17 per cent. Over the same period, imports from the US grew from 9 per cent to 26 per cent.

Vietnam, a war in which Britain refused to participate, strengthened the strategic relationship with Washington. In October 1966, Australia also got its first presidential visit, which generated almost as much enthusiasm and even bigger crowds than the Queen's first excursion to these shores 12 years earlier. In Melbourne, 500,000 people turned out to see the president, Lyndon Baines Johnson – a riotous welcome, in the words of one report, 'that destroyed forever Melbourne's reputation as a sedate city'. His visit to Sydney produced a tickertape storm, and by the time Air Force One flew out of Townsville, where LBJ had been stationed as a naval commander during the war, it was estimated that one million Australians had seen him in the flesh.

Australia's intellectual milieu was changing fast. In 1963, Geoffrey Dutton, an Oxford-educated historian from one of South Australia's most prominent families, published 'British Subject', a short polemic in which he made the case for the republic and the banishment of the word 'British' from national life. Three years later, he edited *Australia and the Monarchy*, a symposium of essays which remarkably was the first book to thrash out the arguments for and against a republic. He was thrown out of the Adelaide Club for his pains. Horne, a lifelong republican, was fast on Dutton's heels. In *The Lucky Country*, he argued that clinging to Britain was a 'delusional structure'. Two years later, partly in response to Britain's closer alignment with the rest of Europe, he exclaimed: 'What use is Britishry to us now?'

Though the glue holding Australia and Britain together was not as strong, the monarchy retained much of its adhesive power. John Gorton, another Oxford graduate who presented himself as a beer-swilling Australian everyman, became the first prime minister to actively distance Australia from Britain, but he only went so far. While he called for 'Waltzing Matilda' to become the national song, he stopped short of demanding that it replace 'God Save the Queen' as the national anthem.

Promising a 'new nationalism', Gough Whitlam dispensed with what he called 'colonial relics', like the word 'British' on Australian passports, but he was in no way anti-British. Though a republican, especially after 1975, he was fond of the royals, got on well with them and was something of a traditionalist. Indeed, it was Whitlam who amended the Royal Style and Titles Act to make Queen Elizabeth the 'Queen of Australia', which implied, rightly as it turned out, that she was going to be around for a long time to come. Even in the absence of Robert Menzies, the monarchy's most slavish advocate, the institution continued to survive.

Further royal visits helped buttress the monarchy's popularity. The dip in public support for a republic in 1970, from 40 per cent in 1968 to 28 per cent, was partly explained by the success of a royal visit in April that year, a tour timed to coincide with the bicentenary of Captain Cook's voyage up the eastern seaboard. Nor did many think it odd that she returned three years later for the opening of the Sydney

Opera House, even though the Queen herself described this revolutionary structure as 'a catalyst for Australia's new and growing national spirit'. Back then it would have been unthinkable to stage such a major national event without the participation of the monarch or her consort.

This was a reminder of how republicanism was hampered by a lingering sense of inferiority and unworthiness: a kind of constitutional cringe whereby a Briton was considered superior as head of state to a homegrown alternative. Of Australians, the then British High Commissioner Charles Johnston wrote in 1970: 'like charity, their disrespect begins at home.'

Just as Whitlam did not advance republicanism, nor did the Dismissal crisis in 1975 end up damaging the monarchy, despite the fact that the Queen's representative, Sir John Kerr, had pulled off a constitutional coup. Horne saw this as an opening, and fired off a telegram to the governor-general at Yarralumla, sarcastically welcoming the Dismissal as the final nail in the coffin of the Australian monarch. Not for the first time, however, Horne's irony was misinterpreted, and his telegram was placed in the pile marked 'congratulations'.

Whitlam, rather than publicly lambasting the anachronisms of a system where the Queen's man in Canberra still had the power to sack the government, privately acquiesced to them. As James Curran and Stuart Ward note in their brilliant study, *The Unknown Nation*, the ousted prime minister even 'actively sought the personal intervention of the Queen to correct the errant ways of her governor-general – the very kind of offshore interference in Australian sovereignty that he had tirelessly toiled to bring to an end'.

Perhaps the Dismissal crisis was another moment when Australia revealed the British side of its character. Historians, in contemplating why Albion failed to be touched by the same monarch-toppling fervour that spread through Europe in 1848, concluded that the bonds of deference, subjection and order were too strong. A revolutionary streak is also lacking in Australians, which goes some way to explaining the lack of outrage at Whitlam's sacking.

If the Queen's regular visits have helped shore up the monarch, her absences have also been cleverly timed. This was especially so in the run-up to the 1999 referendum, when Buckingham Palace feared that she would be drawn into the republican debate merely by stepping foot in the country. Consequently, she made just one visit to Australia in the nineties, compared to five in the previous decade. That came in 1992, a year after the formation of the Australian Republican Movement and seven years before the referendum, a safe distance.

On her first trip after Australia had decided to keep the monarchy, in March 2000, the royal visit was not quite a below-the-radar affair but nonetheless discreet. Avoiding the main urban centres, she focused instead on Wagga Wagga, Ballarat, Bourke, Alice Springs and Busselton. Later that year she watched from Britain, as the then Prime Minister John Howard opened the Sydney Olympics, perhaps the biggest single event in the country's history at which Australia defined itself on its own terms. By now, what the Queen didn't open had become just as symbolic as what she did.

With each passing year of her reign, the 'Elizabeth factor' has proved a progressively bigger problem for republicans. More than 50 years after that first visit, then, she remains central to national life. When the dead from the Victorian bushfires were honoured at a memorial service at the Rod Laver Arena in Melbourne, the first speaker to receive a round of applause was not the state premier, nor a member of the emergency services, but the Princess Royal, who read out a two-week-old message of condolence from her mother. At first the ovation was tentative and slightly stumbling, but quickly it grew in volume and intensity, suggesting to the global television audience that many of these grieving Victorians remained loyal Elizabethans.

The response to the bushfires, such a uniquely Australian disaster, took on a strangely British character. Weeks later, ahead of the bushfire benefit concert held jointly at the MCG and SCG, I was contacted by the public relations team handling the event, who told me, in whispered tones, that its emotional highpoint would come from a dramatic, though highly secret, video presentation. At the appointed hour, the giant screens on either side of the rain-pelted stage crossed to Britain. There, they revealed the headline act: the royal princes, William and Harry.

The ultimate achievement for the Queen, as she marked her Diamond Jubilee, was that her continued presence on the throne had become an insuperable obstacle for republicans to overcome. Perhaps through her longevity alone, the Queen has come to embody some of the very values that Australians hold dear: toughness, resilience and loyalty. Improbable as it sounds, given her extraordinary wealth and privilege, maybe there is also respect for her underdog success: the ability to survive the scandals that have tarnished the family name. People have come to look fondly on a character who, as Christopher Hitchens once remarked, 'rises above the showbiz values, disco ambitions and petty neuroses of her clan and brood'. Besides, Australians have always stood to applaud a long and gritty innings, where the batsman has been bruised by a few bouncers.

Julia Gillard, another lifelong republican whose zeal seemed to desert her as soon as she entered The Lodge, made it Labor Party policy that the question should not be revisited until after the Queen's death. Even Malcolm Turnbull, the one-time head of the republican movement, yielded to the same kind of timetable. After all, to dispense with her services so late in her reign would not be fair dinkum. Few leading politicians have publicly agitated to bring down the curtain on Australia's Elizabethan age.

Ideally, republicans need to decouple the principle of a monarch-free country from the winsome personality of the Queen. Yet this turns on the kind of abstraction that goes against the grain. The 'Elizabeth factor' impacts the debate in other ways, too. Bold rhetoric will surely be required from national leaders to bring about a republic, yet delicacy is the order of the day as long as the Queen remains on the throne. For the politically timid, her presence also provides a rather useful alibi: an excuse for inertia.

The Queen, judging by her response to the outcome of the 1999 referendum, would draw satisfaction from the republican malaise. On what turned out to be a day of two halves for rugby-loving republicans, she was scheduled that day to present the William Webb Ellis trophy to the winner of the World Cup, played between the Wallabies and France in Cardiff. At half-time, Her Majesty confessed she was desperate for the Aussies to beat the French, according to the then Australian High Commissioner Philip Flood, so that she could hand over the trophy to John Eales, a republican. Rarely have moments of regal schadenfreude been placed on the public record, but Flood's disclosure showed that the Queen is hardly a bystander in this debate, willing though she was to accept the judgement of the Australian people (ready that day were three statements from Buckingham Palace, one in case of a Yes vote, another in case of a No, and a further one in the event that a plurality of Australians opted for a republic but could not command majorities in every state).

Doubtless, the polls commissioned at the time of her final visit would also have been to her liking. With support for an Australian republic at its lowest level in 20 years – just 34 per cent – 55 per cent said they preferred the status quo. By strange coincidence, the poll was a near inversion of the surveys leading up to the 1999 referendum, when 54 per cent said they wanted reform and only 38 per cent wanted to retain her services as the head of state.

The Queen's survival has to be seen as a personal victory, not least because so many small-r republicans have essentially become Elizabethans: individuals who reject the institution but who also cannot quite bring themselves to do away with the present incumbent.

The Queen of Australia went through one *annus horribilis* – in 1992, the year of Squidgygate, Camillagate, the publication of Andrew Morton's *Diana: Her True Story in Her Own Words*, the divorce of Princess Anne from Captain Mark Phillips, the separation of Prince Andrew from Sarah Ferguson and the Windsor Castle fire. Since 1999, her republican foes have been reliving them over and over. On the tenth anniversary of the republican referendum, a small group of campaigners gathered in Canberra purporting to 'mend the nation's heart', a reference to Malcolm Turnbull's anguished rebuke to John Howard on the night the vote went against him. Wearing bright yellow baseball caps and carrying small bowls of wattle, a plant that can thrive in the most inhospitable of settings, the representatives of the three main republican groups planned to converge on the portico of Parliament House from all corners of the forecourt, an intricately choreographed liturgy intended to convey the idea that Australians everywhere yearned for change. The task of orchestrating this manoeuvre was left to one of the organisers, who took great pains in outlining his creative vision to the few republicans who had bothered to turn up. But just as they prepared to move from the lawns of the Parliament House to the forecourt, a policeman intervened. Did the campaigners have a permit granting them permission? Alas, the answer was no. So at a time when they were calling for a great constitutional leap of imagination, the campaigners were not even allowed to cross the road.

By contrast, the celebrations that week of Australian monarchists, held in Sydney, Melbourne and Perth, passed off seamlessly. At the lunches marking what the Australians for Constitutional Monarchy called 'Affirmation Day', the anthem was sung, the royal toast was given, and the mainly elderly crowd, grey-haired and pearled, went home smug in the knowledge that the supporters of the Queen were very much in the ascendant. The feline David Flint, the chairman of the ACM, looked like the cat who had got the cream.

Australian republicans have long been outsmarted by their opponents. In 1999, it was a prime minister, John Howard, who knew that the constitutional convention would pit republican against republican, and who framed the question posed in the referendum to exploit their main point of divergence, what the republic would look like. Moreover, it has always been difficult to win a referendum without the support of the prime minister of the day, especially given Australia's constitutional constipation. As Howard himself put it, the referendum failed 'because of the inherent unwillingness on the part of Australians to change something that they haven't been persuaded was no longer working'. Turnbull referred to it as the 'natural conservatism' of the Australian people. It helped explain the stunning turnaround. Whereas a pre-referendum poll in 1999 had revealed that 73 per cent of respondents supported an Australian head of state, only 45.1 per cent ended up voting for one.

Not everything, however, can be explained by the missteps of republicans and the adroitness of their monarchist foes. Deeper factors are at play. If at the end of the 1960s, republicans were hobbled by Australians who thought too little of themselves, a wholly different dynamic emerged over the next three decades. By the end of the 1990s, the republican movement was thwarted by Australians who were deemed to think way too much of themselves. At the referendum, Australians voted to retain a British elite partly to protect them from an Australian elite. One of the most perverse aspects of the republican push is that it is now perceived as an elite cause, which became evident during the republican referendum. As Nick Cater, the author of *The Lucky Culture*, has noted, the 20 parliamentary seats with the highest levels of education voted for the republic, while all but five of the 95 electorates with the lowest education levels voted against. 'Welcome, fellow chardonnay-swilling elitists,' was how Robert Hughes started his speech at a republican rally at Sydney Town Hall in 1996, a self-deprecation that identified one of the movement's greatest hindrances.

Nor has it helped that the country's two longest-serving prime ministers have been such ardent monarchists, or that their republican counterparts haven't shown anywhere near the same dedication. Paul Keating, who placed republicanism high up on the political agenda during the 1993 federal election campaign, made the best fist of it most notably in his June 1995 speech, 'An Australian Republic: the Way Forward'. 'An Australian head of state can embody our modern aspirations,' he argued. 'Our cultural diversity, our evolving relationships with Asia and the Pacific, our quest for reconciliation with Aboriginal Australians, our ambitions to create a society in which women have equal opportunity, equal representation and equal rights.' At the time, however, the country was entering turbulent economic waters, and this was viewed as a debate that the country didn't really have to have.

Kevin Rudd, who promised to 'accelerate' the republican debate, opted instead for a rhetorical go slow. Even though the creation of an Australian republic emerged as the most fervent demand from delegates attending the 2020 summit – the future Attorney-General George Brandis was apparently the only monarchist in attendance – Rudd consistently failed to elucidate the issue. 'We lost the last referendum nearly ten years ago, we don't want to lose the next one,' he cautioned on ABC's *AM* programme in April 2008. 'So we'll be building this one up very carefully.' This was at a time when the leader of the opposition was the one-time leader of the republican movement, and a referendum might have enjoyed a measure of bipartisan support, an essential ingredient for a 'Yes' vote.

Rudd nudged Australia in the direction of a monarch-less future by appointing Quentin Bryce as governor-general. But his fellow Queenslander hardly did much to advance the cause, despite finally coming out as a republican as she prepared to vacate Yarralumla.

For her part, Julia Gillard hoisted the white flag – or knitted that soft kangaroo. In tying the timing of the debate to the longevity of the Queen, she indicated that republicanism has not only been pushed down the national agenda but completely taken off it. Inflicting even more coronary pain for republicans, Gillard also decided to attend the wedding of Prince William and Kate Middleton.

The royal nuptials almost became as much a red letter day in the Australian national calendar as it was the British, and again highlighted the slow death of Anglo-Australia. From the minting of more majestic coinage to the usual line-up of Australian TV anchors perched outside Buckingham Palace, the marriage was another public relations juggernaut, threatening to leave the republican movement flattened, like road kill, in its thundering path. Nothing better illustrated the Australian embrace of the event than to walk into a hotel that Friday night and to see the pub plasma screens switched from the footy to Westminster Abbey. Many young Australians wore royal-themed outfits, as if it were some regal Halloween. For republicans, this must have been particularly alarming because it showed that young Australians had the same enthusiasm for the Windsors as their forebears – not so much Elizabethans as Kate and Williamistas. What chance did a dry and occasionally lifeless narrative of Australian constitutional change have up against a princely love story?

Because of the celebrity of the young royal couple, republicans are being forced to confront not only the magic of monarchy but also its media monopolisation. While they may ultimately be on the right side of history, during the weeks leading up to the wedding they were on the wrong side of rolling news. Every day, the Buckingham Palace press machine served up yet another William and Kate-related puff piece that was gobbled up by the Australian press. The same cycle repeated itself during the royal birth, which again saw the usual phalanx of Australian anchors and correspondents stationed outside the hospital. One even said on air that they were witnessing the birth of a future Australian head of state. Kate and William have also helped fill something of a tabloid void, thus performing the dual role of royals and hot celebrities. In this sense, they have not only become an adornment to Australian national life, but a much-needed addition to a tabloid talent pool that has been looking rather shallow of late.

Just as Buckingham Palace has been clever at deploying the Queen to shore up support for the monarchy, its roll-out of the young generation of new royals has been masterful. Prince William made two successful visits to Australia in the

15 months before the royal wedding. With each visit, the monarchy emerges repackaged and revitalised.

Of course, Australia will not get a King William or Queen Kate without Charles and Camilla coming first, at which point the republican movement will make its move.

Even then, however, a referendum would be by no means clear-cut. A poll in 2008 suggested that 32 per cent of Australians would continue to support the monarchy when Charles becomes the King of Australia, and that 11 per cent were undecided on the question. Over the course of a second referendum campaign that sizeable minority could easily become a slim majority.

For now, republicans are stymied. Like Prince Albert in the movie *The King's Speech* – played with such aplomb by a British republican, Colin Firth – they appear temporarily to have lost their voice.

From the moment that her parents inked the name on her birth certificate, it was surely preordained that Sammi Strange would one day be granted at least 15 minutes of fame, or its megabyte equivalent. Judging from the hyperbolic reaction in the UK press to the then 24-year-old Melburnian's appointment as the Camerons' Downing Street nanny, it appeared she might even qualify for a footnote in the history of British decline. An Aussie placed in charge of the prime minister's offspring? Surely the country must be going to the dogs?

London scribes adopted two lines of attack. The first, naturally, was that the Camerons had entrusted their three children to a prime vulgarian from the antipodes. 'Cameron's new nanny "shoplifts, smokes and swears",' scoffed *The Daily Telegraph*. 'Do I like to swear? F*** yeah,' noted the *Daily Mail*, quoting Ms Strange's teenage response years earlier to an online questionnaire asking whether she used unbecoming language. The other main criticism, so resonant at a time when the UK had descended into a double dip recession, was that the Camerons should have hired a Brit. 'Why on earth couldn't Cameron have found a British nanny to look after his children?' harrumphed a columnist in *The Guardian*.

Ms Strange had evidently introduced a Sherrin ball to the Downing Street playroom – Julia Gillard also took one to the Oval Office, remember – and who knew what might follow next. *Snugglepot and Cuddlepie*? *Bananas in Pyjamas*? Cherry Ripes? But what Ms Strange truly represented was a process in train for years: the 'Aussiefication' of British life. The slow death of British Australia has run in parallel with the inexorable rise of Australian Britain. David Cameron, Sammi's employer, tacitly acknowledged as much in the run-up to the 2010 British election. Asked on morning television whether he preferred *Eastenders* or *Coronation Street*, he did not miss a beat. '*Neighbours*,' he shot back. Ramsay Street had come to Downing Street long before Sammi Strange had stepped through its heavily guarded gates.

In UK popular culture, Australians are pervasive. Successive generations of British students, as Cameron well knows, have sought light relief from their studies with a daily dose of *Neighbours* or *Home and Away*. Kylie Minogue, the Princess of Pop, first introduced as the tomboyish Charlene, has become such a national institution that *The Sun* even mounted a campaign to heritage-list her arse. Rolf Harris not only provided the playschool soundtrack for British toddlers in the 1960s and 1970s, but even got to paint an official portrait of the Queen.

No commentator has chronicled popular culture with such pinpoint accuracy as Clive James. So much so that when *The New Yorker* needed a writer to capture the mood following the death of Princess Diana it commissioned him, rather than a British cultural commentator, to do so. The kid from Kogarah's influence on other British writers has also been immense. His television reviews in *The Observer* alone spawned an entire legion of young imitators hoping that they, too, could one day craft their own version of a sentence incorporating Arnold Schwarzenegger, walnuts and a condom. 'Thank you, Clive James, thank you,' wrote Charlie Brooker of *The Guardian* when James revealed on the BBC that he was 'approaching his terminus', an admission that prompted a rash of pre-emptive eulogies. Brooker also acknowledged the grip of that Schwarzenegger zinger: 'Every TV column I ever wrote consists of me trying and failing to write anything as explosively funny as that, for 650 words.' Germaine Greer has had a similar impact on British feminists.

In high culture, too, Australians proliferate. In an essay entitled 'The Great Aussie Invasion', the British cultural commentator Bryan Appleyard noted that Australians ran London's South Bank, the London Philharmonic Orchestra, the Science Museum, Sadler's Wells Theatre, the Royal College of Music and the Royal Ballet school. 'Strewth, they're all over the place,' he half-jokingly complained. 'The list is endless. Britain is now run by Australians.' That essay, written a decade ago, would not be repeated today, because the participation of Australians in British life is a given. They have also been absorbed into the fabric of the establishment. Robert May, the Sydneysider scientist who served between 2000 and 2005 as president of the Royal Society (the job once occupied by Sir Joseph Banks, the naturalist who was onboard *Endeavour* in 1770 with Captain James Cook), now has the title Baron May of Oxford, and sits on the crossbenches of the House of Lords.

Partly because *Neighbours* and *Home and Away* are now such a part of the teen and undergraduate culture, words and phrases like 'mate' and 'no worries' are heard more frequently, along with Australianisms like 'that's a big ask'. Lexicographers have noticed that Britons between the age of 15 and 35 are ending their sentences with an upward inflexion, which offers yet more proof of the power of Australian soapies – the 'Neighbours effect'. Or perhaps it is because an Aussie army of Sammi Stranges is responsible for the childcare of so many British middle class children. As for electronic childminding, The Wiggles are always there.

Tony Blair has even been called Britain's first Australian prime minister, partly because of his 'please call me Tony' informality and classlessness. Blair lived in Australia as a small child, while his father was lecturing at the University of Adelaide. At Oxford, he counted Australians among his closest friends and mentors, most notably Geoff Gallop, the former premier of Western Australia, and the late Anglican clergyman Peter Thomson, who became his muscular Christian personal trainer.

The New Labour project, of which Blair was a prime architect, owes more to Bob Hawke and Paul Keating than Bill Clinton. Blair has recounted how, as young parliamentarians, he and Gordon Brown sat at the feet of the 'Silver Bodgie' to be schooled in a political credo fusing free market thinking with social justice that originated in Australia.

Before heading to Hayman Island in 1995, where Blair had been invited by Rupert Murdoch to address a gathering of News Corp's executives, he stopped by Kirribilli House for a tutorial from Keating on how to deal with a media mogul known in Britain as the 'Dirty Digger'. Few things spoke more persuasively of the impact of Australians on British life than Blair travelling halfway around the world to essentially kiss the hand of Britain's most powerful press baron.

In recent times, the Labour Party has wondered whether it should adopt the same cutthroat approach as the ALP. Ahead of the 2010 election, which Gordon Brown seemed almost certain to lose, there was talk within Labour Party circles of 'doing a Hayden', and ditching him on the eve of polling. In the end, it turned out to be too squeamish.

On the conservative side of British politics, David Cameron relies heavily on the Australian political consultant Lynton Crosby, or the 'Wizard of Oz' as he is known on Fleet Street. The Conservatives also used him at the 2005 election, hoping he could do for Michael Howard, the then leader of the opposition, what he had done for John Howard. When Boris Johnson overcame Ken Livingstone to become the mayor of London, James McGrath, another implant from the Liberal Party, ran his campaign. McGrath said afterwards he brought some 'true Australianism' into the campaign. Asked what that meant, he replied, 'The first thing we did on the Boris campaign was to bring in some alcohol.' Loutishly stereotypical as it sounded, McGrath was essentially saying that he'd brought an air of informality to the office, a significant Australian contribution to British corporate life. Another is the appearance in the workplace each November of whiskers, bum fluff and fully fledged moustaches, with UK men embracing the 'Movember' movement that first started in Adelaide and Melbourne.

And what of the contribution in sport? The resurgence of British rowing and cycling owes much to coaches poached from Australia. Shane Sutton, a New South Welshman, coaches Bradley Wiggins, the first British winner of the Tour de France. To reclaim the Ashes in 2005, England relied on the Australian bowling coach, Troy Cooley. In 2013, when England won again, David Saker, another Australian, performed the same role. The British have built a national sporting academy modelled on the Australian Institute of Sport.

For the 2012 London Olympics the touchstone was the 2000 Sydney Olympics. *The Australian* even dubbed them the 'Home and Away' Games because of the involvement of so many Aussies. Michael Pirrie, a veteran of the Sydney Games and a native of Melbourne, served as executive assistant to the Games supremo, Sebastian Coe, who made no secret of his design to emulate the success of the 2000 Games. Australians ran the aquatic centre, the equestrian centre, along with the venues for shooting, water polo, volleyball, football and road cycling. When the Aussies who helped organise the Olympics gathered for a celebratory event, it was held at a hotel not on Oxford Street in London but Oxford Street in Sydney. Australians also helped build the economic legacy of the Games. Next to the Olympic Park in London's East End is a giant Westfield. Wembley, the shrine of English football, was constructed by Multiplex, an Australian firm.

Some of the boorishness in British sport, it has been claimed, also derives from Australia. When, during the 2009 Ashes series, spectators at Lord's booed Ricky Ponting as he made his way to the wicket, Ed Smith, a former England batsman and one of the more thoughtful commentators on the game, theorised that they might be trying to 'out-vulgarise Australia'. Then he made the broader argument that, in trying to ape the MCG's Bay 13, the unruly fans were 'merely playing catch-up with English cricket's widespread obsession with Australia-philia'. English cricket, he suggested, had its 'own cultural cringe – that everything Australian should be copied. First sledging, now booing: they do it to us, so let's do it to them.'

Auberon Waugh once claimed that 'the English seem only to copy the worst characteristics of the New World . . . while never emulating its optimism and enthusiasm'. But that is surely no longer the case. The fashion for classlessness in

Britain, a positive development, has Australian overtones. It seeks to emulate the egalitarianism and lack of pretence that so many Brits find attractive about Australia. When Cambridge University was trying in the 1990s to cast off its snooty image, for instance, it appointed as its vice-chancellor an Australian, Sir Alec Broers.

The broadcaster Michael Parkinson, who splits his year between the UK and Sydney, put it well when he became the first 'Pom' to deliver the Australia Day address. 'For someone brought up to conform to the strict boundaries of class and privilege in post-war Britain; to feel inhibited, shackled even, by the limitations imposed by accent, education and the fact of being a miner's son; for this person to encounter fellow human beings to whom none of these things mattered at all, was a joyous revelation.' Parkinson said he 'truly fell in love with Australia' when watching Paul Keating put his arm around the Queen in 1992, an intimacy which led to his tabloid crowning as 'the Lizard of Oz'. 'Those who believed it was a terrible lapse of protocol, that Mr Keating should be sent to the Tower and tried for treason, completely missed the point,' wrote Parkie. 'Mr Keating wasn't being disloyal, he was merely reaching out in friendly gesture, as one human being to another.' He was being Australian.

Parkie's lecture found an echo that same year from the heir to the Australian throne, Prince Charles. During a speech at an Australia Day reception in London, he reflected on the two terms he spent at Geelong Grammar School in the 1960s – Rupert Murdoch and Kerry Packer are fellow alumni – and wistfully recalled, 'I was able to go around relatively privately and find out an awful lot about that part of the world. As you can imagine I have a huge affection as a result. I've been through my fair share of being called a "pommy bastard", I can assure you! Look what it's done to me. My God, it was good for the character. If you want to develop character, go to Australia. As I say, I have a huge affection for it.' Small wonder he urged his son, Harry, to follow the jackaroo trail.

As the coverage of young Samantha Strange reminds us, imperial condescension can still creep into British attitudes towards Australia. My fellow Poms can be breathtakingly patronising – gleefully so, in fact. Weighing in on the black-face skit row, Marina Hyde, another *Guardian* columnist who based her style on Clive James, wrote, 'we thank the nation for yet another important contribution to the annals of human culture'. That same derisive tone was evident in the response to the tragic death of a nurse, Jacintha Saldanha, at King Edward VII's Hospital in London after a prank call from two Australian disc jockeys. Much of Fleet Street went with the hoary line that Aussies are a bunch of uncouth ruffians. Here again, Australians had an unhappy habit of stereotyping themselves. Riding roughshod over the sensibilities of Nurse Saldanha's family, Southern Cross Austereo honoured one of the disc jockeys, Michael Christian, with an 'Australia's Next Top Jock' award. The company's chairman, Max Moore-Wilton told company shareholders, 'shit happens'.

Noticeable in recent years, however, has been the greater sense of parity between Britain and Australia, and a heightened respect for Australians. 'There's been a change in attitude,' says Robert Thomson, the former editor of *The Times*. 'I haven't felt that there was a presumption that you were some escapee from the outback.'

British diplomats have certainly re-evaluated the relationship with Australia, and William Hague, the foreign secretary, has gone out of his way – literally – to forge a closer relationship with Canberra. Not since 1994 had a British foreign secretary – Douglas Hurd – set foot in Australia up until Hague's first visit in 2011. Two years later, he was back again. Bilateral talks between the two nations, which have been given the awkward acronym AUKMIN, now take place annually. This heightened attention, as Hague openly admitted, recognised Australia's enhanced global standing. Worried about its dwindling influence in the most populous and economically active part of the world, Britain has been forced to play catch-up. This also explains why David Cameron's government has placed added emphasis on the Commonwealth, this loose historical alliance of 54 nations of which Australia has proved such a loyal member.

Have not the Ashes also become more important to the English than the Australians as a meter of national prestige? A losing run stretching 16 years explained the joy unleashed in 2005 when Michael Vaughan's charges finally triumphed in what was perhaps the most riveting series ever played between any two cricketing nations. Yet other forces are also at play. In a world where very few British colonies pay the Mother Country close attention, I suspect we are rather flattered that Australians take the contest so seriously. It is especially soothing for a country that lost its empire but failed to find a role, to recycle the American diplomat Dean Acheson's famous putdown, to feel that the Aussies are motivated still by a desire to balance that presumed historical ledger, since it implies an outstanding deficit and a perpetual state of borrowing. In many ways, the repertoire of the Barmy Army, with its ritualistic renditions of 'God Save *Your* Queen', reveals more about us than you.

But will they ever get to sing 'God Save *Your* King'? Will the institution survive past the Elizabethan age? The monarchy is surely a bigger part of Australia's past than its future, and the fondness is now directed more strongly towards an individual than an institution. The republican movement claims with good reason it is very much alive, but alive like a hibernating animal for which a full awakening is still a long way off. After all, Tony Abbott, the first national executive director of Australians for Constitutional Monarchy, is now the prime minister, and the staunchest monarchist to occupy The Lodge since Menzies.

In his much-lampooned speech in 1963, Menzies made a pertinent, if largely unnoticed, point. Talking of the 'joint allegiance' between Australia and Britain, and the centrality of the monarchy to that relationship, he described it as 'an addition to our freedom, not a subtraction from it'. That has proved a resilient thought, and looks set to remain so with or without the presence of the Queen.

Chapter 7

THE RISE OF ASIAN AUSTRALIA

AN ARCH MONARCHIST, AVOWED Thatcherite and alumnus of a Perth private school, St Hilda's, that served the city's Anglophile elite, Gina Rinehart is in many aspects a product of British Australia. To this day she speaks with a plummy, English-sounding accent, more Pimlico than Pilbara. Her first husband was British. When Queen Elizabeth and Prince Philip visited Western Australia in 2012, she occupied pole position on the rope line and wore a hat that would have turned heads, as well as possibly decapitating them, at the Royal Enclosure at Ascot.

Her recent biography, however, exemplifies the rise of Asian Australia. Never would the country's richest and most newsworthy billionaire have become the object of such fascination, or generated so much wealth, had it not been for the coupling of the Australian economy with the rest of Asia. Her family history speaks of the changes that have overtaken the country and its economy. In the early 1960s, after chancing upon the oxidised iron ore deposits of the Pilbara, her buccaneering father, Lang Hancock, ended up signing a lucrative iron ore royalties deal with the British mining giant Rio Tinto at the encouragement of an American, Tom Price, an executive with the US steel giant, Kaiser Steel, who now has both a town and quarry named after him in WA. The gargantuan leaps in Gina Rinehart's personal net wealth, however, have come from deals negotiated with two Asian companies, the South Korean iron and steel giant Posco, and the Indian conglomerate GVK. They made her Asia's richest woman and set her on the path to maybe becoming the wealthiest person in the world.

Only a decade ago, Australia's rich list was dominated by the east coast business elite. The rise of Asia, which has shifted the centre of Australia's economic gravity over the 129th meridian, means that it is now headed by Western Australian mining moguls. First, it was Andrew 'Twiggy' Forrest, who fits the mould of the swashbuckling resources prospector. Then it was Gina herself. Though a beneficiary of her father's royalty deals, she transformed the family business by spotting, earlier than most, the vast potential of the China market. That is why she hates being called a mining heiress. Though she could scarcely be described as a self-made businesswoman, she is personally responsible for much of her financial success and has turned Hancock Prospecting into the behemoth it is today.

Undeterred by the grime and fluorescence of working in the mines, Australians have followed the money. Across Western Australia, average household incomes rose a staggering 35 per cent in just five years. Paid as much as $200,000, truck drivers in the west can earn more than bankers in the east. WA is now the country's fastest-growing state. Perth is the fastest-growing state capital. Once known for its isolation, now it is known for its affluence. It is now pricier, according to *The Economist*, than either London or New York.

More and more, WA is acting like a quasi-independent realm. Its premier, Colin Barnett, boasts that he spends more time in China than Canberra. 'Western Australia's economic development is not focused on what happens in Canberra,' he says. 'It is focused on what happens in Asia.' On a visit to Beijing in 2011, he added his signature to an historic trade and investment agreement with China, the first it had ever negotiated with a state or provincial government. Barnett could be forgiven for acting like a potentate rather than a premier. Western Australia accounts for 70 per cent of the nation's exports to China, attracts 80 per cent of Chinese investment in Australia, and is the home of 97 per cent of the country's iron ore production.

Families on the eastern seaboard that used to head up the rich lists are trying to catch up by harnessing the same Asian winds. James Packer, the billionaire ousted by Twiggy Forrest from his perch at the top of the rich list, revived his dynastic fortunes by switching the focus of his business from America to Asia. After the death of his father, Kerry, Packer was thought to be haemorrhaging $480,000 an hour because of his failed investments in Las Vegas casinos. His gambling resorts in Macau, where a $600 million investment turned into an $8 billion business, helped keep him solvent. After divesting the Packer empire of its media interests, like Channel Nine and *The Bulletin*, his new home-based business model is built on expanding his casino operation in Melbourne, Perth and Sydney to accommodate high-rollers from Asia. His planned skyscraper on Sydney Harbour, with its cloud-level gambling room designed for China's super-rich, the coveted 'whales', could almost serve as an exclamation mark for Australia in the Asian century. Given the ease with which it has bypassed normal planning regulations, it could also become a monument to the divine right of Australia's corporate princes.

Rupert Murdoch, better known for his acquisitions in Britain and America, nonetheless made sure not to neglect Asia. When in 1993 he purchased Star TV – which stands for Satellite Television Asia Region – he was asked to plot the future trajectory of his multinational media company. 'China, China, China and China,' he replied. Star TV broadcast to India, Japan, dozens of other Asian countries, though not all of China, the primary market he wanted to tap. Still, buying Star TV brought him into contact with a Chinese vice-president of the company, Wendi Deng, who became his third wife. The latest scions of the Murdoch dynasty are half-Asian.

Outside of the resources sector, there is no better case study in the Asianisation of the Australian economy than the national flag-carrier, Qantas. From its sponsorship of national sports teams to its theme song, 'I Still Call Australia Home', Qantas has always tried to tweak the patriotic nerve with its sentimental nationalism. Out of commercial necessity, however, the Spirit of Asia has superseded the Spirit of Australia. In 2011, the company announced a major restructure expanding its regional operations, and also heralded the launch of two new Asian airlines, including a budget outfit operating out of Japan. Simultaneously, as if to underscore its geographic reorientation, Qantas cut two unprofitable Kangaroo Routes to London, operating out of Bangkok and Hong Kong.

No Australian company has wedded its corporate identity to national identity to quite the same degree, and few Australian companies, with the possible exception of Telstra, arouse such strong passions. So its new Asian focus was especially emblematic. It also meant the backlash was ferocious. 'I think it's official,' harrumphed Senator Nick Xenophon. 'Qantas can no longer call Australia home.' Queensland MP Bob Katter attacked 'the slithering suits' who had made the decision, calling them 'a bunch of brainless bastards'. For Alan Joyce, Qantas's CEO, the decision was indeed a no-brainer. 'China may already have the world's fourth-largest population of millionaires, and India the 12th,' explained the Irish executive. 'There are many, many millions of premium travellers in waiting.' If Australia could not succeed in Asia, it could not succeed anywhere, Paul Keating observed in the mid-1990s. Qantas was offering a reworking of that aphorism. If an Australian company with global ambition failed in Asia, then it ran the risk of failing in Australia as well.

Qantas's shift reflects broader changes in the tourism industry. When Paul Hogan promised to hurl an extra shrimp on the barbie, his 'Come and Say G'day' campaign was obviously targeted primarily at Americans and Brits. Yet as Tourism Australia learned to its cost from the puzzled response in Asia to its disastrous 'Where the Bloody Hell Are You?' drive, it needs to converse with potential tourists from China, Japan, South Korea and elsewhere in Asia. Its more recent efforts have not been met with such mystification. Australia has become China's most popular destination. Leaving for Australia is increasingly a sign you have arrived in China.

This is just as well. Whereas visitors from New Zealand, the UK and US used to be its core market, now the tourist sector is increasingly reliant on Asia. In 2010, China became Australia's biggest inbound tourism market, and is now the most rapidly expanding sector. Over 500,000 Chinese visited Australia in 2011, an almost 20 per cent increase on 2010. By 2020, Chinese visitors are projected to inject up to $9 billion into the Australian economy, double their present contribution.

The Asian influx is changing the character of Australian tourism. Chinese visitors, rather than heading for the outback or bush, the long-time lure for British and Americans, prefer urban destinations. In New South Wales, 91 per cent of Chinese visitor nights are spent in Sydney. With gambling a magnetic draw, state governments will come under heightened pressure from hoteliers and the entertainment industry to license more casinos. After all, whales are more lucrative than backpackers.

Tourist attractions are trying to become more welcoming to Asian guests. Sovereign Hill, an outdoor museum in Ballarat that recreates the feel of the mid-19th-century gold rush, has Mandarin-speaking guides and even a bespoke China tour. It has attracted over a million Chinese visitors keen to learn how their forebears chased fortunes in Australia.

Higher and tertiary education, Australia's fourth biggest export, has not only benefited from Asia, it is dependent on the region. Overseas students account for 22 per cent of student numbers overall, the highest percentage in the world. Of those, 80 per cent are from Asia, and a third comes from China. Campuses are being transformed to accommodate them, with booze-free dorms, gender-segregated floors, and prayer rooms. Because Asian students expect better digs than Australians, accommodation blocks have been newly built or upgraded, with some now having the sheen, if not quite the luxury, of boutique hotels. The country's most eye-catching new academic building, the UTS Business School in Sydney, which looks like it's collapsing in on itself, may be designed by an American starchitect, Frank Gehry, but it is called the Dr Chau Chak Wing Building, a Chinese-Australian businessman and philanthropist.

Many lecture halls are still unfashionably monocultural given the reliance on traditional teaching methods, but the curriculum is slowly being altered so that courses have more of an Asian bent. In business schools particularly, Chinese and Japanese companies are used as case studies as well as US corporations. Australian universities regularly hold graduation ceremonies in Shanghai, Hong Kong and other Asian cities so that parents can more easily attend.

No sector can afford to be left behind. Whereas Australian sport has traditionally preserved the link with Britain, and occasionally undertaken fruitless forays into America, administrators are making inroads into neighbouring countries. In 2010, the AFL broke new ground by holding an exhibition game in China, a 'Shanghai Showdown' between Melbourne and the Brisbane Lions. Hong Kong and Tokyo have hosted the Bledisloe Cup. Though top golfers compete on the US and European tours, the Australian PGA is now officially part of the OneAsia tour. In tennis, the Australian Open, determined not to lose this blue-ribbon tournament to an Asian rival, markets itself as the grand slam of the Asia Pacific (in 2014, the court-side advertising hoardings for Jacob's Creek, a major brand in China, were also in Mandarin). The Socceroos are now part of the Asian Football Confederation of FIFA rather than the Oceania Football Confederation. Since 2007, A-League clubs have competed in the AFC Champions League, with fixtures against Gamba Osaka, Jeonbuk Hyundai Motors and the Pohang Steelers. The 'Come Play!' campaign, Australia's unsuccessful bid to host the 2022 World Cup, turned the old tyranny of distance idea on its head. Australia, the bid claimed, was the 'gateway to Asia'.

Towards Asian cultural influences, Australia has become more welcoming. Food is the most obvious, whether served up by *MasterChef*'s cohort of Asian-Australian chefs, including Poh Ling Yeow and Adam Liaw, or the Sydney restaurateur Luke Nguyen, whose culinary trips through Vietnam have proved so popular in print and on television. Tetsuya Wakuda, a Japanese-Australian who started his Australian career rolling sushi in Sydney's Taylor Square, is widely viewed as the country's finest chef. Still, it takes more than a handful of wasabi peas and a plate of Pad Thai to bring about a meaningful realignment.

Australian festivals are getting more of an Asian flavour. Joining the crowds to watch the Anzac Day parade pass through the streets of Sydney's CBD in 2013, I was struck by how many Asian-Australians lined the route. Community events, like, say, the annual Granny Smith Festival in northwest Sydney, celebrating Australia's most globally-renowned orchardist, no longer have such a vintage air. The Marching Koalas and the Castle Hill RSL band parade alongside the Sydney Korean Women's Association and the Falun Dafa Association. As well as swirling batons, clarinets, tartan, bagpipes and men in giant kangaroo outfits, there are kimonos, gongs, cymbals and meandering Chinese dragons. The Chinese New Year celebrations in Sydney have become so efflorescent that they have been dubbed 'Mardi Gras goes to China'. It is also the biggest Chinese New Year festival anywhere in the world outside of China.

Intellectually, whereas the dominant influences have typically been British and American, there are signs that Australian thinkers and politicians are being swayed by the philosophical winds blowing in from Asia. When Joe Hockey, the then shadow treasurer, delivered what became known as his 'age of entitlement' speech, Hong Kong was his model for what a smaller welfare safety net might look like, while he also spoke admiringly of the 'concept of filial piety, from the Confucian classic Xiao Jing'. What made the speech all the more noteworthy was that Hockey delivered it in London, where Australian politicians have usually gone to reinforce ties with Britain.

For the Australian right, Singapore has increasingly become the model nation. Rupert Murdoch heralds this city-state as 'the most open and clear society in the world'. Delivering the Lowy Institute lecture in 2013, he praised Taiwan, Hong Kong, as well as Singapore, and issued a challenge for Australia to attract the best Asian graduates to its universities.

Gina Rinehart echoed her friend's praise for Singapore, waxing lyrical about a nation 'which welcomes investment, makes real effort to minimise red tape (even asking its people and businesses to point out time- or money-wasting red tape if they find it), has low taxes, low crime, enables guest labour, and has no debt'. In her plans for northern Australia to become a special economic zone, free from the scourge of what her father derisively labelled Canberraism, Singapore is the blueprint.

Nor is it just the Australian right looking towards Asian countries. When the policy think tank the Grattan Institute published a report on educational standards, it urged Australian educators to learn from East Asia's 'unrelenting focus on learning and teaching', and the Confucian tradition of elevating the teacher. After all, the four top global educational performers, according to the OECD, are Shanghai, Singapore, Hong Kong and South Korea. While the embrace of Asian ideas is by no means novel, it is unquestionably becoming more pronounced. It represents an intellectual pivot of sorts.

Identifying areas of kinship and common ground would be useful, according to Tim Soutphommasane, whose parents were refugees from Laos: 'Might there be value in reflecting on the similarities between Asian concepts of communal obligation and our own value of mateship?' Here, he was echoing Horne, who argued: 'To take our ideology of fraternalism seriously and apply it to Asians could lead to a creative awakening among Australians.'

More and more, Asia is the benchmark. 'I keep alluding to Hong Kong,' explained Joe Hockey during his speech in London, 'because Hong Kong is our direct competition, as is Singapore, as is Korea in different ways, Vietnam, Indonesia.' Likewise, any debate about updating Australia's creaky infrastructure usually begins with how Asia is racing ahead. Michael Wesley's landmark book *There Goes the Neighbourhood: Australia and the Rise of Asia* opens with the incongruity between travelling from Central Station in Hong Kong to the gleaming international airport, and embarking on the same journey from the grubby Central Station in Sydney to the dated Kingsford-Smith terminus. Japan's bullet trains have long been the prototype for those who would like to see a high-speed rail service linking Sydney, Canberra and Melbourne.

Still, for all of Asia's transformative impact, Australia remains hesitant about supplanting its traditional arms-length relationship with a whole-hearted embrace. On the rare occasions that the national conversation focuses on Australia in the Asian century, it is often out of a sense of geopolitical correctness rather than real enthusiasm. It is a dialogue the country feels it ought to be having rather than wants to be having. Lip service is paid, goals are set, white papers are published and there is broad agreement that Australia should be doing more, but nothing much changes unless driven by commerce and profit.

This shortfall between ambition and outcome is evident in the decline of Asian language teaching in Australian schools. The Gillard government announced its intention to make

Australia an Asia-literate society by 2025, but the number of school children learning Asian languages continues to decline. In Victoria a greater number of Year 12 students learns Latin than Chinese (both, admittedly, are paltry, 200 to 150).

Encouraging the learning of Asian languages for their own intrinsic value rather than their commercial usefulness should also be the goal, even if the attractiveness to potential employers of curriculum vitae adorned with a qualification in Mandarin or Japanese acts as a helpful spur. Paradoxically, though, the Asianisation of Australia has created a powerful disincentive effect. A prime reason why the take-up of Asian languages is so low among non-native-speaking Chinese language speakers is because they have to compete in exams against native Chinese speakers who converse in the language at home. Understandably, this competitive disadvantage is putting off many white Australians.

When studying abroad, partly because of the common language, Australian students still prefer America, New Zealand and Britain over Asian universities. German and French institutions are also more popular, despite incentives like the AsiaBound grant programme brought in under Labor to encourage Australians to get a first-hand experience of Asia, and the Coalition's New Colombo Plan, which shares the same aim.

When the old Colombo Plan was launched back in 1950, Percy Spender, the minister for external affairs in the Menzies government, spoke about nurturing closer ties with its neighbours. 'Australia is next door to Asia, and our destiny as a nation is irrevocably conditioned by what takes place in Asia,' he said. 'It is therefore in Asia, and the Pacific, that Australia should make its primary effort in the field of foreign relations.' But to re-read his remarks today is to be reminded that Australian leaders have for decades been delivering these kind of bromides. The difficulty has been bringing about a genuine national reorientation.

Unquestionably, more could be done on the cultural front, which retains still an overwhelmingly Anglocentric leaning. Lamenting the country's 'meat and three veg' culture, Lyndon Terracini, the artistic director of Opera Australia, complained that 'the extraordinary tastes of Asia' routinely were ignored. We still await a cultural version of 'Asian fusion' cuisine that has made dining out in Australia such an exotic and flavoursome adventure. The Chinese-Australian artist Guan Wei, whose work has set Nolanesque Ned Kelly motifs against Chinese landscapes, is a rare but welcome addition.

Indigenous art is also finding an appreciative audience in China. The Tu Di Shen Ti (Land and Body) exhibition, showcasing works collected by the Ngaanyatjarra community from Warburton Ranges in the Western Desert, opened at the Australian Embassy in Beijing in mid-2011 and has been touring the Chinese provinces. More than 85,000 people have seen it.

The Australian movie industry has been notorious for ignoring its neighbours. Peter Weir's *The Year of Living Dangerously* and Robert Connolly's *Balibo*, both of which view Indonesia through the eyes of Australian journalists, are rare standouts. *Japanese Story*, a romance in which Toni Collette's character, Sandy, has a brief but tragic affair with a Japanese businessman, Hiro, visiting the mines of the Pilbara, drew criticism for its clichéd portrayal of both main characters. 'So, tell me about the Japs,' says Sandy, a Perth-based software designer, on learning that she has to be Hiro's guide, as if they are from another galaxy.

Kieran Darcy-Smith's 2012 movie *Wish You Were Here*, which followed a group of Sydneysiders vacationing in Cambodia, rightly drew critical acclaim. But it offered a sophisticated portrayal of tabloid television's paranoid take on southeast Asia: a potentially hostile place where Australians inevitably end up running into trouble.

The Australian news media does a better job of covering Asia, with some of the country's finest journalists, like John Garnaut of *The Sydney Morning Herald*, Mark Willacy of ABC News and Amanda Hodge of *The Australian*, reporting from the region with award-winning distinction. The Lowy Institute's *Interpreter* blog stands out globally for the quality of its regional analysis. Still, the prized posts in all Australian news organisations are not Tokyo, Jakarta or Beijing, but London and Washington. The same is true of diplomatic postings, which is why Kim Beazley is the ambassador to Washington and not Beijing, Mike Rann became the high commissioner in London rather than in Tokyo, Steve Bracks was tapped up for New York not Shanghai and Alexander Downer also headed to Australia's High Commission on the Strand. In *Asia Pacific Focus*, ABC broadcasts a weekly digest of news from the region but it feels like the fourth-ranked programme in the Sunday current affairs roster, behind *Insiders*, *Offsiders* and *Landline*. Again, it feels like a nod rather than an embrace.

Certainly, ABC News 24 regards *Planet America* as a more exciting place to explore. This was especially noticeable in 2012, when the US presidential election coincided with China's leadership transition. Understandably, America's great carnival of democracy garnered far more coverage than the monochrome, heavily stage-managed events in the Great Hall of the People. On the commercial networks, an uneventful visit from Charles and Camilla was also given higher billing than Xi Jinping's rise to power.

This highlights a larger problem in selling the whole 'Australia in the Asian Century' project. The Australian commentariat is still more captivated by American politics, with its motley cast of characters including Barack Obama, George W. Bush and the Clintons, than China's faceless men. Australians, like everyone else in the world, would struggle to name ten Chinese luminaries. Maybe even five. Outside of its Asian ethnic communities, Australia still does not have a close affinity with its neighbours.

Avarice is as big a problem as neglect. The danger for Australia is that its relationship with the rest of Asia becomes purely monetary and transactional, and is defined solely by the corporate sector. Bemoaning the 'mercenary tone' of the national conversation, Tim Soutphommasane fears 'economic self-interest' has become a bar to 'genuine cultural engagement'. Without even noticing it, he writes, 'we've fallen into the habit of making a monetary fetish out of our relationships with Asia, seeing its value only in terms of dollar signs'. Just as persuasively, Michael Wesley notes that 'Australians tend to view the rise of Asia in numerical terms' – GDP figures, investment flows, arms spending and trade levels. Yet '[t]he really important implications of Asia's rise for Australia are not quantitative but qualitative'.

The indictment of Australian academia is that it teaches Asian students but it doesn't learn from them. 'Even those schools and university departments that teach the history of Asian societies (and there is a shrinking number of them) rely almost overwhelmingly on western historiographic frameworks and learning techniques,' says Wesley. His criticism of Australian tourists is that they head to Europe seeking to learn more about the culture and history. When they touch down in Bali and Thailand, they head for the beach, and an Asian version of slip, slop, slap.

On the diplomatic travel front, historians will make much, one suspects, of Tony Abbott jetting off to Jakarta on his first overseas trip as prime minister for a meeting with the Indonesian president – and then on to Bali for an APEC summit. That month he turned down the chance to address the United Nations General Assembly in New York. But, again, the motive behind his trip was primarily transactional: he needed Indonesian help to solve the boat people problem.

Australia's continued suspicion of Indonesia was highlighted again only a few weeks later when Edward Snowden's latest NSA document dump revealed that ASIO had eavesdropped on Susilo Bambang Yudhoyono, and his wife, Ani, in 2009.

The Indonesian spying incident revealed what will be a recurring problem for Australia in the Asian century. It has no natural regional allies, little common heritage to fall back on and sharp, arguably insuperable, differences in national values. China is a one-party, authoritarian state, which maintains a system of gulags and carries out capital punishment on an almost industrial scale. It is a repressive nation. These are not the attributes of a natural friend.

Those seeking closer cultural ties with Beijing, a noble enough aim, would surely have been distressed by the reaction when the Melbourne International Film Festival screened a documentary on Rebiya Kadeer, the Uighur leader once imprisoned by Beijing who has campaigned for her people's greater autonomy from China. When *The 10 Conditions of Love*, by the Australian director Jeff Daniels, appeared on its programme, an angry Chinese cultural attaché visited the festival director, Richard Moore, to demand that it not be screened. When Moore refused, the festival's website came under almost immediate cyber-attack, with its homepage vandalised with a Chinese flag and anti-Kadeer slogans. The same hackers thwarted those wishing to purchase tickets online, which hammered the festival financially. More sinister still was the round-the-clock bombardment of the festival's fax machines, this time with grotesque images of decapitated kangaroos. Moore had intended to screen three Chinese films, but they were pulled by their directors in protest at Kadeer's planned appearance in Melbourne.

With Japan, which used to be Australia's biggest trading partner, it has been hard to nurture genuinely intimate relations while the country continued to send a fleet to the Southern Ocean each year to slaughter whales, and the nations confronted each other in the International Court of Justice. With Indonesia, there will always be differences over the boat people problem and death penalty. Australia's regional alliances are marriages of convenience rather than true romances.

Indecision also goes a long way towards explaining Australia's Asian ambivalence. The question of whether China represents an opportunity or threat is far from settled, and won't be for a long time to come. At the big end of town, the commercial benefits are obvious, but industrial workers understandably view Asian competitors as a threat to their livelihoods. Qantas maintenance staff at Avalon in Victoria or car workers on the Holden production lines in Adelaide and Port Melbourne take a very different view of Australia in the Asian century to Gina Rinehart and her mining mogul friends. Rather than riches, for them it has meant redundancy. In property, first-time buyers especially have bemoaned a spending splurge from wealthy Chinese investors in new homes and apartments that has priced them out of the market.

A sizeable demographic still fears that Australia is in danger of being 'swamped by Asians', hence the appearance of Asian Mall-type stories on current affairs shows. This is arrant nonsense, just as it was when Pauline Hanson first used that phrase. In 2009, the Chinese overtook the UK and New Zealand as Australia's biggest source of immigrants, but the 2011 Australian census found that Chinese was still only the seventh most common self-reported ancestry. Sydney is the home to Australia's largest Chinese community, but just 3.4 per cent of the city's population was born in China. In Melbourne it is 2.3 per cent. In recent years, the most noticeable population trend has been that Australia is becoming more aged rather than Asian.

At the macro-economic level, an obvious worry is the injurious effects of the China-fuelled resources boom, with Australia already showing signs of the 'Dutch disease' in industries, like manufacturing, tourism and fashion, hit by the high dollar. The Dutch variant, first diagnosed by *The Economist* in the late 1970s, proved to be relatively short-lived, because The Netherlands retooled its economy, and revitalised its industrial sector. Because Australian manufacturing has been on such a sharp downward trajectory, with more than 100,000 jobs in that sector lost since 2008, some have already renamed the 'Dutch disease' the 'Australian disease'. Western Australia is having the same distortive effect on the economy that the western suburbs are having on politics.

Even sectors that have benefited from the closer economic alignment with Asia often suffer a flip-side. The China-fuelled boom has made it more expensive for the Chinese to come here. This is especially true in higher education, where Chinese student numbers peaked in 2010. The soaring Australian dollar made US universities more inexpensive – on average $7000 cheaper a year, according to a recent government survey. Australian universities rank still as Asia's top education destination, but now lag behind the US, Britain and Canada. Overall, Australia experienced a 12 per cent drop in overseas student numbers between 2010 and 2012.

In bringing about friendlier ties with the region, a problem also persists at the highest level. Australian leaders recognise intellectually that they are living in the Asian century but continue to act like they are living in the American century, with a sentimental attachment to the British century as well. Their heads comprehend the dualism of Australia's position, but their hearts are firmly with America and Britain. This bias was evident in remarks Tony Abbott made at his old Oxford college in December 2012, in what came to be known as his 'Anglosphere' speech. 'China, Japan, India and Indonesia are countries that are profoundly important to Australia,' he said. 'Size, proximity and economic and military strength matter. Of course they do; but so do the bonds of history, of shared values, and of millions of familiar attachments.' More controversially, Abbott insinuated that Anglo-culture was superior. 'Western civilisation (especially in its English-speaking versions),' he claimed, 'provides our comparative advantage among the cultures of the world.' In *Battlelines*, he used similar language with a similar implication when he described John Howard's foreign policy as a 'kind of neighbourhood watch scheme for Western values'. Again, it implied that Western values were superior to Eastern values, not a particularly helpful view for a modern-day Australian leader to advertise.

Since becoming prime minister, Tony Abbott has described Japan as Australia's best friend in Asia, but it is nowhere near becoming Australia's best friend globally. Likewise during the 2013 campaign, he spoke of 'More Jakarta, less Geneva', an easy slogan to utter because of the Swiss city's strategic irrelevance. But he would never say 'More Beijing, less Washington'. Delivering a speech in the US capital, again before becoming prime minister, Abbott even went as far as to argue that 'few Australians would regard America as a foreign country'.

When American GIs were deployed to Australia in 1943 they were handed a small booklet, a *Pocket Guide to*

Australia, produced by America's War Department. 'You're going to meet a people who like Americans and whom you will like,' it read. 'The Australians have much in common with us – they're a pioneer people: they believe in personal freedom: they love sports . . . But there are a lot of differences too – like tea, central heating, the best way to spend Sunday morning, or saluting officers and such. You'll find out about all those, but the main point is they like us, and we like them.' It is hard to imagine a Chinese or Japanese official ever penning such a flattering text on its southern neighbour – or one being reciprocated. Familial attachments, along the philosophical points of convergence and emotional links that go with them, will grow as the Asian proportion of the population increases. But for now, Australia remains a strongly Anglo-Celtic country.

This aligns with public opinion. Successive surveys from the Lowy Institute have shown that Australians are more positively disposed towards the UK, New Zealand, Canada, America and even France than any of their Asian neighbours. Of those, Singapore and Japan, the most westernised countries, elicit the warmest feelings.

The question for Australia, however, is whether this Anglo-bent is sustainable, especially in the conduct of its foreign affairs, as the rise of Asia continues.

Enemies of Kevin Rudd would later release a video of off-cuts showing him swearing and cursing as he struggled to record a message in Mandarin for a Chinese community group during his first spell as prime minister, but one of the reasons why he was seen as the coming man in 2007 was because of his proficiency in the language.

At the APEC summit in Sydney on the eve of that year's federal election, John Howard hobnobbed with his deeply unpopular friend, the 'Toxic Texan' George W. Bush. Rudd, meanwhile, managed to steal the show by addressing a luncheon for the Chinese delegation in their native tongue. 'My wife and I have a particular love for Beijing,' he said, with the choppy fluency of flawless Mandarin. 'We love the feeling of Beijing. We love the people of Beijing, and of course, its culture. Twenty years later, the little girl that we took to Beijing this April married a young man from the Australian Chinese community. My son has already been to Shanghai's Fudan University to study. I also have a little boy, our youngest, who is in his early years of high school. He is really, really naughty – he doesn't like doing his homework. But he has already begun his study of Chinese.'

Though incomprehensible to most Australians, the speech nonetheless resonated. It bolstered the already overwhelming sense that he was the man for the moment – an Asian moment – and that Howard was, again, lagging behind the times.

For all the warmth exuded at the Sydney luncheon – the Chinese reportedly were dazzled – a diplomatic chill soon descended over Rudd's relations with Beijing. Yet that was partly because he knew the country so well, and believed therefore that he could speak more frankly than his predecessors. He did so on his first prime ministerial visit to the country in 2008, during a speech at Peking University. 'A true friend,' said Rudd, who had decided that China should be his first port of call as PM rather than Tokyo, 'is one who can be a *zhengyou*, that is a partner who sees beyond immediate benefit to the broader and firm basis for continuing, profound and sincere friendship.

'A strong relationship, and a true friendship,' he told the students, 'are built on the ability to engage in a direct, frank and ongoing dialogue about our fundamental interests and future vision.' That was his lead-in to criticise China on Tibet, a subject that the straight-talking John Howard had publicly avoided. China did not want *zhengyou*. It wanted trading partners who bit their lips when it came to discussing human rights violations.

The Stern Hu controversy, involving the imprisonment of a Chinese-Australian Rio Tinto executive over allegations of bribery, also had a souring effect. So, too, did the Copenhagen climate change conference, when the then Chinese President Hu Jintao scuppered a meaningful deal cutting emissions. Rudd went ballistic. 'Those Chinese fuckers are trying to rat-fuck us,' he reportedly fumed.

When the Rudd government brought out its long-awaited defence white paper it also raised Beijing's ire, since it was predicated on the danger of a belligerent China. It noted that 'the pace, scope and structure of China's military modernisation have the potential to give its neighbours cause for concern'. The language was diplomatic, but the implication was clear: China's military build-up posed a threat to regional peace. No national document better exemplified Australia's conflicted response to the emergence of a superpower to the north. To meet the potential threat from China, Australia would invest more heavily in defence, but its new jet-fighters and submarines would be financed by tax revenues generated by selling resources to China.

This contradiction highlighted Australia's overriding geostrategic challenge: of how to maintain its commercial rapport with China, while at the same time extending the defence alliance with Washington. The relationship that underwrote its prosperity was potentially at odds with the relationship underpinning its security.

This quandary was tackled by Hugh White, Australia's pre-eminent defence expert, in his much talked about

Quarterly Essay, 'Power Shift: Australia's Future between Washington and Beijing', published in 2010. White, a professor of strategic studies at the Australian National University and the main author of the Howard government's 2000 defence white paper, posed the nettlesome question of how Australia would manage its international relationships when, for the first time in 200 years, neither of its closest allies, Britain or America, had 'the final say' in Asia. John Howard had 'assured Australians that they did not have to choose between US and China', observed White. Rudd regarded this problem as so distant that it did not need to be confronted. Tony Abbott observed in *Battlelines* that America would still be the dominant economic power in 2020 and that Beijing's rise 'may not mean much change for Australia's international relationships or foreign policy priorities'. Struck by how few political leaders even wanted to address the question, White wryly observed: 'Like climate change, the issue seems too hard for our political system to handle.' Challenging the post-war consensus that the American alliance should remain the foundation of Australian foreign policy, he argued that 'the new Asian order' made the status quo untenable.

The 'power shift' thesis provided the backdrop for Barack Obama's visit in 2012, during which the US president announced that America would make an 'Asian pivot', and focus more attention on the world's most economically dynamic region. During his short stay, Julia Gillard – who had not read White's essay but was familiar with its argument – rejected emphatically the notion that Australia should reposition itself so that it is somehow equidistant between America and China. Rather, Australia would continue to side with America, to be that true mate down under. Much of the media coverage during the visit focused on the tactile relationship between Gillard and Obama, which bordered on the smoochie. More striking, however, were the images and words designed to convey strategic intimacy. Intricately choreographed to lend it a determinedly martial feel, the president's itinerary included the thunder of the 21-gun salute, the solemnity of a wreath-laying ceremony at the Australian War Memorial in Canberra and the quiet poignancy of a visit to the memorial for the USS *Peary*, the American destroyer bombed by the Japanese during the attack on Darwin harbour in February 1942. During his brief stopover in the Top End, he also took part in a campaign-style pep rally for diggers who had recently returned from Afghanistan. 'Aussie, Aussie, Aussie,' he shouted, in an aircraft hangar draped with giant Australian and American flags.

The touchstone for all the speeches from Obama, Gillard and Abbott was the unique experience of shared combat in every major US conflict since American forces entered World War I in 1917. Though the trip lasted just 30 hours, it continually evoked the historical underpinnings and shared sacrifice of a 60-year-old military alliance. Its overriding message was that blood is more binding than ore. Values, too. As Obama put it in one of the most pointed lines of his speech to parliament: 'partnerships can't just be about one nation extracting another's resources'. He also announced that up to 2500 US Marines would be stationed in Darwin by 2017.

China reacted angrily to the deployment of troops, and the deepened ties between Canberra and Washington that it signalled. 'It may not be appropriate to strengthen and extend this military alliance,' noted its foreign ministry spokesman, Liu Weimin, 'and may not be in the interest of countries within this region.' China's *People's Daily*, speaking more bluntly, warned that Australia risked being 'caught in the crossfire'.

For all Beijing's bluster, however, less than six months later Gillard, on her first trip to the People's Republic as prime minister, pulled off the significant coup of an agreement on annual leadership talks with the Chinese. It meant that for the first time relations between Beijing and Canberra were elevated to a 'strategic partnership'. Coming so soon after the announcement of the US marine deployment, it suggested that Australia could have it all: close relations with both Beijing and Washington.

The Gillard deal also came exactly 40 years after Gough Whitlam first established diplomatic ties with China, which served as a reminder that Australia has been tackling this conundrum for decades. Horne, remember, had prefaced *The Lucky Country* with a note of warning about China, and identified a strand of thought 'not widely represented in Australia outside intellectual and left-wing groups': those who would have it that 'Australia will never be trusted by "Asia" unless it withdraws itself from its alliance with America and declares itself to be non-aligned'. As far back as the early 1970s, Hedley Bull, the country's preeminent foreign affairs thinker, argued that Australia would soon have to rethink its relationship with America. Calling for an Australian declaration of independence at the time of the Bicentenary, Phillip Adams noted: 'We're closer to Asia than to Pennsylvania Avenue or W1. We are now well-advanced in weaning ourselves from Britain, but in embracing the US we've simply changed one mammary for another.'

The evidence of the past 40 years, however, is that Australia has played the diplomatic game of counterbalancing its US and Sino relations with considerable skill. Continuing this hedging strategy will doubtless become more challenging, especially as China's military gets bigger and its regional ambitions get bolder. Just how far would Australia go, for example, to back up Japan, its 'best friend in Asia', if the row over the Senkaku Islands in the East China Sea reached the point of near conflict? Yet Canberra should be able to manage this problem, not least because Washington and Beijing, with their co-dependent economies, will need to finesse it, too.

Besides, it is hardly as if Australia is the only country faced with this dilemma. South Korea, Taiwan and Japan also have a security partnership with America but a close trade partnership with China. Nor should Australia's commercial relationship with America be overlooked or undervalued. The US, as well as being the country's fourth largest export market, is also its biggest foreign investor. Britain remains the second.

At the start of the 1960s, Horne argued, 'we're all Asians now', a statement that remains true geographically, but not so intuitively. Instead, the central idea contained in that 1943 American field guide to Australia still resonates: 'they like us, and we like them'. Until the same can be said of China, Indonesia and Japan, with genuine affection and warmth, Australia will continue to locate itself within the Anglosphere as much as it does in Asia, its longstanding default position.

As with regional diplomacy, Australia in the Asian century should be a matter of smart calibration. Canberra should not shun Beijing or Tokyo, but nor should it spurn its long-standing allies. In any case, it is not faced with a hard choice between the two now or in the near future.

What has always struck me about Australia is its ability to absorb many of the attractive aspects of UK and US culture, but to filter out the worst excesses, such as the rigidity of the British class system and America's instinctive mistrust of government. It achieves this while at the same time retaining its distinctiveness. In sifting the good from the bad, there is no reason why it should not be able to be just as choosy as its engagement with Asia intensifies.

So prospering in an age when the locus of the world has shifted eastwards need not involve a radical overhaul of the national identity, or trigger some national identity crisis. Rather, it requires a greater openness to the idea that there is more to good neighbourliness than profitable economic ties, a renewed emphasis on the cross-flow of mutually beneficial cultural influences, and a realisation that its diplomacy will have to be more nimble and less slavish towards America. The people of this country are indeed all Asians now, but they are Australians first and foremost. They should not lose the art of being unselfconsciously themselves.

Chapter 8

THE CULTURAL CREEP

TODAY IT WOULD FEATURE REVOLVING chairs, an online poll, the usual hashtag hieroglyphics and maybe even a competitive cooking element, but in the early 1950s the Australian Broadcasting Commission's talent contest *Incognito* was a more innocent piece of light entertainment. Alas, no recording of the radio programme survives in the corporation's vast audio archive. Nor does it merit a mention in the two-volume authorised history of the ABC. Yet *Incognito* is one of the most influential programmes the national broadcaster has ever put to air, if only because it caught the ear of the Melbourne-based critic A. A. Phillips. The idea, thought Phillips, was quaint enough: to pit a local artist against a foreign guest, with the audience asked to adjudicate. Occasionally, listeners would favour the homegrown performer, thus producing 'a nice glow of patriotic satisfaction'. The programme, however, was founded on the demeaning premise that 'the domestic product will be worse than the imported article'. Phillips coined a neat description for this 'disease of the Australian mind' and immediately his aphorism, described in a 1950 *Meanjin* essay of the same name, took hold: 'the cultural cringe'.

Four years later, the historian Manning Clark issued a rebuttal, arguing that Europe was 'no longer the creative centre'. Nor were Australians philistines who had pitched their tents in the 'Australian Cultural Desert'. In his 1954 lecture 'Rewriting Australian History', he exhorted his compatriots to 'drop the idea that our past has irrevocably condemned us to the role of cultural barbarians'. Clark, however, was swimming against a rip.

By the end of the 1950s, Patrick White's more durable polemic *The Prodigal Son* had been published, which described his miserable return from England after the war to a country where in 'all directions stretched the Great Australian Emptiness, in which the mind is least of possessions'. Robin Boyd weighed in soon after with *The Australian Ugliness*, which bemoaned the craven Americanisation of local culture – Austerica, he called it – and its lazy embrace of the middling standard. 'In all the arts of living, in the shaping of her artefacts, as in politics,' he wrote, 'Australia shuffles along vigorously in the middle . . . of the road, picking up disconnected ideas wherever she finds them.'

Towards Australian culture, Donald Horne was scathing. 'Australia was mindless,' he thought after returning from London in the late 1940s, feeling like a European exile. 'Where were the art museums and theatres, the intellectual debate?' he exclaimed. Here he was amplifying Phillips, who spoke of the 'estrangement of the Australian intellectual'. Struck by the 'sheer dullness of life', Horne opined: 'Intellectual life exists but it is still fugitive.'

The dancer, actor and choreographer Robert Helpmann, speaking in the mid-1960s, delivered the ultimate putdown.

'I don't despair about the cultural scene in Australia,' he scoffed, 'because there isn't one here to despair about.'

It was as if a team of scientists had unlocked the country's DNA and found cultural inferiority imprinted in the molecular code. Bagging Australia became a badge of sophistication: European sophistication. To be cultured in Australia was to deny Australian culture. In the midst of this orgy of self-loathing, it was easy to forget that Mark Twain had described Australia at the turn of the century as a country rich in 'art galleries, libraries, museums, hospitals [and] learned societies'. It was, he declared, 'the hospitable home of every species of culture'. Of 'Ballarat English' he could hardly have been more complimentary, predicting it would sweep the world. It took 'all the hardness and harshness out of the tongue', he gushed, 'and gives to it a delicate whisper and vanishing cadence which charms the ear like the faint rustling of the forest leaves'.

When Bertrand Russell, the great post-war British intellectual, left Australia in 1950, at the end of an eight-week tour, he saw the country as something of a global exemplar. 'I leave your shores with more hope for mankind than when I came among you,' he said during his valedictory broadcast on the ABC. Earlier in his trip he waxed lyrical about an uncrowded country of 'boundless opportunities' not 'shackled by the past' or 'hampered by the achievements of your ancestors'. Though critical of the treatment of Aborigines, he saw Australia as a place 'to lead happy and successful lives' and to 'preserve for the world the great ideals of democracy and freedom'. Long before all those human development indexes and liveability league tables put Australia on top, Russell viewed it as a lodestar nation. Tellingly, however, the Australian press refused to believe that he had formed such a positive view. Some reporters even speculated that he would deliver much harsher judgements on the BBC after returning to Britain – though he never did.

Bill Clinton paid tribute to the Australian arts during a visit to Sydney in 1996. Citing the novels of Patrick White, Thomas Keneally and David Malouf, the paintings of Sidney Nolan and Russell Drysdale, the films of Peter Weir and Baz Luhrmann, and bands like Midnight Oil, he described the nation's cultural contribution as being 'far out of proportion to its population in modern art, in learning, in music, in theatre, in opera, in the cinema'.

Yet just as Lucky Country thinking has endured, so, too, has cringe-thinking. Harold Holt, John Gorton and Gough Whitlam's cultural nationalism, which led to the foundation of the Australia Council and encouraged the homegrown movie and publishing industries, dealt it wounding blows. So, too, did celebrations for the Bicentennial and the Sydney Olympics opening ceremony, with its playful retelling of the Australian story. Nonetheless, vestiges of the cringe still linger, like a virus that has been controlled but not fully cured.

When the new National Museum of Australia opened in Canberra at the turn of the century, its architect, Howard Raggatt, designed it almost as a monument to the cringe by intentionally incorporating a string of reproachful jokes. Part of the building referenced Le Corbusier's celebrated Villa Savoye finished in the 1930s, but Raggatt inverted the original structure and rendered it in black rather than white. Snidely, it recalled the mistake made by an Australian magazine, which published the first photograph seen here of Le Corbusier's modernist masterpiece back to front. Incorporating into the design features from the Opera House, Raggatt made sure to include the glass walls enclosing the shells designed by Peter Hall, Utzon's successor – what he described to a visiting international architectural critic as 'the clunky Australian work'.

Happily, a remedy to the cringe lies beyond these shores, where something more communicable and infectious has taken hold: Australia's cultural creep.

One of the few occasions each year when Australia's artistic success internationally is given mainstream coverage at home, Hollywood's Annual Academy Awards have become a sort of cinematic Olympics. Channel Nine's show-business correspondent, Richard Wilkins, patrols the red carpet and after-parties much like a sports reporter hugs the boundary line and gate-crashes the post-match celebrations in the sheds. His brief beforehand is to catch the Australian celebrities as they enter the Dolby Theatre so that he can pass on the good wishes of the nation. Afterwards, he hopes to bestow its congratulations. Given the patriotic flavour of the coverage, and the yearning for green and gold statuettes, it is surprising that the noun Oscar has not yet been turned into a fully fledged verb, as is the case with 'to podium' or 'to medal'.

In a nation keen to quantify its per capita success, the Academy Awards provides a welter of statistical proof. Prior to the mid-1990s, Peter Finch was the only Australian to be nominated for lead actor, winning, posthumously, in 1977 for *Network* (his widow, Tamara, delivered his acceptance speech, based on watching him rehearse it repeatedly in the mirror). Since then three men, Geoffrey Rush, Russell Crowe (an Aussie when he wins, though a Kiwi when he gets into trouble) and Heath Ledger, have been nominated six times between them, and taken home two gongs: Rush for *Shine* and Crowe for *Gladiator*. Ledger, like Finch, won after his death, for best supporting actor in *The Dark Knight*. During the first 69 years of the Oscars only four Australian actresses were recognised in lead and supporting categories.

In the 16 years since, six have shared a dozen nominations, among them two winners, Nicole Kidman for *The Hours* and Cate Blanchett for *The Aviator* and *Blue Jasmine*. It is still something of a mystery how the saintly Cate missed out for her portrayal of England's virgin Queen in *Elizabeth: The Golden Age*.

The common mistake in measuring Australia's cultural success abroad is to focus singularly on its big-five actors, Blanchett, Kidman, Rush, Crowe and Jackman. Yet Naomi Watts (*21 Grams*), Toni Collette (*The Sixth Sense*), Judy Davis (*Husbands and Wives*), Rachel Griffiths (*Hilary and Jackie*) and, fabulously, Jacki Weaver (*Animal Kingdom* and *Silver Linings Playbook*) have also caught the eye of the Academy. Then there are the hordes of actors and actresses who have not yet received nominations: the brilliant Guy Pearce, Eric Bana, Abbie Cornish, Sam Worthington, Chris Hemsworth, Bryan Brown, Hugo Weaving, David Wenham, Joel Edgerton, Ben Mendelsohn, Richard Roxburgh and the up-and-coming Mia Wasikowska.

On television, Australian stars are ubiquitous – Simon Baker in *The Mentalist*, Rose Byrne in *Damages*, Anthony LaPaglia in *Without a Trace*, Ryan Kwanten in *True Blood* or the comedienne Rebel Wilson in *Super Fun Night*. So many actors now make it in American television and film that the ABC even came up with a reality show, *Next Stop Hollywood*. It inverts the cultural cringe exposed by *Incognito* by giving viewers the patriotic glow of satisfaction at seeing Aussies regularly beat the yanks on *their* home turf.

There has been considerable behind-the-scenes success, with Australians winning Oscars for cinematography, art direction and costume design, and also in the scientific and technical categories. With four Oscars for costume and production design in *Moulin Rouge* and *The Great Gatsby*, the extravagantly gifted Catherine Martin has accumulated more golden statuettes than any other Australian. Three times in the past decade have Australian films won for animation, an area of rising excellence: *Harvie Krumpet* in 2004, *Happy Feet* in 2006 and *The Lost Thing* in 2010. The Australian producer Emile Sherman carried off a Best Picture statuette for *The King's Speech*.

Maybe it would help, in terms of public awareness, if Australia had a *Chariots of Fire* moment akin to the ceremony in 1982 where the film's screenwriter Colin Welland shouted, 'The Brits are coming!' as he held aloft his Oscar like a musket. But it would seem a little after the fact, since the Aussies arrived a long time ago.

With the exception of Mel Gibson who won for *Braveheart*, the Academy has not been so kind to Australian directors. Yet Bruce Beresford, Peter Weir, Fred Schepisi, George Miller, Scott Hicks, Chris Noonan and Baz Luhrmann have all won acclaim in Hollywood. Small wonder, having directed films of the quality of *The Truman Show*, *Moulin Rouge!*, *Shine*, *Babe* and *Dead Poets Society*.

Australia's cultural creep extends well beyond the red carpet in Tinseltown. Following on from the success in 2006 of *Ten Canoes*, the first Australian movie ever to be filmed entirely in Aboriginal languages, the judges at the 2009 Cannes Film Festival presented the Camera d'Or best first feature film award to Warwick Thornton's *Samson and Delilah*. The following year, the Sundance Film Festival presented David Michod's *Animal Kingdom* with the World Cinema Grand Jury prize. Especially noteworthy about Michod and Thornton's success was that their stories, from the underworld of Melbourne and the otherworld of the red centre, were so authentically Australian. More usually, breakthrough Australian movies have either been self-parodies, like *Crocodile Dundee* and *Strictly Ballroom*; or historical dramas, like *Breaker Morant* and *Gallipoli*, that revisited injustices from the imperial past.

On Broadway the Australian crawl is nearing a strut. In recent years Geoffrey Rush has taken two local productions to New York, Eugene Ionesco's absurdist drama *Exit the King* and Nikolai Gogol's *Diary of a Madman*, where theatre-goers paid as much as $700 for a seat. His performance as the 400-year-old King Berenger earned him his first Tony, thus completing the coveted triple crown of acting: Oscar, Tony and Emmy. 'Put simply,' wrote John Heilpern, the theatre critic of *The New York Observer*, 'Mr Rush is giving one of the greatest virtuoso performances I've ever seen.' Yet Australians did not require a New Yorker to tell them that, for they had already recognised his brilliance themselves at the Malthouse Theatre in Melbourne and at the Belvoir in Sydney.

When Hugh Jackman put on his one-man show, *Back on Broadway*, the 'impossibly talented' actor, as one New York critic called him, was likened to Frank Sinatra and Judy Garland. Though the show began with him singing 'Oh What a Beautiful Morning!' from *Oklahoma*, reprising his breakthrough role in the National Theatre's London production, it was principally a celebration of Australiana. He was accompanied in many numbers by an indigenous ensemble. He took the audience through slides from his Sydney scrapbook. The climax came with 'I Still Call Australia Home', the hit from the Peter Allen biopic *The Boy from Oz*, for which he won a Tony. The *New York Times* called it a 'dream date' that delivered.

Cate Blanchett's theatrical success in America has been more significant, for the simple reason that the Sydney Theatre Company's *A Streetcar Named Desire* completely upended the cultural cringe. What chutzpah to take a 'made in Australia' production of the great masterpiece of American theatre to New York and Washington. Again, the reviewers gushed. Blanchett had scaled 'the Everest of modern American drama', wrote John Lahr in *The New Yorker*. 'I don't expect to see a better performance of this role in my lifetime.' He also praised Joel Edgerton's Stanley as 'superb' for his 'low-key roughness'. Again, there was no need for outside validation. Blanchett and her troupe had crossed the Pacific with standing ovations from Sydney audiences ringing in their ears.

Cultural ambassadors, like Cate Blanchett and Hugh Jackman, are raising Australia's profile in wholly unexpected ways. As part of the Rudd government's lobbying campaign for a seat on the Security Council, foreign diplomats were taken to Jackman's one-man show on Broadway and afterwards given the 'hugs and kisses treatment' in his dressing room. With the X-Man lending the bid its X-factor, one senior Western diplomat even went as far as to argue, 'Hugh Jackman won Australia its seat.' Then, in almost the same breath, she rhapsodised about Blanchett's performance in the Woody Allen comedy *Blue Jasmine*, for which she went on to win the Golden Globe and her second, much-deserved Oscar.

The ever-likeable Jackman has become Australia's de facto roaming cultural attaché, a vast improvement on its previous unofficial occupant, Sir Les Patterson. Providing yet more evidence of his Aussie pride and ambassadorial clout, on Australia Day in 2014 Jackman persuaded the Empire State Building to shower its soaring spire with green and gold floodlights.

Australian actors inevitably attract the most attention, but not necessarily the most acclaim. In literature, Thomas Keneally, Peter Carey (twice), D. B. C. Pierre and Aravind Adiga, an Indian-born Australian citizen, have won the

Booker Prize. Tim Winton (twice), David Malouf, Kate Grenville, M. J. Hyland and Steve Toltz have been shortlisted. What makes these writers so culturally relevant is not so much that they were recognised by international juries but that they speak with a uniquely Australian voice.

Despite his foreign residency, Peter Carey's *True History of the Kelly Gang* and *Oscar and Lucinda*, not to mention many of his other works, are insistently homegrown novels. Thomas Keneally won the Booker for *Schindler's Ark*, but he was also nominated for *The Chant of Jimmie Blacksmith*, another distinctly Australian work. Tim Winton is Australia's great laureate of the ocean. Kate Grenville has become the literary custodian of its colonial past. *Cloudstreet* and *The Secret River* could not have come from any other country. Christos Tsiolkas's *The Slap* and Steve Toltz's *A Fraction of the Whole*, two of the more recent books to catch the eye of the Booker judges, have also brought contemporary Australian voices into the international realm.

With Les Murray, who *The New Yorker* adjudged to be one of the three or four leading writers of poetry in English, the metre is singularly, even obstreperously Australian. It combines what *The Oxford Companion to Australian Literature* described as 'respect, even reverence, for the pioneers, the importance of the land and its shaping influence in the Australian character . . . such bush-bred qualities as egalitarianism, practicality, straightforwardness and independence'. Fabulously uncomplicated, Murray has happily embraced his moniker, 'the bush bard' – one he shares with no less a figure than Henry Lawson – and also has described himself as the last of the Jindyworobaks, the literary movement in which white writers promoted indigenous idioms.

Murray, according to Clive James, is the 'king of the stay-at-homes', while the great Peter Porter was the 'king of the stay-aways'. Eulogising his friend in *The Times Literary Supplement*, James told of how Porter spent 'much of his career in a fork, punished in Australia for trying to please the Poms, and punished in the UK for being an Aussie expatriate with a frame of reference above his station'. By the time of Porter's death from cancer in 2010, James reckoned 'he was a living example of the old country's culture reinforcing itself with the energy of the new, and of the new country's culture gaining scope from an expanded context'. To honour his memory, and to welcome him home, the *Australian Book Review* announced it would rename its annual poetry prize, the Peter Porter Poetry Prize.

In music, we could speak of any number of groups or any number of performers. From Geoffrey Gurrumul Yunupingu, the inaugural number one in the newly created world music chart, to Gotye, whose global smash hit 'Somebody That I Used to Know' helped him carry off three Grammys; from the world-renowned jazz trumpeter James Morrison to the great Peter Sculthorpe, Australia's Aaron Copland.

The Australian Chamber Orchestra is a singular success, to classical music what the flair team Barcelona is to soccer. Its leader, the violin virtuoso Richard Tognetti tells a revealing story from the 1970s, of a Japanese agent who wanted to book the ACO but suggested it would help if they discarded a few letters from their name. The Austrian Chamber Orchestra would draw bigger crowds. Nobody makes that request any more. *The Times* has called the ACO 'the best chamber orchestra on earth'.

Dance is an area of growing and glorious strength. The Australian Ballet has performed to sell-out houses at the Lincoln Center in New York. The Melbourne-based troupe Chunky Move has toured America, France, Germany, Lebanon, Hungary, Colombia, Japan, Belgium, Canada and

Russia. The Queensland-based Circa, which has elevated circus to an art form, has appeared in 24 countries on six continents. Circus Oz has performed in 26. In cabaret, there is the avant-garde diva Meow Meow, or Melissa Madden Gray to use her real name, whose sultry and stockinged stage show has been likened to a mix between Sally Bowles, Joan Collins and Lady Gaga.

In the visual arts, we could celebrate the work of the Aboriginal photographer Tracey Moffatt, the Egyptian-born sculptor Hany Armanious, Australia's representative at the 2011 Venice Biennale, the video artist Shaun Gladwell or the Western Australian painter Brian Blanchflower – to name but a few.

Indigenous art may well be haunted still by 'a shining dream' of 'international acceptance and global prestige', as the writer Nicolas Rothwell has argued, but it is on permanent display at the celebrated Musée du Quai Branly in Paris, with paintings, sculptures, boomerangs and barks from eight artists, including Yannima Tommy Watson, John Mawurndjul and Ningura Napurrula. The 1988 *Dreamings* exhibition on Park Avenue in New York was also more of a breakthrough than Rothwell concedes. Featuring more than a hundred works from Central Australia, Arnhem Land and the Cape York Peninsula, it had half a million visitors by the time it had travelled to Chicago and Los Angeles. *Dreamings* also provided the inspiration for the Kluge-Ruhe Aboriginal Art Collection at the University of Virginia, which opened in 1997, the only permanent collection of indigenous Australian art in America. The Museum of Contemporary Aboriginal Art in the Dutch city of Utrecht, another institution devoted solely to Australian work, has just celebrated its tenth anniversary.

In movie animation, Animal Logic, the Sydney-based visual effects company behind *Babe* and *Happy Feet*, is a global centre of excellence. In computer gaming, LA Noire, an homage to film noir produced by Team Bondi, became the first computer game ever to be shown at the Tribeca Film Festival.

In another modish art form, the staging of extravagant spectaculars, opening ceremonies and galas, the world leader is Ric Birch, the executive producer of the opening ceremonies at the Barcelona and Sydney Olympics, and an adviser in Beijing. Another Australian, Ignatius Jones, was the creative director for the opening and closing ceremonies in Sydney, and oversaw the award-winning opening of the Vancouver Winter Olympics.

In product design there is Marc Newson, who is responsible for everything from the reclining seats in business class on Qantas to an even more expensive chair, the aluminium-clad Lockheed Lounge, which has sold for $1.6 million at auction. Not only have his products been exhibited as artwork in New York, but they've been reproduced in a coffee-table tome published by Taschen which sells for $1000.

In arts management, there is Michael Lynch, the former CEO of the Sydney Opera House who ran the South Bank in London and who is now in charge of Hong Kong's arts precinct in Kowloon. In art criticism, Sebastian Smee of *The Boston Globe* won the 2011 Pulitzer Prize for Criticism. The story is repeated in every creative field.

Architecture, which has seen local practices encroaching ever more boldly into foreign markets, such as Britain, America and China, is another area of growing Australian success. The award-winning new ticket booth in the heart of New York's Times Square was designed by John Choi and Tai Ropiha, architects from an up-and-coming Sydney-based firm which has picked up a string of international awards. The Melbourne-based practice Denton Corker Marshall not only won the contract for the Manchester Civil Justice Centre, Britain's first major court complex since the 19th-century Royal Courts of Justice on the Strand, it also pulled off the cheeky coup of winning the international competition to design a visitor centre at Stonehenge, one of Britain's most sacred and sensitive sites. When the courthouse was completed in 2007, *Blueprint*, the design magazine, described the structure, with its cantilevered boxes referencing Mondrian, as among the ten best in Britain over the past decade. So 'remarkable' and 'exhilarating' was the building, wrote the leading architectural critic Stephen Bayley, that it made 'divorce and probate sexy'.

DCM, which is known locally for buildings such as the Melbourne Museum, 'Jeff's Shed', and Macquarie Tower in Sydney, is also designing the new Australian Pavilion at Venice's Giardini della Biennale. This is an especially significant project, since the new gallery space replaces the temporary building designed by Philip Cox in the late-eighties that has been likened, not inaccurately, to a dunny shed. The project, in fairness to Cox, was a rush job completed on the cheap, so that Australia could claim one of the garden's last vacant plots. ('The complaints,' the architect once barked, 'give me the fucking shits.') Now, in its place will sit a cube-shaped structure fashioned from South Australian black granite, a gallery space that can sit more happily alongside pavilions designed by greats such as Alvar Aalto and Josef Hoffmann.

Though DCM's projects tend to be in the European modernist tradition, the Australian architectural aesthetic, along with its two most celebrated practitioners, Glenn Murcutt and Peter Stutchbury, is also winning wider acclaim. For his reworking of the Australian homestead, which combined the corrugated-iron bush vernacular with the Aboriginal ethic of 'touching the ground lightly', Murcutt in 2002 was awarded the Pritzer prize, the profession's highest honour. 'His is an architecture of place,' read the Pritzer jury citation. 'Architecture that responds to the landscape and to the climate.' An Australian pastoral.

Stutchbury has adopted the same organic approach. While Murcutt, his close friend, believes a structure should touch the ground lightly, Stutchbury has developed a building style where it is often almost impossible to delineate between the two. Using sliding doors and collapsible corner windows, he achieved what the architectural writer Lindsay Johnson has called 'the dissolution of inside and out'. Perhaps his most iconic building is the sublime Deepwater Woolshed in Wagga Wagga, which looks like it should more rightly provide a summer home to the Sydney Symphony, an Australian Tanglewood, rather than sheep awaiting shearing. Alain de Botton, the philosopher, is also an admirer, observing that Stutchbury has produced 'a distinctive, modern Australian beauty – an architecture that remembers where it is, what country it is in and what century it is in'. It is a far cry from the decades when Harry Seidler, an Austrian-born immigrant who studied under Walter Gropius, dominated the architectural scene. Seidler, whose elegant towers grace the skylines of Brisbane, Melbourne and Sydney, believed that importing European modernism obviated the need for a distinctive Australian aesthetic.

Partly because of Murcutt and Stutchbury, Australia has become a world leader in residential architecture. Alas, some of the best work is found outside of the cities, and therefore out of view. How many Australians, I wonder, have seen Murcutt's breakthrough Marie Short farmhouse, built in 1975 in the New South Wales town of Kempsey, with its elegant corrugated iron pavilions? Or the Marika-Alderton House in the Northern Territory, which looks like a stilted woolshed? Consequently, the genius behind so many beautiful houses has not himself become a household name. 'In an age obsessed with celebrity [and] the glitz of our "starchitects",' wrote the Pritzker jury chairman, Murcutt was 'a total contrast: our laureate works in a one-person office on the other side of the world from much of the architectural attention'. True to his architectural philosophy, he prefers to touch the ground lightly.

For Murcutt and Stutchbury's work to remain hidden is the architectural equivalent of Sidney Nolan's Ned Kelly paintings being held under lock and key in some private collection or the music of Peter Sculthorpe being rehearsed but never performed. At least coffee-table books and the internet have brought them widespread global recognition. Stutchbury, who has built in Japan, Vanuatu and Russia, is in high demand on the international lecture circuit, and in the past few years has spoken in North and South America, Africa, India, Scandinavia, as well as addressing the Royal Institute of British Architects in London. Murcutt, a sole practitioner who seems positively hermetic compared to the Fosters, Rogers and Hadids of the architectural world, is also sought-after, even though he does not accept foreign commissions. Since 2000, he has, however, run an international master class – at which Stutchbury also teaches – that has been attended by some 500 architects from over 80 nations.

So let us eschew that unlovely phrase heard more commonly in diplomatic and sporting circles that Australia is punching above its weight. But in arts and culture, whether in singing, acting, dancing, designing, writing, sculpting or building, modern-day Australia has exceptional cultural outreach. The problem is not a lack of creativity or talent but rather a failure of self-realisation. That is precisely why the conductor Alexander Briger brought together the Australian

World Orchestra in August 2011, a band made up of 90 or so musicians from 45 foreign ensembles. His intention was to showcase their international success at home. There 'are so many Australian musicians holding these major positions with so many orchestras across the world', he told reporters, 'and I doubt very much that the general public here knows who half these people are. So it's time for them to finally receive their deserved recognition in Australia.' Knowing his audience, Briger, the nephew of Sir Charles Mackerras, drew a sporting analogy: 'You look at Cadel Evans and how he was celebrated recently. These musicians are the same. They really are the top of the top in their field, they have achieved amazing things.' Alas, this is not being acknowledged sufficiently at home.

What makes the cultural creep all the more arresting is not just the proliferation of artists enjoying international success but where they come from, what is their Australian story, and what sort of relationship they have with their homeland. When an Australian had last won the Grammy for record of the year, it was 1975 and the singer was Olivia Newton-John. Blonde, beautiful and bubbly, she was instantly recognisable as Australian. The most recent recipient, Wouter 'Wally' De Backer, who is better known simply as Gotye, is cut from different cloth. For a start, he was born in Bruges, Belgium, and emigrated to Sydney when he was two years old.

Take the author Steve Toltz. *The Wall Street Journal*, in heaping praise on his debut novel *A Fraction of the Whole*, described it as 'Voltaire-meets-Vonnegut'. Yet its rollicking eclecticism is more a product of his multi-ethnic background: his Polish, Lithuanian, New Zealand and Palestinian grandparents. Toltz explained himself more simply when asked on the ABC to characterise his ethnicity: 'I am Australian.' Markus

Zusak might have a central European name, but the author of *The Book Thief*, which has sold more than eight million copies worldwide, is a Sydneysider. His German mother and Austrian father emigrated to Australia in the 1950s.

In *The Slap*, international readers have been introduced to the voice of a Greek-Australian, Christos Tsiolkas, although, again, the 'Greek' seems superfluous. Set in suburban Melbourne at the fag end of the Howard years, *The Slap* was especially audacious, not least because it cast the Anglo family as outcasts. *The Slap* came to be marketed internationally as a discourse on child rearing – should an adult be able to discipline another parent's child? But it was truly a dissertation on Australian multiculturalism.

In another break from the past, Australian artists are no longer so scornful of their country or compatriots, or inhibited by the crippling self-consciousness once the norm. Quite the opposite. Just compare Les Murray, a contender for the Nobel Prize, with the last Australian recipient, Patrick White. Cheltenham- and Cambridge-educated, White modelled his technique on the great Russian and French stylists, and spoke with flinty contempt for his homeland. Murray is defiantly Australian, with a refreshingly gruff disregard for the airs and graces of British and American literary circles.

The international success of the comedian Chris Lilley differs from that of his satirical forebear Barry Humphries. *Summer Heights High*, his bullseye parody of suburban adolescence, proved such a hit on HBO that the American network co-produced the follow-up, *Angry Boys*. Yet Lilley continued to insert gags and references – like naming one of Gran's guinea pigs Kerri-Anne – that only Australians would appreciate. Rather than abandon his home audience, he took it along for the ride, and his humour, though damning, remained affectionate. Humphries, by contrast, was merciless, and his early comedy work betrayed the sourness and superiority of an exile. As Peter Conrad noted, Humphries 'belonged to the first generation of intellectuals for whom the denunciation of Australia counted as an urgent national priority'.

Dame Edna and Sir Les Patterson were creatures of a monocultural country beset by stultifying conservatism and conformism. Lilley's ensemble of characters reveals Australia's modern, multicultural face. Consider Ricky Wong, one of the competitors in Lilley's Australian of the Year parody, *We Can Be Heroes*. This Chinese-Australian overachiever is continually distracted from his studies by the lure of the stage, and his starring role as 'Walkabout Man' in the spoof musical *Indigeridoo*. Or Jonah Takalua from *Summer Heights High*, the indolent teenager of Tongan descent, who daubs his trademark phallus graffiti all over the school.

Nor did Lilley become an expatriate to succeed. There is no longer the same rush to the international departure lounge for promising young artists seeking to advance their careers – what A. A. Phillips called the 'centrifugal pull of the great cultural metropolises'. In the past, Australian artists distanced themselves not just physically but emotionally from their homeland. Nowadays, it is as if they have become artistic missionaries in their own land. The prime example is Cate Blanchett, who combined her Hollywood film career with running the Sydney Theatre Company. Geoffrey Rush and Hugo Weaving make a point of performing in local theatrical productions, as well as appearing in Australian movies. Baz Luhrmann has even gone as far as to bring big budget productions to Sydney, with unexpected results. In *The Great Gatsby*, Jay's Long Island mansion was in Manly; the Valley of Ashes, the stretch between Manhattan and West Egg, was filmed in Balmain; Nick Carraway's cottage was in Centennial Park.

Because the new crop of stars has a more affectionate relationship with Australia, Australians have a more affectionate relationship with them. This has meant that the 'tall poppy syndrome', that lazy journalistic fallback, is no longer such a destructive force in the arts and culture. Rather, Australians appear to be enjoying the international success of their compatriots. Hugh Jackman and Cate Blanchett are hugely popular locally. The political fire she came under for her advocacy on behalf of the carbon tax was because she was seen as a preachy environmentalist rather than an artistic snob, an important distinction. When Russell Crowe appeared with Oprah when she presented her show from the forecourt of the Opera House, he bemoaned the gleefulness with which Australians cut homegrown stars down to size. But Crowe's public standing has risen in recent years, especially since he started hurling footballs with the South Sydney Rabbitohs rather than phones at the Mercer Hotel in SoHo. There was a time when I thought that the tall poppy syndrome should be renamed the 'Nicole Kidman syndrome', since she seemed to be the primary target. Yet her divorce from Tom Cruise and her marriage to Keith Urban, the popular Australian country star, appears to have rehabilitated her public image. That national scythe, rusty through lack of use, no longer eviscerates even Nicole.

Australia's cultural castaways have also become emissaries. Clive James, who left Sydney for Britain in the early 1960s, has often been portrayed in the Australian press as a disloyal knocker. When he wrote in *The Observer*, after seeing the Opera House for the first time, that it resembled a 'typewriter full of oyster shells', it provoked a barrage of negative local headlines. Yet James has long been a cheerleader for the Australian arts, rejecting the ludicrous notion that his homeland cannot be viewed as an artistically mature nation. 'Australian actors and filmmakers and writers and arts people have been colonising the planet for years,' he wrote in a review of Baz Luhrmann's *Australia*, 'and the jokes about Australia's deficiency of culture are old hat, like all the jokes about Australians knowing nothing about wine. Australia killed the wine jokes by producing supertankers full of wine that the whole world wanted to drink and it killed the culture jokes by flooding the world with an outburst of quality remarkable for a country that looks big on the map but has fewer people in it than Mexico City.' The world knows this, wrote James, but Australia's intellectuals 'persist in cherishing an inferiority complex so at odds with the facts that it amounts to a psychosis'.

What makes this cultural impact all the more impressive is that Australia cannot boast a major governmental organisation devoted to touting its wares. There is no equivalent of the British Council, the Alliance Française or China's Confucius Institutes. In the late 1990s the Australia International Cultural Council was created at the prompting of the then foreign affairs minister, Alexander Downer, to promote Australia as a 'stable, sophisticated, innovative and creative nation with a rich and diverse culture'. But it was only a consultative group, with the narrow remit of facilitating exhibitions within Australian embassies, and providing small travel grants for artists. That so few people even know of its existence speaks of its peripheral role – though the Gillard government called for its revamp.

Nor does the Australia Council engage much in what it calls 'international projection'. Its budget to promote the arts abroad is just $2.5 million, less than 2 per cent of its annual spending. This means the arts do not have the financial means to counter the 'dumb blonde' image of Australia. Whereas the 'Where the Bloody Hell Are You?' campaign cost $180 million, the entire annual funding for the Australia Council that year was just $175 million.

Successive governments have been poor in trumpeting artistic achievements. When the Gillard government released its discussion paper on National Cultural Policy, the first such review since the landmark 'Creative Nation' report of the Keating years, it noted that homegrown artists 'need to compete on the world stage'. It neglected the victories achieved already. Thankfully, when its Creative Australia white paper was published, it went some way towards remedying this: 'Australian artists are celebrated at home and are steadily achieving a significant international success,' it noted. 'Our artists are prominent on the world stage.'

This international success has been built on a firmer base at home. The country's cultural infrastructure has never been so strong, and now rivals the country's sporting infrastructure. Set on the banks of the snaking Brisbane River, the Gallery of Modern Art (GOMA) in Brisbane has helped turn the city's South Bank into one of the hottest stretches of cultural real estate. By 2010, less than five years after it opened, it had not only become Australia's most popular gallery, but one of the top 50 in the world. Sydney's arts scene has been enhanced by the opening of a new extension at its harbourside Museum of Contemporary Art Australia, a gallery that had outgrown the Art Deco former maritime building that had been its home since the early 1990s. Melbourne can boast the eye-catching Melbourne Recital Centre and the Melbourne Theatre Company's Southbank Theatre, both of which were designed by Ashton Raggatt McDougall. The new National Portrait Gallery in Canberra which opened in 2008, a low-slung concrete building that complements the brutalist architecture of its neighbour, the High Court, is another elegant structure. Perth has the new State Theatre Centre of Western Australia.

Most thrilling of all is the new Museum of Old and New Art in Tasmania, which *The New York Times* called 'the best museum you've never heard of' – though a long essay in *The New Yorker* penned by Richard Flanagan soon changed that. With exhibits including the dismembered body parts of a suicide bomber rendered in chocolate and a machine that supposedly manufactures excrement, the museum is wilfully shocking. But that has not deterred visitors. MONA has produced something of a mini-Bilbao effect for Tasmania.

Less showy attractions also dot the cultural landscape. The Wheeler Centre, set up after Melbourne became UNESCO's city of literature in 2008, is dedicated to the discussion of writing and ideas. The White Rabbit gallery in Sydney has one of the world's finest collections of Chinese contemporary art. The Brett Whiteley Studio in Surry Hills, which celebrates an artist who helped Australians cast a fresh eye over their landscape, is another hidden gem. Australia's changing digital topography, with its increased availability of high-speed broadband, has also provided a boost for the arts. One-fifth of Opera Australia's audience now listens to its performances online.

Australian art galleries are among the best attended in the world. Many of the blockbuster exhibitions, admittedly, have been imports: alone, the *Masterpieces from Paris* exhibition shown in Canberra attracted a staggering 476,000 visitors. But there has been no shortage of home successes, too, such as the landmark Sidney Nolan exhibition in 2008, and the long overdue Rosalie Gascoigne retrospective that opened in Melbourne the same year. Sydney's Archibald Prize for portraiture breaks new records every year, as does Sculpture by the Sea. It started in 1997 as a one-day event at Bondi that attracted 25,000 people. Now it lures more than half a million visitors, and has travelled to Western Australia and been transplanted to Denmark. The Vivid Festival in Sydney, the night-time carnival which projects dancing images onto the Opera House and other harbourside structures, has been a crowd pleaser, and become the biggest festival of lights in the Southern Hemisphere.

Combining the arts with the landscape, an obvious selling point of Sculpture by the Sea, has become a winning formula. Opera Australia's harbourside productions of *Carmen* and *Madama Butterfly* have been both popular and critical successes. The Sydney Biennale, which is spread over five venues around the harbour, attracted 665,000 people in 2012, an almost 30 per cent rise from two years earlier. It benefits enormously from the lure of its main site at Cockatoo Island, an already brilliant venue with the potential in the hands of the right architect – Peter Stutchbury, perhaps – to become one of the world's most spectacular cultural hubs. Imagine a glorious new gallery there, with the architectural pull of the Opera House.

All this underscores the extent to which the arts are being democratised. The Australia Council's 'More Than Bums on Seats' report in 2010 revealed its surfacing as a mainstream activity. In a previous study conducted in 1999, over half of respondents said that the arts attracted 'the somewhat pretentious and elitist'. A decade later, only a third shared that view. Nearly three-quarters of the population attended at least one artistic event. As *The Australian* noted: 'more Australians are more culturally attuned than at any time in history'. The cultural workforce has also grown, with 5.3 per cent, or 531,000 people, employed in the arts. No-collar workers, perhaps we should call them.

Problems remain aplenty. Canberra is awash with cultural illiterates. Julia Gillard, during her time as prime minister, was not known to have ever attended a cultural event at the

Sydney Opera House. Tony Abbott has ridiculed the more challenging works of the federal parliamentary art collection as 'avant-garde crap', and hung traditional landscapes and a portrait of the Queen in his office. Mark Latham, the one-time Labor leader, described classical music, opera and ballet as 'insufferably boring' with 'no social worth other than in the treatment of sleeping disorders'. Kevin Rudd won tabloid approbation by opting for the same bullying populism during the Bill Henson controversy, even though he had not seen the semi-naked photographs of teenage girls. He squashed the idea that the Sydney Opera House should be renovated, saying that the money would be better spent on hospitals, a false choice. It sounded like another statement of political philistinism targeted at the battlers in the western suburbs who don't have a view of its billowing shells. Among Campbell Newman's first acts in charge of Queensland was to cancel the Premier's Literary Awards, a setback to a state that had looked to the arts to help repair its 'Deep North' image. Even Peter Garrett, the country's most well-credentialled arts minister, tried to end funding for the Australian National Academy of Music, though he reversed the decision following an outcry from the classical music community.

Rare now are art-loving politicians like Malcolm Turnbull, who bravely defended Henson and even tapped out a stream of appreciative tweets during his first visit to MONA – a move that appeared to confirm that he was resigned never to leading the Liberal Party again. The former New South Wales premier and foreign affairs minister Bob Carr, who wrote a book on his love of history and literature called *Thoughtlines*, is another rarity. Carr dealt a commendable blow to the cultural cringe by walking out of Kevin Spacey's *Richard III* in Sydney at the interval and opting instead for a kebab. He simply did not think that the world-famous actor was up to scratch. Most of their colleagues, though, have turned philistinism itself into an art form.

The ABC, the country's preeminent cultural institution, has also scaled back its arts coverage, with the closure of its specialised arts unit, the cancellation of *Art Nation* on ABC1 and *Artworks* on Radio National. Geoffrey Rush, Nick Cave and Tim Winton were among a number of artists who protested that the move would 'diminish the ABC's irreplaceable role as the nation's cultural memory'. Another casualty has been the *Australian Literary Review*, which Clive James once suggested Rupert Murdoch would brandish as he approached the pearly gates.

ABC continues to surrender too much airtime to British-made programming. Equally, the commercial networks air too much American trash. Save for a few exceptions, like *Redfern Now* and *Rake*, television drama tends to disappoint. Australian TV obviously does not have the budgets for a *Mad Men* or *Game of Thrones*, but surely it has more than enough talent to produce a cleverly scripted hit like *Breaking Bad*.

Australian movies still find it hard to get screen time at home – and in 2011 captured only 3.9 per cent of the domestic market. Even that was a slight improvement on the ten-year average of 3.8 per cent. *Burning Man*, one of the best homegrown films of recent years, survived in movie theatres a matter of weeks, despite Margaret and David giving Jonathan Teplitzky's 'stunningly well-made film' nine stars between them. Critical successes, such as Eddie Perfect's masterful *Shane Warne: The Musical*, often end up being commercial flops.

The Australian fashion industry has been decimated through a combination of the high dollar, online shopping and the Treasure Island rapaciousness of international retailers.

The soaring dollar has also made Sydney and Melbourne less attractive as backdrops for Hollywood movie-makers. In the noughties, American film producers spent an average of $137 million each year on big budget films, like *Superman Returns* and *The Chronicles of Narnia*. Now that figure is a derisory $2 million.

For all the country's prosperity, there is a paucity of super-rich patrons of the arts. The Western Australian mining boom has not yet produced a modern-day equivalent of the architectural riches of the Victorian gold rush. Tycoons, like James Packer, are known more for their lack of taste and refinement than cultural appreciation. His Crown Casino in Melbourne, with its mish-mash of Art Deco lounges reached by corridors lined with Roman mosaics, classic Greek columns and mogul-style latticework ordinarily found in Rajasthani palaces, is a temple to bad taste, aptly called 'Vegas on the Yarra'. The mining magnate Clive Palmer is intent on building a replica of the *Titanic* and peppering parkland with dinosaurs. Billionaires, as the journalist Paddy Manning reminds us with the title of his biography of the former mining magnate Nathan Tinkler, also tend to be 'Boganaires'.

There are notable exceptions. The Tasmanian millionaire and professional gambler David Walsh built MONA to showcase his extraordinary private collection in what he has called a 'temple to secularism' and 'subversive Disneyland'. The new wing at the MCA in Sydney received a large share of its funding from investment banker Simon Mordant and his wife, Catriona. Dame Elisabeth Murdoch was another passionate arts philanthropist, honoured with an auditorium named after her at the Melbourne Recital Centre.

Relish is still evident in the media coverage of cultural blips, like Baz Luhrmann's *Australia*, when the cringers go to work. After an early trailer was released for *The Great*

Gatsby, which showed a spelling mistake in one of the computer-generated images of a billboard in Times Square, local reporters were quick to seize upon it. The implication was that an Australian could not be trusted with an American classic. Populist arts shows, like Sculpture by the Sea, often attract snooty reviews for their over-reliance on gimmickry, which seems a rather humourless line of attack.

There remains a tendency, as Peter Conrad, the Oxford-based Australian academic, has argued, to seek comparisons between Australians and international artists rather than judge them on their own intrinsic worth. I have done so myself above, in linking Peter Sculthorpe with Aaron Copland. Conrad was bemoaning how Carol Jerrems, an Australian photographer working in the 1970s, was often compared with Diane Arbus, the New York photographer known for her black and white portraits of dwarves, transvestites and circus performers. 'Must Australians always be matched with some prototype from the wider world, rather than being judged on their own merits?' he asked.

Internationally, there have also been glitches. When in 2013 the Royal Academy hosted the first major exhibition of Australian art in 50 years, it was panned by the London critics. Calling it 'tourist tat', Waldemar Januszczak of the *Sunday Times* was particularly scornful of a piece by John Olsen installed on the ceiling, which created 'the sensation of standing under a cascade of diarrhoea'. Nor was he impressed by Fred Williams, who 50 years ago became the first Australian artist to have a solo exhibition at the Museum of Modern Art in New York. Onto the 'delicate emptiness of desert', Williams had 'splattered thick cowpats of minimalism'. Describing the entire exhibition as 'inadequate', Brian Sewell, the art critic for the *London Evening Standard*, bemoaned the contemporary Aboriginal work that was 'so obviously the stale rejiggings of a half-remembered heritage wrecked by the European alcohol, religion and servitude that have rendered purposeless all relics of their ancient and mysterious past'.

Coming at a moment of national creative strength, I was curious to see how Australia would react to this criticism. Would it be met with spasms of cringe or a shrug of the shoulder? The truth is there were elements of both. The domestic press got a few headlines from this high-brow sledging, but others appeared to take the view that, as with wine, Australia simply had not exported its best stuff.

Can a country that sends so much culture abroad still be hobbled by the cringe? Alas yes, and new forms of this disease of the Australian mind have metastasised. Bestselling international writers are feted at book festivals whereas homegrown writers do not receive anywhere near the same adulation. *Q&A*, by inviting random visiting celebrities onto the show who clearly know nothing about Australia, has also come up with a modern version of the 'What do you think of Australia?' line of questioning asked of starlets as they stepped off the plane. This starstruck guest-booking policy has produced surreal results. A panel discussion bringing together Christopher Pyne, the economist Judith Sloan and, inevitably, Graham Richardson, a panellist who appears so frequently that he must almost qualify for his own chair, also included the gonzo American film director John Waters. In other ways, however, *Q&A* and its erudite host, Tony Jones, have made a valuable cultural contribution by taking the show on the road to the Adelaide Festival and the Melbourne Writers Festival. Occasionally, *Q&A* ends in song, invariably its most watchable part.

Maybe it is cringeworthy to make such a song and dance of Australia's international artistic success. That was a complaint when I argued for the cultural creep in an essay for the *Griffith Review*. This line of thinking, according to the writer Emmett Stinson, placed 'more value and prestige' on 'Australian cultural products which have been validated by well-respected overseas institutions', and sought 'to value Australian cultural products in the mirror of a global market-place'. Yet to demonstrate how Australian arts are more greatly appreciated, it is necessary, it seems to me, to provide evidence. Debating the point further runs the risk of entrapment in a circular argument, in which it becomes almost impossible to discuss Australian arts in a global context without being accused of succumbing to the cringe. To me, that commits the greater felony of yielding to insularity. Besides, the departure point for the cultural creep is the standing ovations and rave reviews delivered by Australian audiences long before plays, books, recitals and the like leave these shores, not the other way around. Australians do not need outsiders to validate their own aesthetic judgements. It was hardly a surprise that the Sydney Theatre Company production of *Uncle Vanya*, bringing together Hugo Weaving, Richard Roxburgh, John Bell and Cate Blanchett, became such a hot ticket at the Lincoln Center. Yet to disregard the commendation of international critics and audiences again seems blinkered – and doubly so when the critics in question are often so miserly in their praise. The cultural cringe requires an obituary, and the narrative of success abroad helps draft it.

My richest Australian cultural experience came not from seeing Cate Blanchett in *Streetcar* – oddly, I happened to be in the audience on the night that she required stitches in her head after being hit by a flying Bakelite radio. Nor was it marvelling at Geoffrey Rush in *Exit the King* at the Belvoir, a setting so intimate that I could almost reach out and touch him. The Sidney Nolan retrospective was a rare treat, as was watching *Samson and Delilah*. That set at the

Opera House from Geoffrey Gurrumul Yunupingu, before he became internationally famous, will live long in the memory. But the performance that still gives me chills was the Sydney Theatre Company's production of *The Secret River*. The drama, adapted from Kate Grenville's bestselling novel, tells the story of William Thornhill, a British convict pardoned in the early 19th century who sets out with his young family to build a new life on the banks of the Hawkesbury River to Sydney's north. For a time, it portrays a spirit of co-existence and acceptance, as the family starts to befriend members of the local indigenous tribe. Yet Thornhill can never banish from his mind the two ideas with which he arrived, that the tribesmen are encroaching on his land, rather than he on theirs, and that the 'blacks' are murderous savages. Brilliantly acted by a multi-racial cast, stunningly staged and directed by Neil Armfield, and adapted from Grenville's masterwork with great skill and power by Andrew Bovell, who co-wrote *Strictly Ballroom*, it distilled into three hours of theatre so much of what is enviable about the Australian arts scene. Hopefully, the production will one day make it to New York, still more London, where it would resonate strongly. But that will not alter in any way its mesmerising effect on Australian audiences. Like so much other art that does not necessarily travel, it will not bolster the case for the cultural creep, but it will help kill off the cultural cringe.

In his seminal essay A. A. Phillips argued that the cringe was a greater enemy to Australia's cultural development than the country's isolation, and warned about a boastful strut from 'I'm-a-better-man-than-you-are' Australian bores. He wanted his compatriots to walk with 'a relaxed erectness of carriage'. Thankfully, homegrown performers assumed that posture years ago, whether on Broadway, at the Booker Prize ceremony, at the Belvoir or Bennelong Point.

This gait was also in evidence on a temporary stage in Canberra when Geoffrey Rush stepped forward to receive the 2012 Australian of the Year award. Much of his acceptance speech read like a rejoinder to a previous recipient, Sir Robert Helpmann, whose quip about Australia not having any culture to speak of caused lasting damage. In just two generations, Rush claimed, Australia had grown from a relative wasteland into a unique species of native tree that only Australian soil could cultivate, and his award was 'an endorsement of our national story of creativity'. He went on: 'We live on an island that boasts the oldest nation on Earth. There is inspiration right there, where performance rituals are at the heart of its being – our dreaming. The stories we tell ourselves as adults and to our children, in the communal dark, have a serious importance.'

Then he likened his fellow Australian artists to spiders, almost invisible and prone to being whacked occasionally with a newspaper. Well, those arachnids are on the march. Dare we call them cultural creepy crawlies.

Conclusion

THROWBACK AUSTRALIA

AUSTRALIAN TELEVISION PRODUCERS HAVE in recent times hit upon a sure-fire formula to guarantee big ratings. Costume designers are instructed to dress the women in above-the-knee skirts. Make-up artists affix Dennis Lillee-style moustaches, styling male cast members as if every month were 'Movember'. Props departments scour second-hand car yards in search of mint condition Ford Falcons and Holdens from the seventies. The fashion is for retro drama, whether it focuses on the 'puberty blues' of teenagers coming of age in beachside suburbs, the publishing wars between feuding media barons like Rupert Murdoch and Kerry Packer, or the birth of World Series cricket, the cradle of so much Australian sporting iconography. Even *Prisoner* has been revived.

In recent times, Australia as a whole has taken on a retro feel, for the country seems to be in regression. Tony Abbott's 19-member cabinet, which included just one woman, looked like a throwback to the seventies. Afghanistan, as was noted when the government was sworn in, had more women in the cabinet. His entire ministry included just four other females. Had she been re-elected, the cabinet would also have featured Sophie Mirabella, but that would still have been less than half the number of women who served under Kevin Rudd. The incoming treasurer, Joe Hockey, had once called for Australian boards to have at least 30 per cent female representation. The Abbott ministry had just 5 per cent.

Ita Buttrose, the 2013 Australian of the Year – whose selection, following the success of one of those seventies period dramas, *Paper Giants: The Birth of Cleo*, underscored the nostalgic air of national life – complained that the absence of women harked back to the days when she was running *Australian Women's Weekly* under Kerry Packer. The prime minister's patronising defence that 'there are some very good and talented women knocking on the door' also sounded like something an executive from that unreconstructed era would say. To assuage feminist concerns about his commitment to gender equality, Abbott appointed himself as minister for women. But his comments during the 2013 campaign that a woman candidate had a 'bit of sex appeal' again betrayed a 1970s mindset.

In sexual equality, a World Economic Forum gender report published shortly after the change of government, and compiled largely beforehand, showed Australia was falling behind. Having ranked 15th in 2006, it had slipped to 24th. In female political empowerment, it was an embarrassing 43rd.

Other areas of national life also appeared ridiculously dated. When the Australian navy held an international fleet review in late 2013 to commemorate the centenary of its ships first entering Sydney Harbour, Prince Harry was flown in from London to take the salute. It felt like a reversion not only to the days when the Queen opened the Opera House because no Australian was considered sufficiently well credentialled, but also to the Federation celebrations in 1901, vested as they were with such tug-of-the-forelock deference.

The royal prince gladly played his part, turning up in a brilliant white tropical dress uniform that belonged more in pre-war Singapore than 21st-century Sydney. With the media decreeing Harrymania had swept the country, Abbott also succumbed. Offering his own variation of Menzies' 'I did but see her passing by' encomium, he proclaimed on the lawns of Kirribilli, 'Prince Harry, I regret to say not everyone in Australia is a monarchist, but today everyone feels like a monarchist.' Writing in *The Bulletin*'s commemorative edition marking the Bicentenary in 1988, Abbott had written: 'Time has killed British Australia but has not yet put much in its place.' Yet his over-the-top welcome for Prince Harry suggested British Australia had staged a Lazarus-like revival.

So, too, did the restoration of dames and knights, an unforeseen move instigated personally by Abbott which was reminiscent of Menzies's gambit to call the Australian pound the royal. The difference was that, for all the guffaws, jokes and renamed Twitter accounts with heraldic handles, the writ of the prime minister this time held sway. Australia's conscious uncoupling from Britain was seemingly being put into reverse.

To buttress the monarchy even further, Abbott chose Peter Cosgrove, the hero of the East Timor expedition in 1999, as the new governor-general. In doing so, he fused the Australian military even more closely with the Australian monarchy, just as John Howard had done, though less conspicuously, when he picked Major General Michael Jeffery to replace the Reverend Peter Hollingworth. It meant that the governor-general's vintage Rolls-Royce, after five years of ferrying around a closet republican, Quentin Bryce, would once more convey a staunch monarchist – and a hugely popular and highly respected one at that.

Lending national life more of a martial feel, Cosgrove's appointment also foreshadowed the centenary of Gallipoli, a solemn anniversary during which Australia would again define itself by revisiting the past rather than focusing on the present day or future. Doubtless during the centenary the country would yield to a welter of Anzac mythmaking of the kind the historian Martin Crotty describes as 'reverence divorced from understanding'. With the government appointing a minister in charge of the First World War commemorations, James Brown, a former officer in the Australian army, warned of a 'four year festival for the dead which in some cases looks like a military Halloween'. In particular, 2015 promised to be a backward-looking year.

In launching Operation Sovereign Borders, the new prime minister turned again to the military to stop the boats, revisiting the more recent past of John Howard and Tampa. In his weekly news conferences – which, staying with the warlike theme, he took to calling 'briefings' – the immigration minister Scott Morrison appeared alongside Lieutenant General Angus Campbell and used the words 'operational matters' to bring down a veil of secrecy on the mission being mounted close to Indonesian waters. As he stonewalled journalists, the unavailing Morrison came across as a modern-day Captain Mainwaring, the blustering and blinkered comic figure from *Dad's Army*. Even Mainwaring's title, the commander of the Home Guard company, seemed to fit. Faced with this media blackout, Australian journalists had to get their information from the Indonesian government, itself hardly a model of openness and transparency. Reporters complained these briefings, with their mix of secrecy and paranoia, belonged not in a contemporary democracy but rather the pages of Orwell.

There were shades of Newspeak in Morrison's injunction to officials within his department to refer to asylum seekers as 'illegals'. Dissenters within the Immigration Department, most notably its senior civil servant Andrew Metcalfe who had argued publicly against turning back the boats, were gotten rid of. In another censorious move, staff Twitter feeds were also silenced.

The policy, in achieving the narrow goal of stopping the boats, had some success. As with the Pacific Solution, however, it came at an incalculable price. Relations with Jakarta plumbed to their worst level since the intervention in East Timor. Again, the UNHCR condemned Australia's detention regime as illegal, and complained of a 'sharp deterioration' in the level of care. Then came further violent disturbances, this time at the detention centre on Manus Island, during which an Iranian asylum seeker, Reza Barati, was so badly beaten that he died of multiple head injuries. A dozen more were seriously injured. The UN once more expressed grave concern that Australia was offering inadequate protections and subjecting detainees to degrading and inhuman conditions. It was the sort of admonishment normally dished out to a rogue rather than First World nation. Heightening the sense that Australia was becoming a rogue state on the question of asylum seekers, even China felt emboldened enough to lambast the abuse of human rights.

Other than stopping the boats, Tony Abbott's priority interest appeared to lie in prosecuting once more the culture wars of the 1990s and 2000s – not so much a trip down memory lane as an incursion. The ABC soon came under fire – here, he seemed to be delivering the 'quo' to Rupert Murdoch's pre-election tabloid quid – for being biased and even traitorous. 'I think it dismays Australians when the national broadcaster appears to take everyone's side but its own,' he told the talk show host Ray Hadley, 'and I think it is a problem.' Evidently, the new prime minister looked upon dissenting and even questioning voices not just as un-Australian but unpatriotic. In coupling the military ever more closely with the government, perhaps the hope was that a blind and unthinking patriotism would prevail.

In education, Christopher Pyne announced a review of the national curriculum, complaining that it did not 'recognise the legacy of Western civilisation'. To conduct this review, he appointed Dr Kevin Donnelly, a soulmate of the prime minister's and former Liberal staffer, who was strongly opposed to the curriculum increasing 'understanding of and acceptance of gay, lesbian, bisexual and transgender people', and also to multiculturalism. Again, this was throwback Australia.

The paradox was that a number of leading conservative politicians came themselves from modern families. Abbott's sister, Christine Forster, a self-styled 'small-l Liberal and big-L lesbian', is a firm advocate of same sex marriage. Much to his horror, Bob Katter's half-brother Carl has become a prominent LGBT activist. But the new government much preferred traditional family values. Senator Cory Bernardi articulated that view most strongly in his controversial polemic *The Conservative Revolution*, when he argued the traditional family model should be in 'prime position', and criticised its nonconformist iterations. Though Bernardi did not speak for the Coalition, these kinds of fringe views were closer than ever before to the conservative mainstream.

Abbott himself was an old-fashioned figure, with a tendency to view Australia through sepia-tinted spectacles – or to be, as Robert Hughes once said of John Howard, 'a visionary with eyes in the back of his head'. Like his Liberal predecessor, often he gave the impression of preferring that the cultural revolution of the 1960s had never occurred. His personal morality reached back to the pre-permissive society, pre-Vatican II era. In his thinking could be traced the formative influence of B. A. Santamaria, the Catholic intellectual and political activist, whose antediluvian philosophy would not have been out of place in Victorian times when piano legs were covered with pantalettes. Abbott once referred to his co-religionist as 'the greatest living Australian' and 'a philosophical star by which you could always steer'. Having joined Santamaria's movement as a teenager, he was especially admiring of his spiritual and political mentor because he was a crusader for 'unfashionable truths'. Abbott revelled in his own unfashionability. He viewed it as an asset, central to his appeal.

As well as Abbott recommencing the culture wars, academics and researchers complained of a war on science, reviving fears that the country was returning to the days described by Horne when Australia represented 'a victory of the anti-mind'. Abbott made good his promise to disband the Climate Commission, which meant sacking the prominent climate change scientist Tim Flannery – although the body quickly resurfaced as the crowd-funded Climate Council. Cuts were made to the Australian Research Council, while he also abolished a number of public health agencies. Again, he was happy to fly in the face of modernity.

For Abbott, like Gillard, the international stage was outside his comfort zone. At the World Economic Forum in Davos, where he gave a keynote speech outlining Australia's plans for the forthcoming G20 summit in Brisbane, delegates delivered an Eartha Kitt-style snub. It was not that they failed to recognise him, more that they were not particularly interested in what he had to say. The new Australian prime minister, as a correspondent for the *Financial Times* reported, had the misfortune to follow the new Iranian president, Hassan Rouhani, and did not have the star power to compete. 'Rouhani packed out the hall,' the man from the *FT* tweeted. 'Everybody is leaving before Tony Abbott explains Australia's ambitions for the G20 in 2014.' Admittedly, Rouhani was a tough act to follow, especially at a time when the international community was still weighing up whether this moderate cleric who sought rapprochement with America was for real. But with Abbott in Davos perhaps it was also a case of his parochialism preceding him.

Overall, Abbott intentionally gave the impression of preferring to be a stay-at-home prime minister. 'I don't think we should be getting ideas above our station,' he had told ABC's *7.30* programme ahead of the election, in response to a question about supporting US airstrikes against the Assad regime. 'I don't think we should be getting above ourselves here,' he said again. 'We are a significant middle power but no more.' That last statement was true. Barring some unforeseen global calamity, Australia will always be in the middle tier of nations. But the tone of his comments also betrayed a dearth of international ambition, and signalled an end to the diplomatic activism of the Hawke, Keating, Howard and Rudd years, which had greatly enhanced Australia's standing.

In a strange fluke of timing, Abbott came to power midway through the month that Australia chaired the Security Council in New York, the fruition of Kevin Rudd's grand diplomatic plan. His election also came on the eve of the UN Leaders' Week, an annual diplomatic jamboree where prime ministers and presidents descend on New York to address the general assembly. Coming so soon after entering The Lodge, Abbott understandably sent Julie Bishop to deputise. But Rudd, once more a former prime minister, also headed to New York, under the pretext of his membership of a UN global sustainability panel. At the height of his popularity, when nurses used to pinch his bottom, Rudd must have thought he had a decade to bestride the region and the world. But in New York he was caught in the telephoto lens of a Fairfax photographer shorn of the trappings of power, walking dejectedly through the city's skyscraper-lined canyons without any aides, without any security detail and without much global influence. If Gough Whitlam going to Beijing signalled the start of a new era of diplomatic engagement, that solitary shot of Rudd alone in New York may well provide its coda.

That day in the foyer of the UN headquarters building I bumped into him, and he greeted me like a long lost friend – a far cry from the surliness of our first encounter in Canberra. It was another sign of a politician on the wane: the greeting for a journalist in a foreign land who granted the relief of recognition.

Such was the Australian public's disdain for politics that the Abbott government never even got to enjoy a honeymoon period. Rather, there were early signs that the marriage would not last. Polls commissioned to mark its first 100 days showed that the Coalition's position had significantly worsened since the September election. Both the Nielsen and Newspoll surveys were damning: no incoming government had ever polled so badly.

In the olive green swivel chair reserved for the opposition leader sat Bill Shorten, whose election not only underscored the dominance of the 'faceless' factional leaders in this age of political speculation, but also represented the triumph of career politicians. Save for a short spell working as a lawyer – at a law firm representing trade unions – Shorten had spent almost his entire working life in union and Labor politics. His was the model curriculum vitae of a modern-day political striver: student activism with the ALP, a couple of part-time jobs with Labor politicians, a union career culminating in his commandeering of the Australian Workers' Union, and a safe parliamentary seat. Ambition appeared to drive him more than belief, a yearning for power unaccompanied by a clear sense of what he wanted to do with it – again, the identikit profile.

The 44th parliament was just as rowdy as the 43rd, despite the exhortations of the new speaker Bronwyn Bishop to uphold a more decorous standard. On her first day in the Speaker's chair, she declared that MPs should henceforth be referred to as 'honourable members', in an attempt to raise the tone. Inevitably, however, her very elevation sparked a partisan fistfight, because of her long-established reputation as a Liberal warrior. Not the kind of politician from whom to take behavioural cues, her appointment provided yet more evidence of the excessive politicisation of public life.

So Australia continued to upend the old maxim that a country gets the politics it deserves. The crankiness of voters suggested they yearned for better. The political cringe showed no sign of abating. If anything, it was getting worse.

Canberra's knack of inflicting harm on the country's international image was also evident following the death of Nelson Mandela, with the refusal of Parliament House officials to lower the flag to half-mast. Once again the bureaucratic mind, paralysed by rigid protocol, seemed incapable of responding to an event of such epic meaning that normal rules were temporarily cast aside.

While the flag controversy swirled, Parliament Hill also served as the backdrop for the country's first gay weddings, with 30 couples taking advantage of the ACT's new law legalising same-sex unions. Briefly, Australia, too, looked like a rainbow nation. Less than a week later, these unions were effectively annulled, after the High Court ruled they violated the 2004 Marriage Act. Federal lawmakers should determine who should get married, the court ruled, and the manner in which they should marry.

On the equality front, Tony Abbott did, though, press hard for the recognition referendum, and spoke with the sincerity of a politician who has spent an impressive amount of time in indigenous communities trying to better acquaint himself with their problems. This was an area where he had a chance to forge something of a legacy. He also displayed a capacity to surprise, as he did when he introduced the ABC *Australian Story* on Lieutenant Colonel Cate McGregor, a friend who was also one of the country's highest profile transgender figures. But any gains in the indigenous and human rights community were squandered by proposed amendments to the Racial Discrimination Act, which weakened the protections against racial vilification. For a nation with a casual racism habit, it was surely unhelpful to hear the attorney-general, George Brandis, argue that Australians had 'the right to be bigots'. Akin to a redneck's charter, the changes seemed to offer greater safeties for racists and chauvinists than the victims of abuse. The move also went against public opinion, which was increasingly intolerant of racist behaviour. Between 66 and 74 per cent either agreed or agreed strongly, according to a recent survey conducted by researchers at the University of Western Sydney, that it should be unlawful to insult, humiliate or offend anyone because of their race.

For economy watchers, there was a swathe of perturbing news. It exacerbated the sense Australia had spent too long in the sun, and come to rely far too heavily on the resources sector. Chinese growth, the harbinger recently of Australia's growth, slowed significantly. Unemployment rose to 6 per cent for the first time in a decade. Even in Western Australia, unemployment climbed to 5 per cent, as the state's economy adjusted to lower levels of mining investment. The WA comfort blanket looked frayed and thinning. The Treasury, largely in response to the slowdown in the resources sector, forecast the next decade would bring the weakest income growth in 50 years.

The worry, once only nagging and intermittent, that Australia had not invested sufficiently smartly during the golden years of the resources boom became received wisdom. Habitual concerns about the housing bubble bursting surfaced again. Manufacturing took another thrashing, with the closure of Ford and Holden and the withdrawal of Toyota. Australia would no longer manufacture cars, a setback which heightened its economic status anxiety. The shedding of a further 5000 jobs at Qantas, the ailing national carrier, dealt a further symbolic blow. The talk was of the 'shrinking kangaroo'. In the face of all these challenges, Joe Hockey seemed a long way from becoming international treasurer of the year.

Perhaps Australia needed another recession to reprioritise political life, so that the economic health of the nation would be the focus of attention and boat people and the culture wars would take their more rightful place as third- or fourth-tier issues. After all the frivolity of the leadership churn, and the complacency of the resources boom, politics needed to get serious again.

Even as the country was forced to navigate choppier waters, George Megalogenis's *The Australian Moment* remained arguably its most talked-about book. Its thesis was as stirring as it was sound: that Australia had become a model nation envied the world over, not through its endowment of resources but rather because of its inventiveness and endeavour. Alas, the title was in danger of becoming unintentionally literal. The Australian moment could be just that, something fleeting and ephemeral. At the end of his book, Megalogenis had asked sardonically: 'Are we in danger of becoming a great country?' Just two years on, however, the national mood was noticeably less buoyant, the future less assured. For all the robustness of the Australian model, it was facing another test of whether it was recession-proof and politician-proof.

All this I watched from afar, having left Australia to take up a new posting three days after Kevin Rudd returned as prime minister. These events, I should stress, were not linked, though it did seem entirely fitting, given the political volatility of the previous six years, that I should witness one more spill for the road.

Flying out of Sydney Airport, the last person I spoke to on Australian soil was Kim Beazley, a man who would have dearly loved to have been prime minister, briefly as he boarded the Qantas flight to Los Angeles en route to Washington. Sorry as I was to leave, I told the ever-affable ambassador I wouldn't miss the politics. 'Not too flash, is it,' he said, providing something of an epitaph for my Australian posting.

Our flight took us eventually to John F. Kennedy International Airport, where I started my new assignment as the BBC's New York and UN correspondent, something of a dream posting. Life in the States, in so many ways, was such a breath of fresh air. No longer did I have to cover Canberra politics, though Washington politics wasn't that flash either. After the insularity of Australian national life, it was good to be based at the UN headquarters in New York's Turtle Bay, surely the world's most internationalist and multicultural workplace. Needless to say, it was a boon to live in what is still the planet's most vibrant metropolis, a place I knew well but always approached with the thrill of the new arrival. As F. Scott Fitzgerald effused: 'The city seen from the

Queensboro Bridge is always the city seen for the first time, in its first wild promise.' It is also a place that welcomes newcomers. 'One belongs to New York instantly,' the novelist Tom Wolfe once opined.

For all that, I found myself missing Australia more than expected, and found that my mind had not yet fully migrated to a different continent. New York may be the greatest city in the world, but it does not have the liveability of Sydney or Melbourne. Beyond the kitchens of its hatted restaurants, the food was not so reliably good. I agreed with the legendary travel writer Jan Morris, when recently she noted of the Big Apple food scene: 'Australian menus are as eclectic.' And where was the beetroot in the burgers? The coffee was appalling, which explained why those sought-after Australian baristas were doing such a frothing trade. Though New York is home to the world's richest collection of modern architecture, I missed the Opera House, a building that had always exerted a near-mesmeric fascination from the first time I glimpsed its shells from the unsightly setting of the traffic lights near the top of Bondi Road. Though nothing in Australia came remotely close to the concentration of theatrical talent on Broadway, its hottest ticket was still Cate Blanchett – in anything. The saintly Cate could read from a New York telephone directory – all five boroughs – and theatregoers would cough up hundreds of dollars for a seat. In raising children, New York's urban jungle made the suburbs of Sydney look like the sunniest of uplands. If there was a better place to bring up kids than Australia, I had not yet been there.

My posting in Sydney had been an unexpected diversion, personal not professional. During a previous appointment in South Asia, I had fallen in love with an Australian. Not long after arriving, I fell in love with Australia, too. When it came to leaving, I was sorrier to go than the beautiful Sydneysider who was now my wife. Further strengthening the bond, we left with two small Australians. It meant that reflecting on Australia was now impossible to divorce from ruminating on what sort of Australians we wished them to be.

My dear hope is that they will never look on their homeland as a country too distant to matter and too small to make a difference, and thus reject the provincialism that so often encages national life. Rather, they will share the impatient sense of wanderlust that packs out the economy seats of long-haul flights with expectant young Australians, flags embroidered on rucksacks and inflatable headrests at the ready. They will embrace the outdoors, and with it the sporty impulse that fills playing fields each Saturday morning with children daubed with zinc cream, and crams beaches with eager nippers.

Preferably, they will reject, or at the very least question, the stereotyped views of their country, even those promulgated by Australians themselves. They will see in their birthplace a land of brilliant colour, from the ochre of the outback to the aquamarine of the oceans, but also countless shades of grey.

They will embrace the fairness doctrine, and believe, too, that the newest arrivals and also those who settled here first, their Aboriginal compatriots, should be its equal beneficiaries. They'll be thankful that they were born in one of the world's most successfully multicultural countries, and reject racism in all its forms, even when it comes with a laugh and a punch to the upper arm. They will embrace diversity rather than be frightened by it. By the time they grow up, I hope that fear and hatred are no longer a permanent feature of politics.

On Anzac Day, they will commemorate the commonness of man and also the commonness of women. They will learn enough about Australian history to know that the early years of the new federation not only gave rise to the White Australia policy but also old age pensions, female suffrage and the minimum wage. They will be open-minded enough to recognise that the Australian story, like the national timeline of so many other countries, contains both the marvellous and malevolent. Ideally, they'll reject the anti-intellectualism that breeds such mistrust of the gifted and talented, but also avoid the kind of pretentiousness and air of superiority that gives rise to those suspicions in the first place. National self-loathing, I hope, will never for them become an article of sophistication.

At the cricket, I hope they will bounce beachballs, and boo the stewards who puncture them – as they barrack for England, naturally. They will appreciate good coffee, share their parents' love of Australian cuisine, in all its innumerable flavours, rise to applaud the Australian Chamber Orchestra but also be able to sing along to Icehouse's 'Great Southern Land'. When talking about Australian culture, or better still creatively pitching in, they will walk with that erectness of carriage.

Over the years, they will develop a keener sense of what it is to be Australian rather than un-Australian, and look at those global maps with the country at the centre without so much as a second thought.

During his trip to Australia in 1950, Bertrand Russell penned a long-forgotten piece for *The West Australian* in which he spoke of a country where the future would surely be better than its past, and that had greatness in its grasp. 'Perhaps you are all too comfortable to take so much trouble,' he cautioned his newfound friends. 'Perhaps you will be content with a moderate and humdrum success, but I hope not. I hope that the more enterprising spirits among you will be inspired by a golden vision of a possible future, and will be content to take the risks involved in aiming at great success rather than acquiesce in the comfortable certainty of a moderate competence.'

Much of this vision already has been realised, but still present is the danger that the country could settle only for moderate success. My hope and expectation is that Australia will always keep aiming for that ever more golden future, and my children will always see in their homeland a nation where the rise continually trumps the fall.

AFTERWORD

EVEN FROM THE DISTANT vantage point of New York City, the rise of Australia was plain to see. It was all around us. At a book-lined apartment building on the Upper West Side, the author Richard Flanagan received a rapturous welcome at the launch party for his novel, *The Narrow Road to the Deep North*. In attendance were some of Manhattan's leading literary luminaries, among them the novelist Lionel Shriver and Robert B. Silvers, the long-time editor of *The New York Review of Books*. This being a city that gravitates towards people of the moment, some no doubt had been drawn to the event after reading the review from *The New York Times* the previous weekend. 'Magnificent' was how it described the story of the Australian surgeon Dorrigo Evans, who battled to maintain his dignity in the degrading surrounds of a Japanese POW camp.

Before this eager crowd, Flanagan delivered an endearingly self-effacing speech. Once in Chicago he had been introduced as Tanzania's great living writer, he recalled. In his thick Tasmanian burr, he also told how he had completed the fifth draft of the book – the previous four had either been burnt on the fire or erased from his computer hard drive – on the day of his father's death. Throughout this 12-year process, doing justice to his dad's wartime experience on the 'Death Railway' had been his spur. Weeks later, at a black-tie gala in London, Flanagan was awarded the Man Booker prize. Because US authors were allowed for the first time to compete, the accolade was doubly significant. The smart money had it going to an American not an Australian. 'In Australia the Man Booker prize is sometimes seen as something of a chicken raffle,' he said that night. 'I didn't expect to end up with the chicken.'

Cate Blanchett completed another victory lap on Broadway, this time appearing in Jean Genet's profane romp *The Maids*. The Sydney Theatre Company's multi-media production, one of the more innovative staged in New York in recent times, drew the customary plaudits. 'I wouldn't have missed it for the world,' wrote a critic in *The New York Times*. 'Once again, she proves herself to be the ruling mutation master among contemporary actresses.' *The Maids* also introduced New York theatregoers to the beautiful young actress Elizabeth Debicki. Perhaps we were watching the flowering of the next Cate Blanchett.

Australian food and coffee received a fawning press. *The New York Times*, ever keen to identify the latest fad, published not one but two pieces on the influx of Australian coffee houses. 'New York is a city of immigrants and their unofficial embassies offering a taste of home: the French bistro, the English pub, the California juice bar,' its correspondent wrote. 'Add to that list the Australian café. What started as an expedition a few years ago has become an invasion.' The *Times* devoted a separate piece to Toby's Estate's speedy colonisation of the hipster suburbs: 'The coffee is rich and intense, and so very Australian.' *The New Yorker* opined about the new Australian restaurants opening up, even though ordinary by Sydney and Melbourne standards. Even *Starbucks*, the mainstay of the caffeine industrial complex, unleashed the flat white on the American market.

Over at the United Nations, Australia ended its two-year term on the Security Council with another push to increase the flow of humanitarian aid to Syria, the signature issue of its tenure. That Syrian mothers and children now ate food rather than grass in once-besieged cities like Aleppo owed much to the efforts of the Australian ambassador Gary Quinlan and his team. In pushing for new resolutions allowing aid convoys to cross the Syrian border, without the permission of the Assad regime in Damascus, Quinlan placed himself in the unusual position for an Australian diplomat of facing down Washington. The Americans argued that the political process should take precedence, but the Australian ambassador prosecuted the argument, patiently and successfully, that thousands were starving while peace talks remained stalled.

As a result of its efforts on Syria, and also its lead role dealing with other problems like Afghanistan and Al-Qaeda, Australia carved out a unique role on the Security Council. It could never rival the Permanent Five members, the United States, Russia, China, Britain and France. Yet it exercised vastly more influence than the other nine rotating nations, and emerged as what might be called a 'Temporary Member Plus'. For all that, senior figures within the Department of Foreign Affairs and Trade, perhaps out of envy perhaps out of small-mindedness, continued to question the practical and strategic value of the venture. Seemingly they preferred the shilling table to global diplomacy's famed horseshoe table. Bizarrely, Quinlan was even prevented from speaking publicly to the media, which meant that one of Australia's diplomatic success stories went under-reported at home.

During a speech to the UN General Assembly in September 2014, Tony Abbott also failed to mention his country's humanitarian efforts (in pushing Syrian aid, Quinlan had acted largely on his own initiative rather than being guided by Canberra). But even sceptical Liberals, who not inaccurately once looked on Security Council membership as a Rudd vanity project, came to realise the value of membership. Never was it more useful than when Russian-backed rebels blasted a Malaysia Airlines Boeing 777 out of the skies above Ukraine, killing 298 passengers and crew, among them 27 Australians. Abbott pushed for a Security Council resolution demanding an international investigation. The Australian mission's experience of negotiating with the notoriously obstructionist Russians helped get it passed.

The shooting down of MH17 showed that on occasions Tony Abbott had the capacity to exercise forceful global leadership. His initial rhetorical response, when he told parliament 'this looks less like an accident than a crime', was strong. His speedy decision to seek UN action was also a shrewd move, since it isolated Moscow and paved the way for an independent international investigation. Julie Bishop, the new government's undoubted star, also burnished her reputation as a formidable foreign affairs minister. Pressing the case for a UN resolution in New York, she reduced Russia's ambassador Vitaly Churkin to tears when she reminded him of the children murdered.

Only a few months later, however, Abbott undid much of his good work when he announced that he planned to 'shirtfront' the Russian president, Vladimir Putin, at the G20 summit in Brisbane. Even Australia's closest diplomatic friends thought these remarks were risible. Western diplomats at the UN guffawed. After the statesmanship displayed in the aftermath of MH17, he sounded again like a backwoodsman.

The Brisbane summit, the highest-ranking gathering ever convened on home soil, had been intended by Kevin Rudd to showcase the rise of Australia, and to underscore its enhanced global role. Abbott took a more municipal view. Addressing Barack Obama, Angela Merkel, Xi Jinping, David Cameron et al in a private retreat, his rambling opening remarks, which included a whinge about the unpopularity of his proposed $7 co-payment for Medicare, sounded more like parish notices than global agenda-setting. Again, Australia's leaders took the aphorism 'all politics is local' to the point of absurdity. Self-satirising and self-sabotaging, the prime minister looked more like the Mayor of Warringah than a top-tier international leader.

At a summit originally envisioned to emphasise the country's newfound centrality, the Abbott government found itself marginalised on climate change. Australia was cast not just as an outlier but also as a near pariah. Before arriving in Queensland, Obama ambushed Abbott by announcing a landmark global-warming deal with Xi Jinping during a stop-off in Beijing. Then, in an unexpectedly reproachful speech at the University of Queensland, Obama delivered a stinging putdown. 'Here in the Asia Pacific, nobody has more at stake when it comes to thinking about and then acting on climate change,' he warned. Never before had an American president given an Australian leader such a public dressing down on home soil. And, as with the Beijing deal, the Abbott government was blindsided.

In the wings of the summit, US and European Union officials also battled to insert meaningful references to climate change into the summit's formal communiqué, over fierce objections from the host government. Abbott had been determined to downplay what other leaders regarded as the world's most pressing issue. Eventually, however, the other G20 members browbeat him into submission. 'Trench warfare' was how one European Union spokesman characterised the fraught negotiations.

Australia continued to be vilified for its asylum seeker policies, too. In his maiden speech as the UN's High Commissioner for Human Rights, Zeid Ra'ad Al Hussein complained that the policy of sending boat arrivals to Papua New Guinea or Nauru, or returning them to Indonesia, was 'leading to a chain of human rights violations'. The UNHCR complained it violated the refugee convention. 'If every state in the region decides they'll close the door,' warned a high-ranking UN official, 'then there will be nowhere safe for people to go.'

The boat stoppage meant that, thankfully, there were no more drownings at sea. This gave the government a defence. Scott Morrison repeatedly claimed that, rather than the conditions in the offshore detention centres, Australia's 'national shame' on the issue was 'almost 1200 people dead'. But the altruistic goal of stopping the drownings always seemed secondary to the political goal of stopping the boats.

The politicisation of this question was underscored once more when the Australian Human Rights Commission produced a report focusing on the children held in indefinite detention. It documented more than 230 assaults involving children and 33 incidents of alleged sexual assault. One Iranian girl likened being kept in indefinite detention to 'suffocating like a fish that is kept out of water'. Her two younger brothers had been detainees from birth, and separated from their father for over a year. 'We have been threatened, mentally tortured, discriminated and provoked against all the time we have been in this dark cage,' she said. Tony Abbott, seemingly unmoved by this kind of testimony, dismissed the report as a 'blatantly partisan politicised exercise', and said the Commission, led by the eminent law professor Gillian Triggs, should be 'ashamed of itself'. He also suggested it send a congratulatory letter to Scott Morrison for ending the drownings at sea. Even when confronted with evidence of inhumanity, his response was combative and political.

A massive $3.7 billion cut to the foreign aid budget and Abbott's refusal initially to dispatch Australian health workers to battle the Ebola outbreak in West Africa further undermined Australia's reputation for good international citizenship. Traditionally, Australians have rushed to the frontlines of humanitarian disasters – tsunamis, tornados, earthquakes, disease outbreaks – earning a near-unrivalled reputation in the international NGO community for volunteerism. Abbott's policy of non-intervention, combined with the withdrawal of so much foreign aid, signalled a more hands-off and hard-hearted approach.

Moves in Canberra to force Muslim women wearing burkas to sit in a specially sealed-off area when visiting the House or Senate also heightened the perception internationally that Australia had become the nasty country. In all my years in Australia, I had never once seen a woman dressed in a burka. Yet the House speaker Bronwyn Bishop claimed that segregating the public galleries was an urgent security measure, even though it meant relegating burka-clad women to second-class citizenship. Abbott opposed the policy, which was quickly dumped, but confessed he found the burka 'a fairly confronting form of attire', hardly the language of inclusiveness. He had used a similar formulation in regard to homosexuality, saying he felt 'threatened' by it.

Ham-fisted remarks from Abbott about a 'Team Australia' dealt another blow to community relations. 'Everyone has got to be on Team Australia,' he said, when outlining the threat posed by Islamist fighters returning from Syria and Iraq, adding: 'don't migrate to this country unless you want to join our team.' Muslim Australians, the vast majority of whom regarded ISIS as psychopathic thugs, understandably felt that the prime minister had unfairly brought their national loyalty into question. The Islamic Council of Victoria immediately cancelled a meeting with the prime minister. As police and intelligence chiefs would attest, Australia has not suffered more deadly attacks largely because of the cooperation from Muslim community leaders in identifying potential Jihadists.

The public and political response to the Sydney siege, when a deranged Islamic fanatic took 18 hostages at the Lindt Chocolate Café in Martin Place, was more measured. The aftermath of the 16-hour siege underscored that the nobler impulses of Australians were stronger than the malign forces of racism or Islamaphobia. Though there was an uptick in anti-Muslim messages on social media, there was no violent backlash against the Muslim community. Nor was there a repeat of a Cronulla-style disturbance or any online entreaty to #killallmuslims, which was the response to the attacks in Paris.

Like all Australians, Muslims mourned the murder of the café manager Tori Johnson and the death of barrister Katrina Dawson, and were quick to disavow the actions of Man Haron Monis. Tens of thousands embraced the social media hashtag #Illridewithyou, which offered good neighbourly reassurance to any Muslim fearing reprisals. As it was, there weren't any.

Unsurprisingly, given the guilelessness of public debate, it was not long before the #Illridewithyou hashtag became ensnared in the culture wars. Liberal backbencher George Christensen complained it created 'false victims' and detracted from those who had truly suffered at the hands of the gunman. It was a 'typical pathetic left-wing black armband brigade campaign, casting Aussies as racists who will endanger Muslims', he blasted on Twitter. Though hashtag activism can be facile, these hieroglyphics seemed like a well-meaning gesture intended to convey a sense of community, just as Australians had done a few days before with the 'Put Out Your Bats' tribute to the cricketer Phillip Hughes. The overriding message was 'We're not racists', rather than 'We fear what the racists in our midst will do'. In a phone call with Tony Abbott, Barack Obama singled out this online initiative for praise.

National moments like the Sydney siege can have a transformative effect on political leaders, revealing strong and previously unappreciated strengths. Because in the aftermath of the attacks of September 11 he immediately summoned words to express the country's anguish, Rudy Giuliani became 'America's Mayor'. Bill Clinton, a president written off as irrelevant following the Republican Revolution only a few months earlier, did much the same following the Oklahoma bomb attack in 1995. Yet Abbott's response seemed only adequate. His comments sounded stock rather than rousing. Years of scripted sloganeering, during which he lived on the advice of spin doctors, had seemingly robbed him of the ability to speak naturally. Like Julia Gillard, his delivery had become halting and robotic, which meant that even the heartfelt sounded manufactured.

In Canberra, where few senior political figures managed to connect with the public, it was a common affliction. The second most powerful man in the country, Joe Hockey, who had set great store in his chummy likeability, proved a turn-off as treasurer. Ahead of delivering what polls measured to be the most unpopular budget in four decades, he was photographed sucking on a fat cigar, like some billionaire shipping tycoon cruising the Mediterranean. Hockey committed an even more egregious gaffe in claiming that the poorest Australians 'don't have cars or don't actually drive very far'. With the job seemingly beyond him, he did not look like he would ever trouble the judges who award the International Treasurer of the Year.

Scott Morrison, the stopper of the boats and the frontbencher most admired by Abbott, came across as callous and unfeeling. A poll of GPs in *Australian Doctor* magazine suggested Peter Dutton was the most unpopular health minister in 35 years. Christopher Pyne, the accident-prone education minister, seemed especially hapless.

On the opposition benches, Bill Shorten, who tended to speak in political jargon and message-of-the-day soundbites, hardly looked like a prime minister in waiting. His lacklustre approval ratings were only marginally better than Abbott's. As with the Liberals, his female deputy, Tanya Plibersek, drew a more favourable press, partly because she spoke more plainly and thus came across as more authentic.

Not just at the federal but the state level, too, anti-incumbency was fast becoming the dominant theme in Australian politics. In Victoria, voter unrest led to the ejection of an unpopular Coalition government after just a single term. Still more stunning was the defeat in Queensland of Premier Campbell Newman's LNP government. After winning a landslide victory in 2012, which left Labor with a rump of just seven seats in parliament, Newman was forced from office less than three years later. Short-lived premierships were now commonplace. Colin Barnett was the only premier to have served more than five years in office. On the morning after the Queensland state election, only two, Barnett and Jay Weatherill in South Australia, had been in office for more than a year. COAG meetings started to take on the feel of a speed-dating convention, where strangers would make quick introductions never quite sure if they would meet each other again.

The scale of public disaffection with the political class became apparent when academics at the Australian National University brought out their Election Study. For the first time since the late 1980s, when ANU conducted its inaugural survey, none of the nation's leaders scored above an average of five on a scale of 0 to 10. The Nationals leader Warren Truss, who scored 4.34, was the most popular, maybe because he kept a relatively low profile.

The government's unpopularity was especially noteworthy because it had delivered on its three 'Party of No' promises: to stop the boats, abolish the carbon tax and eliminate the mining tax. But these did not align with voter concerns, and again highlighted the breach between lawmakers and the public. As the ANU's election study found, the most important issues for voters were the economy (28.1 per cent), healthcare (19 per cent), education (15 per cent), tax (11 per cent), and only then asylum seekers (10 per cent).

Likewise, there was a stark discrepancy between how the Abbott government looked upon its own achievements, and how they were perceived abroad. The Coalition trumpeted eliminating the carbon tax and blocking the boats as its two great domestic triumphs. Internationally, however, they tarnished Australia's standing, and weakened its moral authority in the region.

By lavishing so much attention on medium-sized or minor problems, ministers themselves seemed small – like student politicians who had never quite reached full adulthood. An outsider landing in Australia would be forgiven for thinking, for example, that the profligacy of its public broadcasters, the ABC and SBS, was its most pressing national problem. The onslaught against the ABC seemed especially petty and politically motivated. Moreover, polls repeatedly showed that the public trusted the national broadcaster more than the national government.

The decision to withdraw funding for ABC's Australia Network, which seemed like payback for Rupert Murdoch's support during the election, was not merely vindictive but also counter-productive. International broadcasting is widely seen as the most cost-effective form of soft power diplomacy. Worse still, the screens went dark at the very moment that ABC executives were due to sign a prized deal giving it the most extensive access to Chinese audiences of any western broadcaster, with greater penetration than the BBC or CNN. What the former foreign affairs minister Alexander Downer had once proudly called 'a window on Australia' had been shuttered for good.

Maybe the blackout was just as well, given the spectacle in Canberra. Parliament House continued to attract its usual assortment of oddballs. Ricky Muir of the Australian Motoring Enthusiast Party did not inspire much confidence when, during an interview with Mike Willesee of Channel Seven, he could not define what was meant by the Senate 'balance of power'. This was especially worrying since he was about to wield it himself.

At least Muir redeemed himself, with a refreshingly honest maiden speech, eight months in the making, in which he admitted his mistakes and made virtue of his frailties. By contrast, Jacqui Lambie, the newly elected senator for Tasmania, continued to sound plain weird. The former military policewoman described supporters of Sharia law as 'maniacs and depraved human beings', who would not stop committing 'cold-blooded butchery and rapes until every woman in Australia wears a burka'. Yet when asked to elucidate Sharia law, she was at a loss. 'It obviously involves terrorism,' she flustered. Lambie, another made-for-YouTube politician, warned that China could invade Australia, and praised Vladimir Putin, post-MH17, for his 'great values'. Asked on talkback radio to describe her ideal man, the senator said he must have 'heaps of cash' and a 'package between his legs'. Though Muir and Lambie were fringe figures, the parliamentary arithmetic of the Senate meant that they were by no means peripheral players.

Clive Palmer eclipsed both of them, whether it was storming out of broadcast interviews or staging photo-ops with improbable props, like the former Vice-President Al Gore. The billionaire's rise was a direct consequence of the dismal state of Australian politics. At a time of rising discontentment with the two major parties, he spotted a gap in the market and barged through. 'Clive is not a cause of our current fractured politics,' wrote Guy Rundle in the *Quarterly Essay* 'Clivosaurus', 'he is one of its most spectacular effects.' After winning the parliamentary seat of Fairfax, this product of the malaise only heightened the sense of malaise. There was something vaudevillian about his every action. Canberra became a circus in which he saw himself as the ringmaster.

The recurring problem for Tony Abbott was that he was also seen as a comic figure. Less than 12 months after he took office, speculation started about how long he would survive. After the 'Winkgate' affair, when he smirked and winked as a cash-strapped pensioner described in a radio call-in how she worked on an adult sex line to make ends meet, *The Washington Post* observed that Abbott was 'quickly becoming one of the world's most hated prime ministers'. The *Post*'s piece showed again that, even in the serious press, international coverage of Australian politics usually meant international disparagement of Australian politics. Even a senior fellow at the prestigious Council on Foreign Relations in New York asked: 'Is Australian Prime Minister Tony Abbott the most incompetent leader of any industrialised democracy?'

When asked to identify his greatest success in his dual role as minister for women, Abbott opened himself up to more mockery. 'As many of you know, women are particularly focused on the household budget,' he said, 'and the repeal of the carbon tax means a $550-a-year benefit for the average family.' Ray Hadley, one of the government's favourite shock jocks, gave him a grade of D minus. In coup-addicted Canberra, the backbenches became restless.

Restlessness turned into open rebellion after Abbott decided to confer a knighthood upon Prince Philip, the Duke of Edinburgh. The shock announcement – the 'Knightmare', as it inevitably came to be described – gave Australia Day even more of an 18th-century feel. Abbott described it as a 'captain's call', the worst from an Australian skipper, arguably, since Greg Chappell ordered his brother Trevor to bowl underarm to New Zealand's Brian McKechnie. Fleet Street relished the story, partly because it allowed them to publish lists of Prince Philip's greatest gaffes. But the decision made Abbott look just as cartoonish. Rupert Murdoch tweeted that it was 'a joke and embarrassment'. Peter Costello called it 'the barbeque stopper of the century', adding, 'Rarely have I heard such ridicule.' Andrew Bolt called it near fatal. Such criticism was hard to write off as 'electronic graffiti'.

In a mea culpa speech at the National Press Club, Abbott's central argument for keeping his job was the chaos that a leadership challenge would unleash. 'The Rudd-Gillard-Rudd years cannot become the new normal lest Australia join the weak government club and become a second-rate country living off its luck,' he said, echoing Donald Horne's most famous line. It had come to this: a speech supposedly intended to set out a new vision for the country was more noteworthy for its warnings of political dystopia in Canberra.

Abbott's devotion to his chief of staff, Peta Credlin, whose control freakery infuriated even senior members of the Cabinet, compounded his problems. But the prime minister regarded his consigliore as indispensable. She was, in his estimation, 'the fiercest political warrior I've ever worked with'.

In modern-day Canberra, there was no higher compliment.

Just a week after his stab at redemption at the National Press Club, Abbott suffered the ignominy of a first-term spill motion. Even more ingloriously, it attracted the support of a majority of Liberal backbenchers, even though he was not up against any challenger. Stunned by the groundswell of opposition in his own party room, Abbott described it as a 'near death experience', and vowed to change. By now, however, he was so closely associated with the worst traits of a failed politics – its negativity, aggression, short-termism and vapidity – that his position appeared irredeemable. He personified the political crisis.

In the week following the spill motion, he became even more aggressively partisan. That is when he launched his attack on the Australian Human Rights Commission and Gillian Triggs. That is when he tore into Labor for causing a 'holocaust of jobs'. In a bid to save his wounded prime ministership, he snarled and lunged like that junkyard dog.

It is small wonder that in a capital inhabited in the main by pygmies, figures from the past have come to loom like giants. This was especially apparent in June 2014 when John Howard and Bob Hawke, the two longest-serving prime ministers of the modern era, appeared together on stage at the National Press Club to celebrate its 50th birthday. Both expressed disgruntlement at the pitiful state of contemporary politics. 'I think we have sometimes lost the capacity to respect the ability of the Australian people to absorb a detailed argument,' Howard told a rapt audience. He also bewailed the rise of the political class 'whose life experience has only been about political combat' and 'the disease of factionalism'. During this unlikely double act, Hawke opined that parliament was held 'if not in contempt, in disdain, and I do think that something ought to be done to lift the quality of performance'.

Veterans in the press gallery also vented their dismay. In his new book *The Adolescent Country*, Peter Hartcher came up with an apt description for the small-mindedness that bedevilled national life. 'The provincial reflex,' he called it. 'Australia is seriously underperforming and it is underperforming because of the pathology of parochialism.' The political historian Paul Kelly, in his study of the Rudd-Gillard-Rudd years, spoke now of an 'Australian crisis'. Complained Kelly: 'The process of debate, competition and elections leading to national progress has broken down. The business of politics is too de-coupled from the interests of Australia and its citizens. This de-coupling constitutes the Australian crisis.' Two new driving forces had corrupted the political culture, he reckoned, 'volatility and fragmentation'.

Nothing brought home the public's hankering for a politics that was bigger and bolder than the death of Gough Whitlam. In mourning his death, Australians were also lamenting the dearth of modern-day politicians of his eloquence, intelligence and vision. 'The popular response to Gough Whitlam's death tells us more about the politics of the present than the past,' wrote the academic Geoffrey Robinson of Deakin University. According to the democracy guru Professor John Keane, the obituaries were a reminder 'how, once upon a time, Australian politics produced world class leaders courageously committed to the public good'. Tellingly, the most memorable eulogies came from outside the political class: Cate Blanchett and the indigenous leader Noel Pearson, intoning lovingly about 'this old man' in a voice that echoed the cadences of the Reverend Dr Martin Luther King Jr.

By bringing out a 707-page tome on the legacy of Robert Menzies, *The Menzies Era*, John Howard sought to harness this political and ideological wistfulness. Even Tony Abbott tacitly acknowledged that prime ministerial greatness might be a thing of the past when, speaking on the 70th anniversary of the Liberal Party, he described Menzies as 'a colossus we might never see again'. The passing of John Howard, whenever it comes, will arouse strong emotions on the right, if not quite the same romanticised feelings as Whitlam. Hawke and Keating will receive loud Hosannas. So did Malcolm Fraser, a champion of multiculturalism and anti-racism, whose death again exposed the calibre gap between politicians of the past and those of the forgettable present.

Powerful though their legacy is, the country cannot rely unendingly on the Australian model created by the reformist prime ministers in what now looks like a golden age. Australia will not be politician-proof forever. New challenges are multiplying. The depletion of its mineral resources, the slowdown of the Chinese economy, the concomitant fall in commodity prices, heavier public borrowing, an ageing population, an antique constitution, the overcrowding of its major cities, and the ravaging effects of global warming. Before the next great reform era can commence, Australian democracy itself might need an overhaul, with reforms aimed perhaps at lengthening the terms of governments, minimising the chances of minuscule parties and marginal figures gaining seats in the Senate, extending the duration of parliamentary sessions and limiting the participation of prime ministers during Question Time.

Nearly 10 years have passed since the leadership spat between Peter Costello and Howard launched this madcap period of volatility, and soon we will be talking about a lost decade. Australia is undoubtedly experiencing a political crisis, which runs so very deep that it will take more than yet another change in leadership to halt the downward spiral.

ACKNOWLEDGEMENTS

THE FIRST TIME I experienced Australians en masse was in a giant tent at the Munich Beer Festival, crowded as well with New Zealanders, where the incessant chant of 'Aussie, Aussie, Aussie' carried on until late in the night, punctuated only by the ping pong cries of 'Kiwi, Kiwi'. You could almost have hung a neon sign at the entrance reading 'Assumed Australia'. All those beer advertisements seemed true. The national colour really was amber. So my first visit to the country, in the late 1990s, came as something of a shock. I had expected a cartoon, but instead encountered the confounding and complex country that hopefully I have described in this book.

So perhaps the first person whom I should thank is the BBC editor who sent me to Australia on what turned out to be an unexpectedly impressionable trip, Rik Morris, a member of the rolling diaspora now back in Adelaide after his sojourn in London. Happily the thing that I left with, along with the mandatory soft kangaroo for my newborn niece, was a yearning to return.

When I came back as the BBC's correspondent in 2006, other editors at the mother ship in London encouraged me to report on the country not only in the traditional manner, on radio and TV, but also to blog, then still something of a departure for buttoned-down British reporters. Initially, the idea was to post online a few random thoughts during the 2007 election campaign, but real estate on the BBC website was soon found to accommodate something more permanent. My thanks to Kate McGeown, Philippa Fogarty and Steve Herrmann for making that happen, and also to Julian Duplain, whose middle-of-the-night sub-editing in London saved me innumerable blushes. The comments of my readers not only vastly increased my understanding of Australia, but also helped me to explore the lesser-known reaches of the Aussie vernacular.

Staying with the BBC, I need to thank my cameramen Andrew Kilrain and Matt Leiper, who are supremely talented shooters and also great travelling companions. My cameraman in South Asia, Nik Millard, one of Western Australia's most valuable exports, was also part of the Aussie brain trust.

My BBC bosses, Paul Danahar, Jon Williams, Jo Floto, Andrew Roy, Jonathan Baker, Jonathan Paterson and Jonathan Chapman, were not just supportive, but allowed me to prolong my posting so long that colleagues marvelled at my limpet-like ability to remain in Sydney. In New York, where would I be without my BBC colleagues Nada Tawfik and Barin Masoud?

Internationally, Australia gets reported by a happy band of Sydney-based foreign correspondents that included Enda Curran of *The Wall Street Journal*, Kathy Marks of *The Independent*, Andrew Thomas of Al Jazeera English, Bonnie Malkin of *The Daily Telegraph*, Steve Marshall of TVNZ, Jonathan Samuels of Sky News, and his predecessor, my good mate and friendliest of rivals, Ian Woods.

There are also scores of local journalists, commentators and academics, friends now as well as colleagues, who shaped my thinking: Peter Hartcher, James Curran, Michael Wesley, Gideon Haigh, George Megalogenis, Julian Morrow, Geoff Thompson, Jane Hutcheon, Tony Jones, Linda Mottram, Antony Green, Michael Fullilove, Chris Reason, Annabel Crabb, Ray Martin, Hugh White, Leigh Sales, Lisa Millar, Troy Bramston, Barbie Dutter, Michael Cox, Sarah Ferguson, Richard Glover, Jen Brockie and the great Mark Colvin, or Colvinius as he better known to his legion of followers on Twitter.

Over the years, an ecumenical group of editors have encouraged my writing, and been kind enough to offer it a home. Tom Switzer at *The Spectator Australia*, Rebecca Weiser, Nick Cater, John Zubrzycki and Stephen Romei at *The Australian*, John van Tiggelen and Ben Naparstek at *The Monthly*, Lisa Pryor at *The Sydney Morning Herald*, Julianne Schultz at the *Griffith Review*, Bryce Corbett and Helen McCabe at *Australian Women's Weekly*, Monica Attard and Lauren Martin at *The Global Mail*, and Sam Roggeveen at *The Interpreter*.

This book, though over 80,000 words long, is also faithful to this the age of Twitter. The idea for it was condensed into 140 characters, and sent, via direct message, to my publisher, Nikki Christer. My thanks to Nikki for seeing in that abbreviated note the potential for something more expansive. Without her, the rise and fall would never have gotten off the ground.

My editor, Patrick Mangan, was not only painstaking but also a valuable sounding board. It has been good to work again with the ever-delightful Peri Wilson, Random House's publicist.

My agent, Pippa Masson, was her usual proficient self, this time getting everything done and dusted well in time before taking maternity leave.

A number of people were kind enough to read parts of the manuscript and to offer their thoughts: Angus Paull, who persuaded me to pull a few punches about the decline of Australian sport; Tim Soutphommasane, a friend and fellow Balliol man, who has written the best book on Australian multiculturalism, *Don't Go Back to Where You Came from*; Peter Brent, whose encyclopaedic knowledge of Australian politics was invaluable; and Sam Roggeveen, whose regional analysis is second to none.

I should also thank the baristas of Sydney, who not only provided a steady stream of caffeine but also corners of their cafés in which to write.

My deep affection for Australia stems from an even deeper affection for Australians, and my time in the country was made even more pleasurable by having such a close-knit group of friends, among them Morna Seres and Ian Hill, Angus Paull and Kristina Ammitzboll, Nick Glozier and Suzy Berry, Schaan Anderson and Gavin Cadwell, Rob Laurie and Kat Vidovic, Calvin and Tess O'Brien, and Michael 'Mod' O'Dwyer.

A shout-out, as well, to the members of my book club, fellow travellers in a journey, via various Sydney hostelries, through the Australian literary canon: Nick Glozier, Simon Nearn, Matt Whale, Huw Turner, Graham Brook, Daoud Edris and the sole Australian representative, Dan Zammit.

My Australian family, confronted with a Pom in their midst, could not have been more welcoming or encouraging. My thanks to Lorraine Wood, one of the proudest Aussies I know. A special thank you to Lee Hansen – or Auntie E, as she is affectionately known – for helping a sleep-deprived author catch some extra pre-dawn hours in bed. Sue Bath also feels like family, as does Julia – or Ju Ju, as she is known to the kids.

As well as thanks, I often feel like I owe my British family an apology for spending so many years so far away. But that is where Australia's new virtual proximity to everywhere has helped. Thanks, as ever, to Sarah, Rod, Rory, Milly, Katie and Ellie, the recipient of that soft kangaroo all those years ago. My dear mum and dad, Janet and Colin Bryant, could not be more loving, supportive or encouraging of my writing.

The kids, Billy and Wren, are our pride and joy. By the time they are old enough to read this, I hope they will have forgotten the sight of their father hunched over his laptop, or, if not, forgiven it. At least the years spent writing in the midst of noisy newsrooms meant that I had no need to closet myself away, and could tap away in the middle of their play. Life's richest pleasure is watching them grow up.

None of this would have happened had it not been for the good fortune of meeting Fleur Wood, in the courtyard of a restaurant in Delhi a decade ago. Legend has it that nothing grows under a banyan tree, but our ongoing love, and everything that has flowed from it, disproves that. What started out as an unexpected detour to Australia has ended up being the happiest journey of my life.

INDEX

Adventures in Correspondentland

As a foreign correspondent for the BBC, Nick Bryant has reported from the wilds of Afghanistan, Pakistan, London, Washington and, for five years, Australia.

Adventures in Correspondentland – his account of these experiences – is part memoir, part travelogue and part polemic. More than anything, however, it is the inside story of the dangers and delights of seeing the world through this unique, sometimes privileged and often strange perspective.

How did Bill Clinton react when, in front of a ballroom of over 2000 people, he had to present the award for 'Journalist of the Year' to the reporter who had discovered the existence of Monica Lewinsky's little blue dress? Why did the media report on the night that Princess Diana was killed in a Paris underpass that she was alive when correspondents knew she was dead? How did Bono help save the Northern Ireland peace process? What were international journalists really saying about Prime Minister Rudd?

In *Adventures in Correspondentland*, Nick Bryant takes us around the world and back home to Australia, where he covered events such as the death of Steve Irwin, the national apology to Indigenous Australians and the 2011 Queensland floods. In being an Englishman abroad, he gives us a fresh, funny and revealing insight into how the world sees Australia at the start of the twenty-first century.

Available Now